THE HISTORY
OF THE
JAPANESE
CAMERA

Calligraphy by the Honorable Mrs. Mayumi Moriyama.

Kunichika — *The Photographer Hanawa Yoshino,* ca. 1878.

Hanawa Yoshino was one of the first women to practice
the new profession of photography in Japan.

Kunichika was one of the best known Ukiyo-e artists
of the late Takugawa and early Meiji periods.

Courtesy of the Pentax Gallery

THE HISTORY
OF THE
JAPANESE
CAMERA

Edited by
Gordon Lewis

From a translation by
William and Amy Fujimura
of *Nihon Camera No Rekishi*

Published by
THE INTERNATIONAL MUSEUM OF PHOTOGRAPHY AT GEORGE EASTMAN HOUSE
For
THE JAPAN CAMERA AND OPTICAL INSTRUMENTS INSPECTION AND TESTING INSTITUTE

Rochester • Tokyo

Edited, Designed and Produced by Gordon Lewis
for the International Museum of Photography
at George Eastman House, Rochester, New York.

Graphic Design by Paul Rossmann.

Manufactured in the United States of America.

Library of Congress Cataloging-in-Publication Data

The History of the Japanese camera/edited by Gordon Lewis from a translation
    by William and Amy Fujimura of Nihon camera no rekishi.
      p. cm.
    Extensively rev and enl. ed. of: Nihon camera no rekishi.
    Includes index.
    ISBN 0-935398-16-3: — ISBN 0-935398-17-1:
    1. Cameras—Japan—History. 2. Photographic industry—Japan—History.
I. Lewis, Gordon, 1945-   . II. Nihon camera no rekishi.
TR250.H56 1990
338.4′7681418′0952—dc20   89-85077
                                             rev. CIP

Contents

Foreword

Industrial history offers no more dramatic example of the massive shift of a production technology from one region to another than the rise of the Japanese camera industry. Germany and the United States, and to a lesser extent, France and the U.K., had been the dominant forces in the design and manufacture of photographic apparatus for more than a century, from the beginnings of the industry in the 1840s until after the Second World War. Precision cameras of the types used by professionals and serious amateurs were primarily of European origin, while the mass consumer market, characterized by the classic snapshot camera, was dominated by American firms. The preeminence of European and U.S. firms was based on their accumulated design and manufacturing experience, and their strengths in existing markets. In less than two decades, world camera manufacturing changed entirely. Japanese photographic enterprises, rebuilding immediately after World War II, first challenged and then surpassed the entire industry, becoming the largest supplier of photographic equipment of all types in the world.

An essential prerequisite to world wide acceptance of Japanese cameras was a system of strict quality control. To address this issue, the Japan Camera and Optical Instruments Inspection and Testing Institute (JCII) was founded in 1954. JCII's founding president, the Hon. Kinji Moriyama, created an organization that established and enforced such an effective system of quality standards that it was able to change completely the international perception of Japanese cameras.

The Japanese photographic industry began in the last century as a group of essentially domestic enterprises which were generally regarded, even in Japan, as producers of inexpensive, largely unsatisfactory copies of European and American designs. But the Japanese reconstruction progressed rapidly after World War II, and by 1950 an era of innovation in design and production methods was underway. The 35mm single lens reflex originated in Europe before the war, but so many technical problems remained unresolved, it was only a limited success. In the 1950s, Japanese firms completely re-engineered the design, making it both reliable and affordable, and the 35mm single lens reflex became the camera of choice for both professionals and advanced amateurs. By the 1970's, Japan had become the world leader in the production of photographic equipment.

In 1984 the International Museum of Photography at George Eastman House, in conjunction with JCII, produced *The Evolution of the Japanese Camera*, an exhibition of four hundred instruments representing more than 80 years of Japanese camera design. After travelling in the United States, the exhibition appeared in slightly modified form in Tokyo.

The late Hon. Kinji Moriyama had always hoped to publish a book in English detailing the history of the Japanese photographic industry. It was left to the tireless efforts of his wife, the Hon. Mrs. Mayumi Moriyama, who succeeded him as president of JCII, to make his wish come true.

This volume is based on fourteen essays by seven writers, from the exceptional translation William and Amy Fujimura did for this book of the two-volume *Nihon Camera No Rekishi*, published in Japanese by Mainichi Newspaper in May, 1975. The Fujimuras then translated a third volume which JCII had published in Japan concurrently with the opening of the *Evolution* exhibition in Tokyo in 1986. This work provided material for the years from 1975 through 1986. The Museum then called on Gordon Lewis, who was founder and Director of Polaroid Archives, and that company's first historian. While serving as series editor at a university press and curator at two other museums, he undertook on behalf of the Museum to correct and completely rewrite the text, add two chapters, and design and produce this volume, *The History of the Japanese Camera*.

The International Museum of Photography at George Eastman House is honored to have been able to publish this book in the U.S. for the Japan Camera and Optical Instruments Inspection and Testing Institute. It is the aspiration of everyone who worked on the project that this book be a fitting tribute to the late Honorable Kinji Moriyama, who profoundly influenced the enterprise of photography, and who played such a decisive role in this latter-day industrial and technological revolution.

Philip L. Condax

Senior Curator
Technology Collections
International Museum of Photography
at George Eastman House
Rochester, New York

March 1991

The History of the Japanese Camera
is respectfully dedicated to the memory of
the late Honorable Kinji Moriyama

Chapter One

It Began With Cabinet Makers

from an article by Yoshiro Tanaka

Avid Photo Pioneers of The Latter Tokugawa Era.

Relatively little is known about photography in Japan before 1868, the first year of the Meiji Dynasty and the beginning of "modern" Japan. Daguerreotype cameras were imported, and there are records of wet plate cameras in Japan around 1857, but the country was isolated from the West during much of the industrial revolution, under a policy enforced by the Tokugawa Shogunate. Photography was practiced by a small group of "Dutch scholars", Japanese intellectuals who pursued the western sciences imported by Dutch merchant ships — the only foreign vessels allowed to enter Nagasaki harbor during the Tokugawa isolation. The few feudal lords who pursued photography did so as an avocation, much in the idiom of the gentleman amateur in the West. Between 1840 and 1860, European nations who sought colonies in the Far East appear to have introduced first daguerreotype, then wet plate cameras into Japan through the port of Nagasaki.

A woodcut print of Lord Shimazu taking photographs. From the Terukuni-ko Kankyuroku collection of Takeo Otake.

The rapid acceptance of photography among the intellectually curious in Japan was due in part to a fascination with all newly imported Western culture. The post-isolationist, latter Tokugawa era was a period of cultural revolution in Japan, during which pioneers such as Lord Nariakira Shimazu, Lord Yoshinoby Tokugawa and Shozan Sakuma devoted significant effort to the new science of photography.

For years it was believed that only four daguerreotypes of the Japanese existed in Japan. Three had been taken by E. A. Brown, who came to Hakodate with Commodore Perry in 1854. All three contain Brown's signature on the obverse, and are inscribed by Perry. The fourth is a picture of a priest in Shimoda, taken by a photographer from a passing Russian fleet in 1853.

In October 1975, an 8 x 11 cm. daguerreotype portrait of Lord Shimazu was found in the Shimazu family vault. It appears to have been taken in 1857 by one of his subjects, who assisted him in his photographic experiments. Their notes indicate that after several hundred trials, they had succeeded in making daguerreotypes, but no others have been found, and this is the only daguerreotype made by a Japanese known to exist today. Neither Lord Shimazu's, nor any other daguerreotype camera, has been found.

Yoshinobu Tokugawa (1837-1913), the last Tokugawa shogun.

Nariakira Shimazu (1809-1858), a feudal lord. Reproduction of a daguerreotype, 1857.

In addition to the daguerreotype, there were two other photographic systems imported into Japan during the last 30 years of the Tokugawa dynasty: William Henry Fox Talbot's calotype, and the wet plate, invented by Frederick Scott Archer.

Wet plate cameras were introduced into Japan around 1857, and unlike daguerreotype cameras, several have been identified and preserved.

Around 1925, ten 10 x 12 inch paper negative photographs, including a picture of the central structure of Kagoshima castle, were found in Shimazu castle. They are presumed to have been taken by Lord Shimazu with his "beloved *In-Ei-Kyo*". Lord Shimazu's name for his daguerreotype camera is the combination of three forms: *In*, which means a print or an impression of a seal; *Ei*, which is shadow, or image, and *Kyo*, which is mirror. Since the daguerreotype appears to be an image printed on a mirrored surface, the name is logically descriptive. From various sources, *In-Ei-Kyo*, which has never been found, is assumed to have resembled one of Fox Talbot's cameras in the collection of the Fox Talbot Museum in Lacock, Wiltshire, England.

Tsurumaru Castle, the keep of Kagoshima Castle. Paper negative made by Lord Nariakira Shimazu between 1854 and 1859.

A positive from the paper negative.

Wet Plate Cameras.

Tsuishu camera, collection of Keishichi Ishiguro. Tsuishu is elaborate red lacquer-ware with relief patterns.

Two types of wet plate cameras are known to have existed in Japan before the beginning of the Meiji era in 1868. The box shape, patterned after the early Daguerreotype cameras, was a design which originated with the camera obscura, before photography itself. Two surviving examples are a wooden camera made by the photographer Kuichi Uchida during the first year of the Meiji era, and the Tsuishu camera, now in the collection of Keishichi Ishiguro.

The other wet plate camera design used folding bellows. The origins of bellows cameras are unclear, but there was one among Niepce's cameras when he died in 1833, and de Seguier designed a bellows camera which Voigtlander produced around 1842. There is an example of this type of camera in the collection of the Prefectural Library of Nagasaki, in Kyushu. It is cabinet format, 12 x 16.5 cm., and fitted with a lens made by St. Meyer, Philadelphia. It was used by Hikoma Ueno, who is generally considered the founder of photography in Japan.

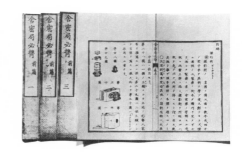

Seimi-kyoku Hikkei, *Handbook of Chemistry, 1862. Translated into Japanese by Hikoma Ueno.*

Hikoma Ueno (1838-1904).

Renjo Shimooka (1823-1914).

The First Commercial Photographers. Early Meiji.

Before Meiji, cameras were used and treasured by a small number of daimyos — feudal lords — and scholars to whom they were expensive, curious inventions from the West. In the feudal society of the time, with little opportunity for common people to become acquainted with cameras or photography, there was a popular superstition that being photographed would shorten one's life. The public viewed photography with a mixture of fear, awe and curiosity.

In the context of modern Japan, and Japanese technology, it is difficult to imagine the degree of superstitious resistance to photography in early Meiji Japan. When Kuichi Uchida, a student of Hikoma Ueno, opened a studio in Tokyo's Asakusa district in 1869, he tried to counteract the popular superstition by naming it Kuichido Manju — the Kuichi Studio of Everlasting Life.

After the Emperor Meiji had a portrait photograph taken in 1872, the ladies and gentlemen of the nobility, various government officials and wealthy businessmen soon sought out portrait photographers for themselves. Among the students of Ueno, and of Renjo Shimooka, who opened successful studios in various parts of Japan were Uchida, Raizo Morita, Matsusaburo Yokoyama, Shinichi Suzuki, Reiji Ezaka, Matsuchi Nakajima, and Tsukuba Kitaniwa.

The Emperor Meiji, by Kuichi Uchida in 1873.

A photography studio in the Meiji era.

The Ezaki Photo Studio. This Meiji era photography studio in Tokyo is believed to be Japan's first Western-style structure, 1889.

Asanuma Shokai and Konishi Honten. 1871 to 1873.

Rokuemon Sugiura (1847-1921), founder of Konishi Honten.

At first, all photographic supplies in Japan were imported, and were sold only through the large, Western-owned import houses in Yokohama. The first Japanese photographic manufacturing firms were pharmaceutical stores, which began by stocking photographic chemicals, then expanding into the manufacture and sale of mount papers, plate holders, camera stands, and finally cameras.

The first such store was opened by Tokichi Asanuma, in Gofuku-cho, Nihon-bashi, Tokyo in 1871. Konishi Honten opened in 1873 in Koji-machi, Tokyo, and moved in 1876 to Hon-cho, Nihon-bashi, where the store began to sell photographic goods.

There are no definite records of the number of cameras made in Japan during the first 15 years of Meiji, from 1868 to 1883. Since there was no optical manufacturing in Japan, all 19th Century Japanese cameras were fitted with imported lenses, and Asanuma Shokai and Konishi Honten sold imported lenses mainly to the commercial studios.

Tokichi Asanuma (1852-1929), founder of Asanuma Shokai.

Asanuma Shokai workshop, ca. 1907.

Konishi Honten ca. 1904.

Among their products, mount papers were the easiest to produce. Both Asanuma and Konishi began to make mount papers around 1877, and soon replaced the imports with their own brands. But at that time they neither sold nor made cameras; only a small number of domestic cameras were being built, by a few master craftsmen and their apprentices, and imported cameras, which were more expensive, were available only through the Western trading houses.

During the Meiji era, two English Ross Dallmeyer lenses were imported in some quantity into Japan, an A-2 portrait and a landscape lens. Two French lenses were available, a Hermagis portrait lens, and a Clement & Gilmer portrait lens, and a Steinheil general purpose lens was imported from Germany.

Asanuma and Konishi, both established in early Meiji, competed as friendly rivals for half a century, and were the foundation of the Japanese photographic industry.

Dallmeyer (U.K.) and Clement and Gilmer (France) portrait lenses. From an 1899 Tokyo Photo Studio catalogue.

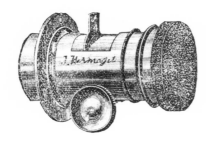

Imported lenses of the early Meiji era.

Hermagis portrait lens. From an 1899 Tokyo Photo Studio catalogue.

Early Box Cameras Made by Craftsmen. 1877.

Wooden box cameras, tripods, and wet plate holders were soon made domestically by cabinetmakers and skilled carpenters. Some began by repairing imported cameras, and later copying them, while others set out simply to duplicate successful products. The imitations were poorly designed and not particularly well made. With the exception of some custom models made by well-known craftsmen, the only advantage of the early Japanese cameras was their low price.

Simple box cameras for commercial photography were made of domestic cherrywood, imported mahogany and teak, and assembled with hand-crafted brass fittings. All the cameras of this time were either box or bellows, or a combination of the two, and all were designed for use inside studios.

In the old Kanda, Asakusa, Honjo, and Fukagawa districts in Tokyo, furniture makers and other craftsmen took orders from studios for custom cameras, and from photographic stores for small quantities of stock cameras. Master photographers, including H. Ueno, K. Uchida, and T. Nakajima, ordered cameras for their former students, who by then operated studios throughout Japan. Two men, Matusuaburo Tamaya during Meiji, and Matsunosuke Ishibashi in 1878, had proposed volume production and sales of box cameras. But the majority of the Japanese public had not yet seen photographs, many of those who had were superstitiously opposed to them, camera making remained a cottage industry.

An early Meiji era wet-plate camera, ca. 1870.

Dry Plates. 1884.

In 1851, when the English sculptor Fredrick Scott Archer invented the wet-collodion process, the practice of photography changed greatly. The medium was no longer bound to the studio, and photographers began to work in the natural landscape, to photograph buildings and cities, even to make documentary photographs of war. Twenty years later, when the Englishman Richard Leach Maddox invented the dry-plate process, the practice of photography was again simplified and enlarged. In 1877, Joseph Wilson Swan marketed dry plates in England, where Charles Bennet introduced a higher speed dry plate the following year. In 1881, the Monckhoven dry plate was manufactured in Belgium, and George Eastman produced and marketed the Eastman Dry Plate in the United States.

Joseph Wilson Swan (1828-1914).

Richard Leach Maddox (1816-1902).

A photographic chemical industry in Japan was far behind Europe and the United States. Hikoma Ueno, using dry plates purchased from a foreigner, took a first experimental photograph in 1881. In 1883, Reiji Ezaki, a photographer in the Asakusa district in Tokyo, used imported dry plates to take photographs of an Imperial Navy torpedo detonation exercise in the Sumida River. The photographs froze the motion of a plume of water rising from the river, and he became known as the "rapid photographer". While commercial dry plates were common in the West, they were a novelty in Japan, and even though there was little foundation for such an industry, many Japanese attempted their manufacture. In 1884, Yokitsu Fukazawa, Katsunosuke Yoshida, Shinji Matsuzaki, and Isshin Ogawa tried to produce commercial dry plates. All failed.

Reiji Ezaki photograph of a torpedo explosion during Imperial Navy exercises on the Sumida River, 1883.

Founders of the Nippon Kanpan Kaisha (Japan Dry Plate Company), 1889. Shozaburo Kuwata, Shiho Katsuragi, Isshin Ogawa and Tajiro Ichioka.

Camera Design Requirements. 1885.

By 1885, Japanese camera designers were aware of dry plates and awaiting their commercial availability. Wet-plate photography required pouring collodion over a glass plate, in light-tight conditions, and, as the name suggests, exposing before it dried. To make pictures outside the studio, the photographer required a portable darkroom — glass plates, chemicals, and a large, lightproof enclosure. Wet-plate emulsions were also slow, typically requiring 2 to 3 second exposures.

Prepackaged, dry photographic plates of substantially greater light sensitivity had influenced both the practice of photography and the design of the cameras in which they were used.

Frederick Scott Archer (1813-1857).

Dry Plates, Roll Film and the Kodak. 1885 to 1888.

The introduction of dry plates, the manufacture of smaller and lighter cameras, and the introduction of shutters to obtain shorter exposure times were all components of a more portable, more flexible and potentially easier photography. One design frequently became the predicate for the next; folding hand cameras influenced dry plate manufacturers to make lighter and smaller sensitized plates.

The first roll film was a collodion emulsion coated on a paper base. After being developed and fixed, the emulsion was peeled off the paper base and transferred to a glass plate. Sometimes called Peel Film, this early roll film demonstrated the obvious advantages over dry plates, but was cumbersome and difficult to process.

(right) George Eastman holding the No. 2 Kodak, 1890.

The Kodak Camera George Eastman introduced in 1888 was a box camera with a single control, the shutter button. Eastman's design premise was simplicity: if the photographer had no other controls, he had no other duties.

But cameras don't make pictures, they expose film. The importance of the Kodak Camera lay in the system that accompanied it. The advertising slogan, which became famous, was: *You press the button, we do the rest*. It was Eastman's company "doing the rest" that revolutionized photography, and made possible a new class of photographer, the amateur.

In May of 1889, enthusiasts from Tokyo and Yokohama, professional photographers and photographic retailers formed the Nihon Shashin Kai, the Japan Photographic Society. Although it lasted only seven years, it was the first in a long succession of both professional and amateur organizations designed to promote the study and practice of photography in Japan. The Society popularized the medium, held the first photography contest, with prizes, in 1890, and significantly increased the public awareness of amateur photography.

Towards a Popular Photography.

A hand camera, with the initials T. S. K. From an 1899 Tokyo Photo Studio catalogue.

A fold-in camera, bearing the signature of its manufacturer, K. Arita. From an 1899 Tokyo Photo Studio catalogue.

A cabinet format dry-plate camera, made by Asanuma Shokai in the 1890's. From the collection of Yoshiro Tanaka.

Members of Japan Photographic Society and avocational photographers throughout Japan frequented the Konishi and Asanuma stores, where they bought high quality, expensive cameras and studied photography in earnest.

But a photography for the general public awaited a greater degree of technical simplicity, not just in camera operation, but in the handling and processing of light sensitive materials. The introduction of dry plates increased the number and kind of circumstances under which photographs could be made. It also greatly simplified the process, making photography appealing to a wider range of the public. In turn, the greater public interest in the medium soon led to the development of a *keiben shashinki*, a light and convenient camera, which was easier and less expensive to use.

One popular wooden *keiben shashinki* was introduced by Jiro Arita. It was half the Tefuda format, which by the terms of the day made it a lightweight, hand camera. Arita opened a store in Tokyo at Tadokoro-cho, in Nihonbashi district, which he moved in December of 1897 to Hatago-cho in the Kanda district. There, he also manufactured and sold a toy-like camera for his amateur customers, whom he would also teach how to take pictures, process film, and make prints.

In February of 1891, Arita's store was renamed Tokyo Shashin Kan, and it continued to sell cameras and photographic products until the middle of the Taisho Era (1918). *Shashin* means photography, *shashin kan* means photographic store or studio, and *shashinki* means a photographic instrument or camera. Around 1899, the company was run by Kisaburo Arita, who wrote under the pen name Sanshu. In the Tokyo Shashin Kan catalog, many of the camera illustrations are signed K. Arita.

The 1899 catalog listed five hand cameras. The first was a simple box camera. The second was a simplified studio camera which focused with a movable film plane; the lens mount and baseplate were part of a single, rigid L-shaped frame which covered the front and bottom of the camera. There was a double box sliding camera similar to the Giroux camera, and two folding bellows cameras — one a view camera, one a hand camera.

Most Japanese cameras were copies of imports, and the Tokyo Shashin Kan catalogue also contained a number of advertisements for foreign products, for which the company asserted itself to be the exclusive agent. By the turn of the century, manufacturers from England, France, and the United States had begun to engage the growing market for photographic equipment and sensitized materials in Japan.

Chapter Two

The Origins of the Modern Camera

from an article by Yoshiro Tanaka

Detective Cameras. Mid-Meiji Era.

By the turn of the century, because of the invention of new photosensitive materials, there were three new photographic formats in the West. Eastman's roll film Kodak camera, which made amateur photography possible, the new detective cameras, and the invention of moving pictures were all predicated on new kinds of light sensitive materials. But in 1900, in mid-Meiji Japan, photography was practiced predominately with box and bellows designs of dry plate cameras.

A variety of detective cameras appeared in the West around 1885. They were clever objects that captured the popular imagination and made the general public increasingly aware of photography. The intriguing concept of the detective camera encouraged some to create their own variations, while commercial detective cameras ranged from the clever to the farfetched. There were cameras that could be worn, including hat cameras, pocket watch cameras, vest, muffler and scarf cameras. To carry, there were book cameras, monocular and binocular cameras, walking stick and cane cameras, and parcel or package cameras. For shooting pictures, there were rifle and revolver cameras. Some 20 years later, copies of these detective cameras began appearing in Japan. Around 1910 the Ueda Camera Store marketed the Memo book camera, and in 1912, a pocket watch camera called the Radio. Sone Shunsui Do introduced a monocular camera called the "Secrette" in 1923.

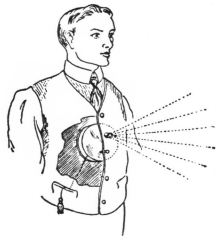

Adams & Co. hat detective camera, 1891, U.K., 3.25 x 4.25 in., dry plate.

Physiographe monocular stereo detective camera, 1896, France.

C. P. Stirn concealed vest camera, 1886, Germany, 45 mm., circular dry plate.

The Development of Motion Pictures.

Muybridge Zoopraxiscope, 1880. Continuous projection of the frames in sequence produces an illusion of movement.

A series of pictures in which movement is divided.

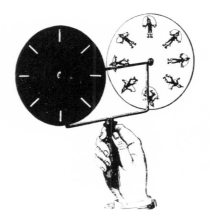

Gaumont pocket cinematographic camera, 1900.

The first toys that showed animated pictures were made in the seventeenth century. In 1852, photographs were used instead of drawings to depict motion. In 1853, various mechanical devices were built into hand painted lantern slides to simulate motion. There were levers which could be moved to create the appearance of a man sawing or chopping wood, and circular wheels which, when turned, caused a moon and stars to pass across a sky. In 1880, the Zoopraxiscope, invented by Eadweard Muybridge, created the illusion of motion by rapidly displaying a series of sequential still photographs on a screen.

In 1874, to take photographs of the transit of Venus, Pierre-Jules-Cesar Ganssen devised a photorevolver which operated at one frame per second. In 1876, Wordworth Dornithorpe invented a drop-plate mechanism for wet plates, which could operate at eight frames per second. In 1877, Eadweard Muybridge used 24 cameras to make sequential photographs of a running horse. Muybridge's photographs gave the impression of motion when displayed on a Zoetrope, at speeds of up to 24 frames per second. In 1882, Etienne Marey succeeded in taking photographs of flying seagulls at 12 frames per second using a photorevolver with a rotary shutter. In 1888, he invented the Chronophotographie, which operated at 20 frames per second.

While the component photographs in sequences became increasingly close, the next logical step towards a motion picture, a mechanism for the continuous projection of arrested-motion photographs, had to await George Eastman's 1889 invention of a flexible, transparent film base.

Among the various innovations in motion picture devices were William Friese-Greene's 1889 Machine Camera; Thomas A. Edison's 1899 Kinetoscope; Charles Frances Jenkins' Phantascope in 1894; the Cinematographe of Auguste and Louis Lumiere in 1895; the Vitascope, also made by Charles Frances Jenkins, but introduced in the name of Thomas A. Edison in 1896; Robert William Paul's Animatograph in 1895; and the 1894 Bioskope, made by Max and Ernst Skladanowsky. A related invention, Demeny's 1891 Phonoscope, was an early application of motion picture technology designed to teach lip reading to the hearing impaired.

Many other new motion picture devices were produced during the last decade of the 19th Century. Some were the result of original, innovative effort,

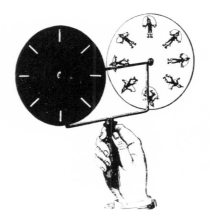

Plateau Phenakistoscope, 1832, Belgium.

The Lumiere Cinematographe, 1896.

others evident copies and imitations. Competition was intense and bitter, and accompanied by frequent accusations of piracy by rival inventors. For the medium at large, it was an undeniably fruitful period. In an 1898 survey, Charles Frances Jenkins reported at least 175 various motion picture devices, including cameras, projectors and dual-purpose mechanisms which could serve as either.

Lumiere Projector, 1896.

Interior of Edison's Kinetoscope, 1891.

The Great Motion Picture Shows in Japan. 1897.

Two Cinematographes, devices which were both motion picture cameras and projectors, made by the Lumiere brothers in France in 1895, were imported into Japan in late 1896. One was brought in by Katsutaro Inahata, a Kyoto businessman, and the other was purchased from an Italian by Yoshizawa Shokai, a firm in Shinbashi, Tokyo.

Similarly, two of Jenkins and Edison's Vitascopes were introduced into Japan concurrently. Both were purchased from the United States, one by Arai Shokai, a firm in Kobayashi, Tokyo, and the other by Waichi Araki, an Osaka retailer of Western goods.

Japan's first motion picture shows began in February 1897, using those four projectors in five theaters: the Kabukiza, Asakusa Hanayashiki, Yokohama Minato-za, Kanda Kinki-kan and Kawakami-za, all in the Tokyo-Yokohama area. Posters advertising the showing read: "New Invention by Dr. Edison of the United States. Electrically Operated Grand Kinematography (originally the Vitascope). Admission: 50 sen first-class seats, 30 sen second-class seats, and 20 sen third class." Billboard posters of other motion picture exhibitions used similar wording.

In late September 1887, Konishi Honten imported a set consisting of a motion-picture camera and a projector, the first of its kind in Japan. The equipment, made by Baxter in Britain, was used by Shiro Asano of Konishi Honten to make the first Japanese motion pictures.

Projector, ca. 1900.

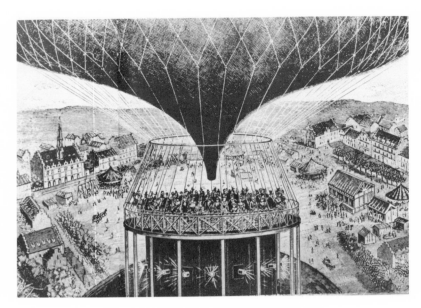

Grimoin Sanson's Cineorama at the Paris Exposition, 1900.

The Cineorama, a system of motion pictures taken by 10 cameras operated by three engineers.

The 20th Century. The Paris World's Fair. 1900.

In 1900, the World Exposition in Paris was an international display of photography, electricity, and modern travel. New cameras were shown by Carpentier of Paris, Lancaster & Son, Birmingham, England, and Rochester Optical of the United States. Motion pictures, by then in their fourth year, were used extensively at the exposition site.

The Lumieres, inventors of the first motion-picture projector, used an astonishingly large 25 x 18 meter screen. Raoul Grimoin-Sanson introduced the Cineorama, a 360 degree projection using ten projectors. Spectators were seated in the center of the theater, ostensibly to replicate the view from the balloon gondola on which the ten cameras had been mounted. Although the concept was well received, heat from the projectors became so intense the projectionists passed out, and the Paris Police, concerned about the possibility of a fire, closed the theatre.

The Mareorama used projection, sound, and rolling and swaying motions to enhance sensation, and the show included two productions of unprecedented grandeur and scale, "Siberian Transcontinental Railway Trip" and "Cruising the Mediterranean".

The Paris Exposition, held at the height of the Art Nouveau era's popularity, included a number of mahogany and teakwood view cameras. Asanuma Shokai exhibited an exotic, lightweight camera made of paulownia wood, which won a second place, silver cup. While Japan was a relatively unknown and small Far Eastern country, its victory over China in the Sino-Japanese War had brought it recent Western attention. At the Paris Exposition, Japan's interest in photography was made evident, and European manufacturers began to concern themselves with Japan as an export market.

Originally, European and American wet plate cameras were imitated quite closely by Japanese cabinet makers. But after the 1885 introduction of hand cameras, Western products displayed advanced designs, new fabrication processes, and precision machined components. The handcrafted, wooden Marion Field Camera was redesigned and manufactured with new metal precision parts for its rack and pinion, hinges, and trim. Machined components significantly improved the camera, and Japanese camera manufacturers immediately began to imitate the Marion.

No. 1 Folding Pocket Kodak, 1898.

Dry Plate Cameras and Roll Film.

Box cameras which loaded magazines of dry plates were quite popular in Japan, because of the improved quality of the plates, and because each magazine made a group of exposures.

In much the same way magazine cameras superceded single plate holders, roll film would eventually overshadow dry plate magazines. The 1898 Folding Pocket Kodak, and the larger, No. 1 Folding Pocket Kodak introduced in 1899, were the first mass-market, folding roll film cameras. The slim, leather-covered aluminum cameras were lighter, more compact, and more convenient to use than the magazine plate cameras they ultimately replaced.

At the turn of the century in Japan, very different standards were being defined for handmade view cameras for professionals, and for mass-produced hand cameras for amateurs. Issues of quality and application had become clear enough that two separate camera industries were beginning to operate side by side in Japan: one serving the commercial and professional market, one the amateur and hobbyist.

Around 1901, both the small distributors of cameras and the major importers such as Konishi Honten and Asanuma Shokai, began to import a wide range of general photographic equipment. The overall market expanded substantially as a series of new cameras and sensitized materials were imported from England, France, the U.S. and Germany.

As the market for photographic equipment grew, Ueda Camera Store in Osaka, Hakushin-do in Tokyo, Sone Shunsui-do and smaller stores such as Tokyo Photo Studio, Shinshin-do, and Naito Shoten began to market box cameras for commercial photographic studios. The cameras were made to order by an increasing number of local workshops, some of which were subsidized by the retailers. Konishi Honten built its supplier and subcontractor network by providing them with both working capital and operational financial assistance.

Popular Cameras. 1901 to 1903.

The first amateur cameras were the varnished wooden box cameras of the 1890s. These cameras, their use sustained largely by the general public, improved only gradually until the turn of the century, when popular interest in photography began to grow. The most popular cameras were no longer mere toys. They had come to be regarded as educational equipment and miniature scientific models. When the Ministry of Education introduced photography and motion pictures into the classroom, these simple cameras came into widespread use.

When the Ueda Camera Store introduced the Britannia No. O in Japan in 1901, the advertisement read: "This camera is the lowest-priced, complete camera. It is aimed at the popularization of photography. It is an extremely effective educational instrument and is most suitable as a gift." The price was 50 sen for the camera, 50 sen for the accessories. The Number 0 format, which was a quarter of the Tefuda format, was also known as the Sweet format.

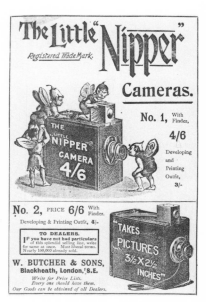

Nippon Camera for children, Asanuma Shokai, 1902   *Ad for the Little Nipper, British Journal Almanac, 1902.*

The Little Nipper camera, an Atom format, dry plate box camera with a drop-plate magazine, was made by W. Butcher and Sons in the U.K. It was first imported in 1901 by the Ueda Camera Store, where it was sold under the name VVV. In 1902, it was imported by Asanuma Shokai, where it was sold as the Nippon Camera for Children.

In 1902, Ginza Hakushindo camera store introduced a domestic box camera called the Saar Hand Camera No. 3, later marketed by Tokyo Photo Studio as the King Camera. In 1907, Tokyo Photo Studio introduced the Sun Camera in both Meishi and Tefuda formats. It is unclear whether these were actually imported Little Nipper cameras, or extremely close copies made in Japan. The origins and identification of a number of cameras in use in Japan between 1901 and 1907 are equally unclear.

In general, quality Japanese cameras and imported cameras were sold by Kohishi Honten and Asanuma Shokai, while popular and educational cameras were sold by the smaller stores. But in response to a growing public interest in photography, the two major stores soon began to manufacture and sell popular cameras.

Cherry Portable Camera.

The Cherry Portable Hand Camera. 1903 to 1907.

In September 1903, Konishi Honten introduced an "educational photographic device," a Meishi size camera called the Cherry Portable. An advertisement for this two yen amateur camera, manufactured at the subsidiary Kubo factory, said: "We have produced a low cost camera by eliminating decorative features otherwise unnecessary in the function of the camera since the more elaborate, completely equipped cameras are costly and not appropriate for teaching children. Our camera is thus aimed at the expansion of education and is entirely different from mere toy cameras."

The Cherry, the first Konishi Honten hand camera, was identical to the Little Nipper. It had a large reflex finder on the top, called the viewing mirror, similar to the optional viewfinder of the Brownie box camera, the one-dollar Kodak camera introduced in the U.S. in 1900.

Three months after the introduction of the first model, a larger, Tefuda format Cherry Portable was introduced. It had a vertical and horizontal viewfinder, and an unusual rotating aperture plate on the front of the camera. Its design was heavily influenced by the 1898 German Krugener Teddy camera.

(left) Aperture plate of the Krugener Teddy, Germany.

(right) Tefuda Format Cherry Portable Camera.

The Meishi format Cherry Portable proved to be short-lived. Some historians believe that Meishi format contact prints were too small to serve as prints, so the Tefuda format was quickly introduced as a replacement. Others believe that because the cameras were only three months apart, Konishi had already designed and begun production of the larger camera before the problem became evident. In any case, Konishi Honten made no more Meishi cameras until the 1911 Minimum Idea in 1911.

Champion Portable.   *Sakura Binocular Prano.*

Both Cherry Portable cameras were drop-plate box cameras, their internal mechanisms similar to A. C. Jackson cameras from the U.K. Among the Jackson cameras imported into Japan were the Champion Portable, introduced in January, 1904, and the June, 1905, Navy Portable.

Konishi Honten introduced the Sakura Army Portable in August 1907. It was the last of that style of box camera — the design was giving way to folding cameras — and at 35 yen it was Konishi Honten's most expensive. Another Sakura camera was introduced in the same year, the Binocular Prano, a stereo camera which used two dry plates for each exposure.

The Sakura Pocket Prano Portable was one of two Sakura cameras copied from the Rochester Optical Pocket Premo C.

Early Rokuosha Portable Cameras. 1906 to 1908.

Japan underwent an economic resurgence after victory in the Russo-Japanese War of 1904-1905. Konishi Honten had established the Rokuosha subsidiary in 1902 in Yodobashi, Tokyo, to manufacture high quality, low cost photosensitive materials. After the war, in 1906, a modern factory was established on the Rokuosha site. Under the direction of Toshinosuke Hasegawa, an engineer, camera manufacturing began there and in several subsidiary factories in the Tokyo area. Over the next thirteen years, all of those plants were gradually absorbed into the Rokuosha facility.

In July, 1906, the first Rokuosha camera was introduced. The 26-yen Sakura Brand Portable was a copy of the Rochester Optical Pocket Premo C. In October, 1907, a 15-yen version was introduced as the Sakura Pocket Prano Portable. Both were made of wood, covered with leather, and had guiderails on which the lensboard slid for focusing.

The Sakura Owner Portable, a copy of the Newman & Guardia Special Patern-B.

The Sakura Owner Portable, a direct copy of the British Newman wooden box camera, was introduced in January, 1907. It had a black, light tight bag attached to the camera body for changing plates in daylight. The Owner Portable was supplied in the Cabinet and Two Plate formats. The Sakura Reflex Prano, the first Japanese-made large format SLR camera, was introduced in April, 1907. The 4 x 5 inch format reflex camera, a copy of the Rochester Optical Premo Reflecting Camera, had a folding focusing hood and a focal plane shutter with speeds of 1/65 to 1/1200 sec.

In January, 1908, the Sakura Prano Portable was introduced. It was a copy of the Rochester Optical Pony Premo, with rack-and-pinion focus. A total of four

The Sakura Prano Portable and the Rochester Optical Pony Premo, from which it was copied.

cabinet and 4 x 5 inch format Prano cameras were introduced in January, 1908, including the Sakura Prano Improved, and the Sakura Noble Portable, a high-quality hand camera.

The Sakura Owner and Reflex Prano were unusual among Konishi Honten cameras, and so closely resembled the Western originals there is some question whether they were really Japanese copies, or whether they were imported cameras sold under the Sakura name. Similarly unclear are the records of two other cameras which closely resembled imports: the Mizu Portable, introduced in September, 1907, and the Palace Portable, June, 1908.

Independent Design. 1909.

Idea Tele-Photo.

The Sakura Prano was renamed the Idea in February, 1909. The name Prano was from Rochester Optical's Premo, while Idea was from Huttig's Ideal cameras. The Idea Telephoto, introduced in April, 1909, was designed to specifications of the Balloon Research Group of the Imperial Japanese Army. The premise of the camera was taken from the Zeiss Magnar Telephoto, and its bellows extension section was copied from the Press Graflex. The camera was equipped with both a frame finder and a Newtonian finder.

The Idea Telephoto was unique in many respects, and it is generally regarded as the first Japanese-made camera with significant elements of original design.

Minimum Idea.

Photographs taken with Minimum Idea cameras.

Mass Production. 1911 to 1919.

In 1911, the last year of Meiji, roll-film and miniature cameras were popular in the West. A growing popular interest in photography had been stimulated by newly invented cameras and photosensitive materials, and the introduction of mass production techniques was making cameras, lenses and precision components more reliable and less expensive.

The Japanese camera industry was behind U.S. and European manufacturers in developing mass production techniques. It took more than eight years for

Konishi Honten, the industry leader, to introduce contemporary mass production techniques into their manufacturing. In 1919, the reorganization of Rokuosha and its subsidiaries was completed, and firms such as Nippon Kogaku, Asahi Optical and Takachihi Seisakusho were founded.

In 1911, at the beginning of this period of development, Konishi Honten introduced two cameras made possible by new manufacturing techniques, the Minimum Pearl and the Minimum Idea. The Minimum Pearl was a smaller, improved version of the 1909 Pearl Portable. The Minimum Idea was a Meishi format camera, with metal struts copied from the No. 1 Folding Pocket Kodak camera, a pop-out front lensboard, and a shutter mechanism, copied from the No. 3 Folding Pocket Kodak. Although in part imitative, there were also novel and ingenious aspects to the Minimum Idea, which proved quite successful.

From the 1903 Cherry Portable to the 1911 Minimum Idea, the changes in Konishi Hointen cameras in many ways represented the evolutionary changes taking place in the Japanese camera industry. In the upcoming Taisho Era, new developments were to come at a more rapid and interesting pace, as the photographic products industry moved from workshops into modern factories. Meiji, from 1868 to 1911, was a bridge between the dawn of photography in Japan, at the end of the Tokugawa dynasty, and the growth of photography into a popular enterprise during the modernization of Japan in Taisho, between 1912 and 1925.

No. 3 Folding Pocket Kodak, Minimum Idea, No. 1 Folding Pocket Kodak.

Chapter Three

Made in Japan

from an article by Hachiro Suzuki

The Taisho Era. 1911 to 1925.

Japanese Expeditionary Force in Siberia. Soldiers sawing a pig carcass in -50 degree weather.

T he Taisho Era was a brief, significant 15 year transition between the 45 years of Meiji and the 62 years of Showa, which ended in 1988. In the third year of Taisho, when World War I began in 1914, imports of both raw materials and industrial products from Europe, particularly Germany, stopped immediately. Japanese industries were forced to develop their own resources, Japan's exports increased, and as a chronic trade deficit was transformed into a surplus, Japan developed from a debtor to a creditor nation.

Japan's economic growth during Taisho provided a fragile prosperity; as a nouveau riche class began to speculate in commodities, the price of staple goods rose sharply. The result was the Rice Riots, in which a public outcry against rising prices became public protest. They were followed by the 1923 Tokyo Earthquake, an economic depression, and a period of severe unemployment.

During the Taisho Era, a growing public awareness of democratic ideals brought about an egalitarianism which differed greatly from the perceptions of the Meiji Era. "Taisho Era Democracy" mixed new notions of freedom, individuality, and equality with a contemporary popular culture and a developing consumer economy. Attendance at music halls and motion picture theaters rose to record levels, and the motion picture, the automobile and the coffee house became symbols of the era.

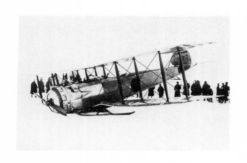

Sopwith military plane with ski landing gear. Japanese Expeditionary Force in Siberia, 1918-1922.

Between 1918 and 1923, a Japanese Expeditionary Force was dispatched to Siberia at enormous expense, and with heavy casualties. Stark, dramatic photographs captured the public attention and provided an intensely visual awareness of tragic events that was new in Japan. Recorded photographically, the Nikolaevsk massacre and Japan's first May Day, in 1920, were part of the complex pattern of light and dark years, of fortune and misfortune, by which the Taisho era is remembered.

The 15 years of Taisho were above all an irreversible beginning of mass consumerism in Japan. The design and character of products introduced during Taisho reflect the country's growing industrialization, as machine-made goods began to appear in a wide range of markets. Photography was becoming a public pastime as well as a professionally practiced graphic art, dry plate cameras were being replaced by easier, more convenient roll film models, and camera production was shifting from small workshops to large factories.

Hand Cameras.

By the latter part of the Meiji Era, the Japanese were manufacturing handcrafted wooden view cameras and studio cameras. Hand camera production had just begun, and would mature by the beginning of Showa in 1926. The distinction between the hand camera, meaning one which is portable and hand operated, and the tripod-mounted view camera, is less exact than the terms suggest. Hand cameras had folding bellows, hinged front covers and a rail on which the lens board and bellows were extended. While the most popular hand cameras used the 65 x 90 mm Dai Meishi format dry plate, by the end of Taisho a number had been made in the larger Tefuda format.

Most domestic cameras were manufactured by Konishi Honten. The Idea hand cameras, with leather covered wooden bodies, came in four different models: A, B, Snap, and 1. They were copies of the Kodak Pony Premo and Premoette cameras. The Idea A had double extension bellows, the B, single, and both were available in Dai Meishi or Tefuda formats. Idea A came equipped with a Trinar f/6.3, a Voltas f/8.0, a Deltas f/6.8 or a Velostigmat f/4.5 on the Dai Meishi format; and a Deltas f/6.8 or Velostigmat f/6.3 on the Tefuda. The Idea B came with a meniscus lens for the Dai Meishi size, and either a meniscus or a Deltas f/6.8 on the Tefuda. The Dai Meishi format Idea Snap, designed for the general public, had a meniscus lens and sold for eight yen.

The Idea No. 1, a new model with a metal lensboard, was sold in both formats, at prices ranging from 33 to 70 yen. The No. 1 was sold either with U.S. lenses: the Voltas f/8, Deltas f/6.8, or Velostigmat Series IV f/6.3 with Woco, Deltas, Victo, or Grammax shutters; or with a German lens, the Trinar f/6.3, in a Prontor shutter.

Idea Snap.

Lily II.

There were three models of the Lily, Konishi Honten's leading hand camera: the Lily II, the Neat Lily, and the Special Lily. The Lily II, patterned after the Voigtlander Alpin, had an unusual horizontal, side opening construction, double extension bellows and rack and pinion focusing. It was the first Japanese camera to have rise and cross front movements, and a Newtonian direct view-finder built into the camera body. In the Dai Meishi format, it was equipped with the Voltas f/8, Deltas f/6.8, or Velostigmat Series IV f/6.8 lens mounted in a Victo or Betas shutter; the Tefuda format came with a Voltas f/8.0, Velostigmat Series II f/4.5 or Velostigmat Series IV f/6.3 mounted in an Optima shutter. The f/4.5 model cost 90 yen. One version, which opened vertically, was strongly reminiscent of the German Bergheil Voigtlander and Maximar Ica cameras.

The Tefuda format Neat Lily was marketed in 1923 with any of the Wollensak lens/shutter combinations available on the Model II, and a large selection of European lenses, including Cooke, Eurynar, Dynar, and Tessar, mounted in Compur shutters. Two of the most popular lenses were functional opposites: the soft focus Verito, and the famously sharp Zeiss Tessar.

The Special Lily was an upgraded version of the Lily II. Introduced in 1919, it was supplied with most of the same European lenses in Compur shutters. With a Heliar lens it sold for 185 yen; a similarly equipped Voigtlander Alpin cost 250 yen. The Special Lily was also available in Dai Meishi format.

The Lily camera used a rack and pinion to extend the bellows and lensboard for focusing. Although gear cutting machines were not yet available in Japan, the gears Konishi Honten machinists made on lathes were quite precise. Similarly, Konishi Honten's Noble was a sophisticated Cabinet format hand camera supplied with Carl Zeiss lenses mounted in Compound shutters, or Bausch & Lomb lenses mounted in the Automatic shutter.

A Japanese Camera Exported to the U. K. 1916.

The 1916 Konishi Honten catalogue refers to a large order from Britain for Lily II cameras. Because of the War, Britain had little remaining capacity to produce cameras. For the first time, Japan began to export cameras, ironically, to the country that, for decades, had exported highly regarded, and frequently copied, cameras and lenses to Japan.

Asanuma Shokai, Konishi Honten's leading rival, concentrated on the manufacture of studio and view cameras. The only hand cameras in the 1915 catalogue were the Eagle series, produced in the Meishi, Tefuda, Postcard and 4 x 5 formats. Among the Tefuda format Eagle cameras were the popular models A, which sold for 9 yen 50 sen; B, 12 yen; and C, 18 yen. The body was also supplied without a lens.

Domestic Cameras, Imported Lenses.

The Compur shutter was introduced in Germany in 1912 by Friedrich Deckel. Except for a small number of high quality focal plane shutters with speeds of $^1/_{500}$ or $^1/_{1000}$, Japanese shutters at the time were simple Time, Bulb, Instant mechanisms.

Through Taisho, Japanese cameras were sold with imported lenses. Japanese production of lenses began with the 1931 Rokuosha Hexar (made with optical glass imported from Jena, Germany), and the first sophisticated shutter of its kind in Japan was the 1932 Lidex, made by Molta Ltd.

An advertisement for the Konishi Honten Idea camera, which was awarded a gold metal at the Anglo-Japanese Exhibition, addressed the issue: "This camera is based on the Pony Premo of Rochester, on which improvements have been made, and for this camera, selected imported lenses as well as the finest material have been used. This the most exquisite, sturdy, and handsome portable camera, is better than foreign cameras on many points as well as being much lower in price, which eliminates the need to purchase expensive imported cameras. It is extremely deplorable that Japanese have a tendency to worship foreign products and belittle domestic goods. This Idea Camera is superior to imported cameras and will certainly satisfy the needs of discriminating photographers, so we urge you to give it a try."

In the booklet *Introduction to Photography*, published by Ueda Camera Store, the section on Star and Idea Portable cameras includes similar assertions: "These cameras are inexpensive, ingenious and well built portable models which incorporate essential features of foreign models and are manufactured by the most skillful craftsmen in eastern Japan. Due to the tariff structure, imported cameras have been subject to high customs duties. This may be taken as a trade measure to protect and encourage domestic manufacture of cameras to copy good foreign designs and import only the lenses and shutters, which were not yet domestically manufactured...and to produce a Japanese-made camera with imported lens and shutter. These cameras are in no sense inferior to foreign cameras and will be welcomed by amateur photographers in preference to the imported products."

The admission, in literature like this, that Japanese camera manufacturers were copying foreign camera bodies, and using foreign lenses and shutters, is less significant than the attempt to persuade the Japanese public that domestic cameras were not inferior. The Japanese felt imported products were likely to be better made, an impression the tariffs, by assuring the imports would cost more than domestic competition, appeared to confirm.

Imported Lenses and Shutters.

Most lenses were imported into Japan mounted in between-the-lens shutters. Even single meniscus and Rapid Rectilinear lenses had built-in shutters: the Konishiroku Pearlette, for example, was available with either a meniscus or an f/6.8 lens mounted in a Wollensak WOCO shutter.

Because there were no domestic lenses, a relatively large group of imported lenses were offered with Japanese and imported cameras. German lenses available in Japan at the time included Zeiss Tessar and Protar; Voigtlander Heliar, Colinear, and Dynar; Schneider Xenar, Angulon, Radionar; Rodenstock Trinar, Eurynar, Trioplan and Helioplan; Goerz Dagor and Dogmar; Ernemann Ernoplast and Ernotar; and Plaubel Anticomar and Aristostigmat.

American lenses included Wollensak Voltas, Deltas, Velostigmat and Verito; and Bausch and Lomb Tessar.

Lenses imported from the U. K. included Cooke; Dallmeyer Pentac, Soft Focus, Speedy, and Adon; and Ross Xpres, Homocentric, Tele Ross, and Telecentric. Tele Ross and Tele Adon lenses were used primarily on large format, single-lens reflex cameras.

French imported lenses included the Krauss Zeiss Tessar and Protar, and the Tirinar.

Medium priced cameras were generally fitted with f/6.3 to f/6.8 lenses. Better cameras were supplied with f/3.5 and f/4.5 optics, and some special purpose lenses were available with f/2.7 to f/2.9. maximum apertures.

There were a number of imported shutters available. The self-cocking Prontor shutters, including the Prontor, Vario, Koilos, Deltas, and Woco had speeds of $^1/_{25}$, $^1/_{50}$, $^1/_{100}$, B and T. The Grammax and Victo were the same, with an additional speed of $^1/_{10}$. Ibsor, Isbo and Betax shutters added speeds of 1, $^1/_2$, and $^1/_5$, and $^1/_{125}$ on some models. Dial Set Compur shutters, including Compur, Compound, and Optimo, had speeds of 1, $^1/_2$, $^1/_5$, $^1/_{10}$, $^1/_{25}$, $^1/_{50}$, $^1/_{100}$, $^1/_{250}$ (or $^1/_{300}$), B and T. The Optimo omitted $^1/_{10}$, and added $^1/_{200}$. Ibso, Compound, and Optimo shutters were pneumatic.

At the time, lenses and shutters were imported principally from Germany and the United States, somewhat fewer from the U. K. Wollensak was the most successful U. S. manufacturer in Japan, because of a distribution contract with Konishi Honten.

Popular Snapshot Cameras.

T he 1911 Minimum Idea camera, although it used dry plates, was designed to take snapshots. A copy of the No. 0 and No. 1 Folding Pocket Kodak cameras, it sold at a popular price and became quite successful in the Taisho Era.

The Minimum Idea Study Society was formed in 1912, for owners of the camera who wished to hold study and picture taking sessions. While it was unusual for such an organization to be formed around a product, it is an indication of the enthusiasm of the new amateur photographers.

No. 1 Brownie.

Konishi Honten began to publish *Hobby of Photography* magazine in 1917, and Minimum Idea camera owners were able to exchange ideas and photographs through the magazine.

In 1918, a Japanese one-minute tintype camera, the Flex, was introduced by the FMP Society Company.

In February, 1900, Eastman Kodak introduced the cardboard Brownie box camera. It sold for one dollar, and was intended primarily for children. While it was manufactured by Frank Brownell, as all of Eastman's cameras were at the time, the name Brownie came from the small, elfin figures drawn by Palmer Cox for a series of popular children's books. Cox's figures appeared in the original advertising for the cameras, and decorated the first packaging. The Brownie became increasingly popular, developed a broad commercial appeal beyond young people, and was followed by more than 70 Brownie cameras of various types and sizes over the next 70 years.

Initially, there were several Brownies, including the No. 2 Folding Pocket Brownie (model B), No. 0 Brownie, and the No. 3A folding Brownie. The No. 2 was 6 x 9 cm. on 120 film, the No.0 was 40 x 65 mm. format on 127 film. In Japan, 120 film was called Brownie film and 127 was called Vest film.

In the later Meiji and early Taisho eras, merchants imitated Kodak's marketing strategy by producing and selling box cameras for beginners as children's or educational cameras. Ueda Camera Store introduced the Star Nipper in 1914 for 1 yen 50 sen, expecting to sell 10,000 per year to elementary school children. The camera was an exact copy of the Little Nipper produced by W. Butcher & Sons in the U. K., and the marketing strategy was exactly that of Kodak's one-dollar Brownie.

In 1918, Sone Shunsui-do introduced the Adam camera, which sold for one yen, or was given away with the purchase of a group of accessories. Like the Brownie, the cardboard Adam had no viewfinder. The Adam and Star Nipper one yen cameras were of no particular technical merit, but were significant in popularizing photography among the general public.

Many people, as they became more acquainted with photography, grew dissatisfied with the yen cameras with which they began, and bought more sophisticated products. Frequently, their next step was the Sweet camera.

The Sweet Camera for Beginners. 1918.

The Sweet camera, introduced by Sone Shunsui-do in 1918, was designed for beginners. It resembled a standard hand camera, was simple to operate and was supplied with a meniscus lens with Time and Instant shutter speeds. The Sweet camera was reasonably priced at eight yen, produced excellent pictures, and became quite popular.

The Sweet format was also called the No. 0. The 1901 Ueda Camera Store catalogue offered two imported cameras, the Britannia No. 0, and the 1896 Pocket Kodak, in the same format. The Sweet format (1 $^5/_8$ x 2 $^1/_8$) is one-fourth of the Japanese Tefuda, Anglo-American Wallet format (3 $^1/_4$ x 4 $^1/_4$). The Atom format (45 x 60 mm.) is one-fourth of the Continental wallet size (90 x 120 mm.).

The Togos were roll film, yen cameras of the 1930s. Earlier yen cameras, the Adam and Star Nipper, used dry plates because during Taisho, the Japanese photographic industry was not able to make or store roll films successfully in the Japanese climate. Because of the heat and humidity problems with roll films in Japan, a number of popular cameras, including the Minimum Idea and the Koroku, were copies of newer, roll film designs modified back to use the earlier, dry plate format.

Sweet.

Ueda Camera Store and Sone Shunsui-Do.

There were two major camera stores in Tokyo, Konishi Honten and Asanuma Shokai, and two in Osaka, Kuwata Shokai and Ueda Camera Store.

Ueda introduced a number of cameras with the Star name and insignia, including the Star Poco, a popularly priced Tefuda format camera; the Star, a higher priced Tefuda camera that closely resembled the Goerz Manufoc Tenax; a postcard sized camera that competed with Konishi Honten's Noble; and a high-quality, 5 in x 7 in. hand camera. Ueda also made the Starette, an exact copy of the British Ensignette, and snapshot and detective cameras. Ads for Ueda's Memo Book detective camera read: "Folded, it looks like a book with golden lettering engraved on the all leather cover. Opened, it becomes a bellows camera with a vertical/horizontal finder and a Time and Instant shutter..." The lens was built into the Ueda Camera Store star insignia on the cover.

Ueda Radio camera, also called the Ueda Star Watch Camera.

The Ueda Radio Camera was a copy of the Lancaster Watch Camera. Shaped like a pocket watch, the front cover opened when the winding stem was pushed. It had a T. & I. shutter, and made 3 cm. circular negatives for which a special developing tank and an enlarger were available. The camera was 5.3 cm. in diameter and 1.3 cm. thick, and sold for eight yen in silver plate, nine yen in brushed silver plate, and twenty yen in sterling silver.

Ueda Camera Store began publishing *Shashin Yo-ho (Essence of Photography)* magazine in the Meiji Era, and subsequently published a number of books.

Sone Shunsui-do was founded in 1902 in the Kanda district of Tokyo to import, manufacture, and retail photographic equipment. The Adam and Sweet were influential examples of the new, inexpensive, amateur cameras. In 1923, Sone Shunsui-do manufactured the Secrette, a copy of the German Contessa-Nettel camera. The Secrette was designed to resemble a monocular telescope, and actually made pictures at right angles to the apparent direction the instrument was pointed. It was a No. 0, Sweet format camera with a meniscus lens, and sold for 24 yen, while the deluxe, Special Secrette was Atom format, and supplied with an f/4.5 Testar lens. Secrette cameras were popular, as was the Tokio-scope, Sone Shunsui-do's copy of the French Glyphoscope stereoscopic camera. The Tokio-scope used conventional dry plates rather than the thin plates required for many stereo cameras, and it also served as a stereo viewer for its 45 x 107 mm. format.

Sone Shunsui-do cameras were ingenious mechanisms which appealed to amateurs, and the owner of the company frequently went to the store to meet customers and give technical advice. Sone Shunsui-do, Kuwata Shokai and Ueda Camera Store were the prime movers of amateur photography in Japan from the late Meiji to the Taisho Era.

Secrette.

World War I. 1914 to 1918.

When Japan declared war on Germany in August of 1914, and the import of German goods halted, there were immediate and severe commercial consequences. Pharmaceuticals and chemicals, even ordinary drugs and products such as aspirin, phenol and salicylic acid were not yet produced in Japan. By September, the Japanese government, seriously concerned, had established a chemical industry committee within the Ministry of Agriculture and Commerce. Under the direction of that committee, various research and technical agencies were started to manufacture drugs, chemicals and dyes. Those agencies were the beginning of the chemical industry in Japan.

A similar situation developed for photography. While there were some stocks of German cameras and lenses, supplies of expendable German goods, photographic chemicals and flash powder, dwindled quickly. Even photographic products from the U. K., Japan's ally, became scarce because of the German submarine blockade.

The best film developing agents of the time were metol, hydroquinone, and pyrogallol, all made in Germany by Agfa, Merck, and Schelling. While these were replaced by Johnson and Marion developers from the U.K., Afga metol, especially, was hoarded and used only for the most important photographs.

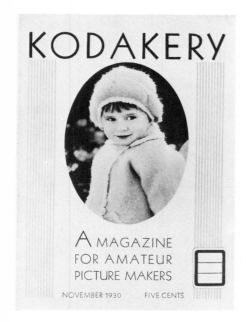

1930.

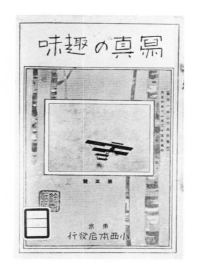

Hobby of Photography, *Konishi Honten, 1917.*

Japan was able to import from the U. S. during the war, and Japanese photographers began to use American products. Kodak roll film was considered among the best in the world, but American dry plates, particularly Eastman products, were thought to be inferior to comparable British products.

The conventional Japanese perceptions of photography were either academic or artistic, and in both cases concerned the activities of trained practitioners of the craft. The notion of photography as a casual activity for the enjoyment of the general public, clearly influenced by America, was new to Japan but somehow in keeping with the attitudes of Taisho. The magazine *Shashin no Shumi (Hobby of Photography)* began in 1917 as an exponent of the new amateur photography. It was a Japanese version of *Kodakery,* a magazine Eastman Kodak had published for many years.

Chapter Four

The Reappearance Of European Influence

from an article by Hachiro Suzuki

The Dawn of the Japanese Photographic Industry. 1919.

World War I created severe supply shortages which had a profound effect on Japanese industrial planning. Because Japan was determined to become less reliant on imported goods and materials, mass production techniques were being introduced into the country at the same time modern photographic and optical industries were being founded.

In 1919, Konishi Honten consolidated all of its subsidiaries into a single factory in the Yodobashi district of Tokyo. The enlarged Rokuosha plant produced all of Konishi Honten's photosensitive materials, cameras, and other photographic products. Initially, the staff consisted of traditional Japanese craftsmen, young graduate engineers and German ex-prisoners of war, who had been retained for their technical experience. Subsequent Konishi Honten cameras carried the factory name as the brand name Rokuosha.

Nippon Kogaku, now Nikon, was formed in 1917 to produce optical devices for the war effort. In 1919, Asahi Optical Company was established to manufacture ophthalmic and projection lenses, and Takachiho Seisakusho, now Olympus Optical Industries, began to produce microscopes. Tokyo Kikuchi established Oriental Photo Industry in 1919, and by 1922 marketed the first Japanese photographic paper under the trade names Orient, Peacock, and OK. In 1921, the Ministry of Agriculture and Commerce established the Osaka Industrial Research Institute to develop optical glass.

German Imports in the Late Taisho Era.

After World War I, the Japanese photographic market was well stocked with U. S. goods. Germany, burdened by wartime reparations and a significant devaluation of the Reichsmark, was trying to increase exports of its highly regarded cameras and lenses. A sudden influx of Voigtlander, Ernemann, Goerz, Contessa Nettel, and Carl Zeiss products in Japan further enlarged an already growing market for imported photographic equipment.

Ernemann Ermanox, Germany.

Goerz Pocket Tenax, Germany.

German lenses were particularly well regarded in Japan, and Voigtlander Heliar, Carl Zeiss Tessar, and Goerz Dagor lenses sold well. In 1924, Ernemann introduced the Ermanox, an Atom format folding camera supplied with Ludwig Bertele's revolutionary, wide aperture 100 mm. f/2.0 Ernostar lens. With the new, higher speed dry plates, the f/2.0 lens permitted the Ermanox to make photographs in quite low light levels, which contributed to new kinds of photojournalism.

During the 1920s in Japan, far more cameras were imported from Germany than from the U. K. or the U. S. Among the large format reflex cameras were the Miroflex, Mentor Folding Reflex, Ihagee Patent Folding Reflex, Ernoflex, Simplex, and Curt Bentzin Reflex. German hand and Klapp cameras included the Tenax, the Patent Etui, Plaubel Makina, Taxo, Maximar, Trona, Ideal, Sonnette, Onito, Donata, Heag, Bergheil, Avus, Alpen, Glunz, Curt Bentzin Primar, Thowe, Linhof, Ango, Nettel, New Klapp, and Palmos.

In addition to the Ermanox, other Atom format cameras included the Ica Bebe, Argus, Miniature Klapp, Minimum Palmos, Pocket Tenax, Ica Atom, Duchessa, Nettix, and Victorix. Among the German roll film cameras imported at the time were the Cocarette, the Icarette, Roll Tenax, Roll Tip, Piccolette, Luxus Piccolette, Bob, Unette, Bobette, and Box Tengor.

Ernemann Simplex, Germany.

British, American and French Cameras.

Among the large format reflex cameras imported from the U. K. were the Soho Reflex, Thornton Reflex, Ensign Folding Reflex, Pressman Reflex, Adams Reflex, Minex, and the Newman and Guardia Folding Reflex. British folding cameras included the Dallmeyer Speed, Panros, Ensign Focal and Thornton Focal Primer. Among British hand cameras were the Sinclair Una, Sanderson, Verto, and the Sibyl, while roll film imports included the Ensign Roll Film Reflex, Ensignette, and Cupid cameras.

British cameras were of excellent quality. While their fine hand craftsmanship had won a small group of Japanese admirers, their sales were far below those of the German cameras. British tropical cameras, hand crafted from teak or mahogany, with red or green leather bellows and gold-plated brass fittings, appealed to the Japanese more as art objects than cameras.

American imports at the time included Graflex and Auto Graflex single lens reflex cameras and Premo and Speed Kodak hand cameras. There were a number of roll film cameras, including the original, the Model B and the Series

Ensign Ensignette, U.K.

Newman & Guardia Sibyl, U.K.

Newman & Guardia Folding Reflex, U.K.

Pocket Kodak Series III.

III Vest Pocket Kodak cameras; the No. 2 Brownie, the Cartridge Premo, and the Numbers 1, 1A, 3 and 3A Special Kodak cameras; Series II and III Pocket Kodak cameras, the Numbers 1, 2 and 3 Ansco cameras, and the Ansco Speedex.

While French cameras were frequently novel designs, they were not as popular in Japan as German and British cameras. At the peak of their pre-War popularity, the Physiographe, Photo Jumelle, and the Gaumont were successfully imported from France. But after World War I, when roll film was becoming popular in Japan, the French continued to make plate cameras, which were of little interest in Japan. French Krauss Tessar and Protar lenses, although made under German patents, proved significantly inferior to German Zeiss Tessar and Protar lenses. There was also an Italian camera sold in Japan, the Murer Single Lens Reflex, which was marketed in both 6 x 9 cm. and Atom format. It appears the Italian camera was influenced more by the French than by German camera designs, and it sold accordingly.

Compact Graflex.

No. 1 Ansco, U.S.

Dual Format Cameras.

The first roll film was imported into Japan in 1894, but the material did not become regularly, or commercially available until 1901. The first Japanese cameras which accomodated roll film were dual format, and also took dry plates. One of the earliest of these transition cameras was the Sakura Palace Portable, a Tefuda format roll film/dry plate camera marketed in 1907 by Konishi Honten.

Konishi Honten introduced the name Pearl with the 1909 Pearl Portable, and used the name continuously until shortly after the Second World War. Many models of cameras were marketed under that name for almost half a century, making it one of the longest trademarks in the camera industry.

The 1909 Pearl Portable and Special Pearl cameras were also Tefuda format, roll film/dry plate cameras. They were exact copies of the No. 3 Folding Pocket Kodak cameras, which could be adapted to use plates. Cameras which used the two materials interchangeably either had two separate backs, or an integral plate holder.

The No. 3 and No. 4 models Pearl Portable were Tefuda format. The No. 3 Pearl was supplied with a Rapid Rectilinear mounted in a Simplex, while the No. 4 had a Zeiss Protar mounted in an Automatic, or a IIB Tessar mounted in a Compound shutter.

The Special Pearl, equipped with a folding direct viewfinder, came with a Deltas f/6.8 or a Velostigmat Series IV f/6.3 lens for the Tefuda camera, and a Velostigmat Series IV f/6.3 or f/7.5 for the postcard-format camera.

In 1923, Konishi Honten introduced the Pearl II, the first Japanese camera designed entirely to use roll film. The camera offered two formats on 120 film, 60 x 90 mm. and 45 x 60 mm. It was supplied with either a Wollensak Deltas f/6.8 or a Rodenstock Trinar f/6.3 lens.

Konishi Honten continued to make Pearl cameras for almost fifty years after the Portable, and the name became one of the longest continuous models of Japanese camera.

Pearl II.   *Advertisement for Vest Pocket Kodak.*

During the years of transition to roll film, Japanese photographers preferred to use domestic and imported dual format cameras. While roll film was lighter to carry than glass plates, and of course shatterproof, it was generally of inferior photographic quality, costly, and seemed at first difficult to process. And while it permitted photographers to more easily make pictures in rapid sequence, in the context of dry plates it was resisted by photographers who wanted to develop and print a picture after each exposure.

Vest Pocket Kokak, U.S.   *Contessa-Nettel Piccolette, Germany.*

The Popular Vest Pocket Kodak Camera. 1914.

Before World War I, the Vest Pocket Kodak was influential in popularizing roll film. Folded, the camera was 4 3/4 x 2 1/2 x 1″, small enough to fit into the pocket for which it was named. It made eight 40 x 65 mm. exposures on 127 film, which came to be called the Vest format in Japan, somewhat smaller than the 60 x 90 mm. negative on 120 film, which was called the Brownie format. After 1915, the Vest Pocket Autographic Kodak camera was fitted with a narrow opening through which the photographer could write with a steel pencil on the back side of the film. A sheet of carbon wound between the film and backing paper transferred the writing to the film.

The Vest Pocket Kodak was a considerable success, and soon after it appeared, a number of similar cameras were introduced in Germany. The most notable European vest camera was the Contessa Nettel Piccolette.

In Japan, the Vest Pocket Autographic was called *bestan*, from *bes*, which was used to mean Vest Pocket Kodak, and *tan*, from *tangyoku*, meaning single meniscus lens. The earlier model was called *tsurutan*, which means, literally, slippery body single meniscus lens, and the smooth, enamel bodied earlier camera is more valuable to Japanese camera collectors today than the Autographic.

Vest Pocket Kodaks were popular in Japan for decades. By removing a diaphragm which restricted the maximum aperture to f/11, the lens operated at an aperture equivalent to its physical size, and produced the very popular soft image for which it still remains desirable today. In 1914, the *Bestan* sold for 15 yen, and a roll of 8 exposure film, 50 sen. The 6-exposure Brownie film was 60 sen at the time. The low prices of the camera and film were partly responsible for the popularity of this camera.

The Korok Hand Camera, introduced in 1914, was a commercially unsuccessful plate camera copied after the Vest Pocket Kodak. Announced as an improved version of the Minimum Idea, it was actually less sturdy, and somewhat ungainly looking. The folding struts were copied from, but weaker than, those of the No. O folding Kodak, and the lightweight lensboard copied from the Vest Pocket Kodak appeared mismatched. The all-metal body was of some significance, and the name *Korok* is of some interest: it was coined from the name of the founder of Konishi Honten, *Konishi Rokuemon*, in imitation of Eastman's *Kodak*.

While the Korok, with its 57 x 83 mm. plate format, was no improvement over the Minimum Idea it was designed to replace, that attempt to redesign the Vest Pocket Kodak led to the Pearlette. Introduced by Konishi Honten in 1925, the year Leitz introduced the model A Leica in Germany, the Pearlette was the first metal Japanese roll film camera, and it was very successful.

Korok hand camera.

Pearlette, the Best Selling Camera in Pre-War Japan. 1925.

The Pearlette was Japan's first vest format roll film camera, as it was Japan's first mass-produced camera. It incorporated popular features of both the Vest Pocket Kodak and the Contessa Nettel Piccolette. Over the years, the Pearlette evolved through innovations and improvements until the Japanese considered the camera to have been reborn as an original Japanese design. The Pearlette league was formed, and remained active for many years; and the Pearlette was the first camera for many Japanese photographers who began in early Showa.

The outstanding attribute of the camera was its metal body, the first camera body to be mass produced in Japan. Rokuosha, a pioneer Japanese manufacturer, began by producing 200 to 300 a month. By the time World War II broke out, it was the best selling camera in Japan. The Pearlette originally sold for 17 yen with a meniscus lens, 25 yen with an f/6.8 Deltas, both in a Woco shutter. The lens and shutter were imported from Wollensak in the United States.

Pearlette.

A Quality Single Lens Reflex Plate Camera. 1926.

In 1926, the last year of Taisho, Konishi Honten introduced a copy of the Ernemann Unette camera called the Record. Designed for beginners, it used paper-backed, unperforated 35 mm. film. Its early commercial failure was due largely to the small negative, and the unusual film it required. Several new models of plate cameras were introduced, even though the industry was converting to roll film. Konishi Honten also introduced the Neat Reflex, a Tefuda format camera, and the Idea Spring, a Cabinet format camera almost identical to the German Goerz Ango.

The Ango was a classic camera supplied in Cabinet, Dai Meishi and Tefuda formats. The body was made of wood covered in black leather, four arms supported the lensboard and connected it to the body, and focusing was done by a helicoid ring. The Ango was supplied with a choice of three Voigtlander lenses, an f/4.5 Heliar, f/6.3 Collinear, or f/5.5 Dynar. With a focal plane shutter with speeds from 1/10-1/2000 second plus T. & B., and a Goerz Dogmar f/4.5 lens, the Ango cost 285 yen, while an Idea Spring with Heliar f/4.5 lens cost 295

Record.

Idea Spring.

Speed Reflex.

yen. The higher price of the domestic camera reflected the reputation the Heilar lens enjoyed, and Konishi Honten's confidence in the camera.

Although Konishi Honten had introduced a reflex camera, the Sakura Plano, as early as 1907, their 1926 Neat Reflex was a copy of the English Soho Reflex, with double extension bellows and a revolving back. Two years after its introduction in Tefuda format, a Dai Meishi Neat was introduced in 1928. The Neat was supplied with Voigtlander optics, of which the f/3.5 Heliar was the most popular.

In 1919, Sone Shunsui-do and Sanei-do marketed the Speed Reflex. Manufactured by Kuribayashi Seisakusho (later Petri Camera Company), it resembled the British Thornton-Pickard Reflex, and sold without lens for 80 yen in Tefuda format, 75 yen in Dai Meishi. Among the imported lenses available for the Speed Reflex were the f/4.5 Ernoplast; f/4.5 Kengott; f/4.5 Xenar; and the f/4.5, 3.5 or 2.7 Tessar.

As Showa began in 1926, several Japanese large format single lens reflex cameras appeared on the market. These cameras, including the Leinflex, SYK Simplex, and the Hardflex, were fabricated in limited quantities and sold with imported lenses. There is some doubt as to the accuracy of published specifications for these cameras, which claimed maximum shutter speeds of 1/500 or even 1/1000 second.

Camera, *published by Ars, 1921.*

Amateur, *published by Kinseido, 1922.*

Photographic Publishing in Japan in the Early Taisho Era.

During Taisho (1912-1925), a number of photography books were published for amateurs, among them several notable how-to books by Katsumi Miyake.

Miyake was a noted painter infatuated with photography, who made frequent trips to Europe and brought back new technical information and new and rare cameras. One of his favorite cameras was the Contessa Nettel Argus, shaped like a monocular opera glass. Miyake's candid pictures, called sketch photographs, were quite popular among amateur photographers.

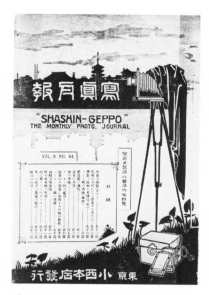

The Monthly Photo Journal, *published by Knoishi Honten.*

The Photographic News, *published by Asanuma Shokai.*

In *Shashin no Utsushikata (How to Take Pictures)*, published by ARS Publishing Company in 1916, Miyake explained photography in a straightforward manner for the amateur. While most contemporary books on photography were too academic for a general reader, Miyake's simply written, popular titles included *Shumi no Shashinjutsu (Photography as a Hobby)*, and in 1920, *Shashinjutsu Ko-shu-roku (Instructions on Photography)*, Volumes 1-4.

Katsuo Takakuwa, who edited Konishi Honten's magazine *Shashin no shumi (Hobby of Photography)*, wrote a book for Konishi Honten entitled *Film Shashinjutsu (Film Photography)*. ARS Publishing Company produced more than 100 editions of the book by 1926.

In April, 1924, Takakuwa founded *Camera* magazine, also published by ARS. The other two periodicals, *Shashin Shinpo (Photographic News)*, published by Asanuma Shokai, and *Shashin Geppo (Monthly Photographic Report)*, published by Konishi Hoten, were product magazines published by manufacturers for studio photographers and advanced amateurs. Camera was the country's first photography magazine, an innovative journal of photography printed on art paper, issued by a publishing firm and distributed throughout Japan by bookstores and newsstands. In 1926, the *Asahi Shimbun (Asahi Newspaper)*, began publication of *Asahi Camera* magazine. For many years, *Camera* and *Asahi Camera* were the standard Japanese photographic periodicals.

In 1922, two new periodicals addressed a renewed interest in artistic photography, *Geijustsu Shashin Kenkyu (Study of Art Photography)*, edited by Minoru Minami and published by ARS, and *Shashin Geijutsu (Photographic Art)*, by the publications division of Toshin Shoten. Shino Fukuhara, who had made a famous photograph of *Paris and the Seine*, stimulated a popular dialogue with a theory of the importance of light and gradation in photography.

In 1924, a year after the Tokyo earthquake, substantial import duties were levied on luxury items, including a 100 percent duty on photographic equipment. In 1925, Asahi Shimbun sponsored what they called a Centennial of Photography festival. In those years, photography became more popular in spite of the increasing cost, and Japanese photographers began organizing groups such as the All Kansai Photographic League in the Osaka area, and the All Kanto Photographic League in the Tokyo area.

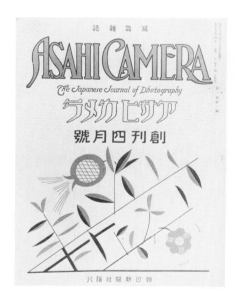

Asahi Camera *published by Asahi Shimbun, 1926.*

The Photo Journal, *1896. The first photography magazine in Japan.*

Chapter Five

Smaller, Lighter Cameras

from an article by Masao Tanaka and Hajimu Miyabe

The First Japanese Roll Film Cameras. 1928, 1929.

Kiku film box.

The Japanese photographic industry grew significantly during the first years of Showa, which began in 1926. Factories were modernized, new companies were formed, roll film finally began to replace dry plates, and new dry plate cameras began to appear in the smaller, Dai Meishi format. Japanese cameras were lighter, more compact and more versatile, and a new group of imported German cameras, the Leica, Ikonta and Rollei, were becoming influential in Japan.

In 1928, Kazuo Tashima founded the Nichi-Doku (Japanese-German) Camera Store, which is now Minolta. In the same year, Asahi Photo Industry Co. made the first Japanese roll film, Kiku, which was marketed through Omiya Photo Products. The following year, Konishi Honten introduced Sakura film.

The Rolleiflex Twin Lens Reflex. 1929.

Franke & Heidecke Rolleidoscop, Germany.

The Rolleiflex, made in Germany by Franke & Heidecke, was a profoundly important camera. It influenced the practice of professional photography in Europe and the U.S. as it began to replace cut film press cameras, and, in subsequent years, it was a highly influential design prototype for the Japanese camera industry.

In 1925, Franke and Heideke had made the Rolleidoscop, a reflex, roll film stereo camera. Horizontally configured, with the reflex viewing lens between the two taking lenses, it was both the best and most expensive stereo camera of its day. The Rolleiflex was a twin lens reflex developed out of a vertical reconfiguration of the stereo Rolleidoscop.

Having chosen the 6 x 6 cm. square format for the vertical twin lens reflex Rolleiflex, the designers of the first model were forced to use 117 rather than 120 film. The roll film advance protocol of the time was to watch for frame numbers on the paper backing, which appeared in a small, circular red window as the film was wound. The paper backing of 120 film was numbered only for the rectangular 6 x 9 cm. format; numbering for the square 6 x 6 cm. format was supplied only on 117 film, which had been introduced with the Brownie in 1900.

Franke & Heidecke Rolleiflex, Germany.   *Franke & Heidecke Rolleicord, Germany.*

The 1929 Rolleiflex used 117 film, and fared badly because of it. By 1930, distribution of 117 roll film was so limited that in most markets the Rolleiflex sold poorly, if at all. Although the elusive 117 roll film remained in production until 1949, the 117 Rolleiflex was such an obscure camera that Franke and Heidecke were faced with the choice of replacing it or going out of business.

In 1932, after three years, an improved Rolleiflex was introduced. It was a 6 x 6 cm. format, 120 roll film camera that is clearly the predecessor to the contemporary Rolleiflex. It had a Tessar 7.5 cm. f/3.5 taking lens and a Compur Rapid shutter. Most important, it had a crank operated, fixed-distance film advance coupled to a mechanical exposure counter. The second Rolleiflex was designed to correctly space exposures mechanically, which allowed the camera to use the ubiquitous 120 roll film. Shutter speed and aperture scales were visible as the photographer looked down into the screen, and the shutter release could be operated as the photographer looked into the viewfinder.

A less expensive camera, the Rolleicord, was introduced in 1933 and it, too, was extremely successful. After the United States, Japan was the second largest overseas market for Rolleiflex, and the influence of the Rolleiflex on the Japanese camera industry was comparable to that of the Leica. The first Japanese twin lens reflexes were the 1937 Minoltaflex and Princeflex, followed by the Lyraflex, Firstflex and Taroflex.

A number of other twin lens reflex cameras were imported into Japan, including the Zeiss Ikoflex; two folding twin lens reflex cameras, the Welta Perfekta and the Zeca-Flex; two focal plane shutter cameras, the Mentorett and Foth-Flex; and the Voigtlander Superb, which had an unusual parallax correction device.

Zeiss Ikon Ikoflex, Germany.

The Ikonta Folding Camera. 1929.

The German photographic industry enjoyed a period of significant growth in the early 1920s, but by the end of Japan's Taisho Era in 1925, markets had shrunk and the competition in them had increased. The Japanese, perceiving this situation from their unique perspective, characterized it as having "upset the supply and demand balance and heavy overproduction flooded the market with too many cameras causing suicidal competition."

As the markets became more resistant to their products, German manufacturers began to reorganize and consolidate. Carl Zeiss formed Zeiss Ikon by merging with four other manufacturers: Ica, Contess-Nettel, Goerz and Ernemann. The merger, and the increasing preference for roll film rather than dry plates, brought about a group of new camera designs. One of the most influential was the 1929 Ikonta; from that camera, Zeiss introduced a steady succession of Ikonta and Super Ikonta folding cameras with self-locking struts supporting the front lens standard behind a spring-loaded front cover. The configuration became the worldwide standard for folding roll film cameras, and Zeiss soon became the world's predominant camera manufacturer.

Zeiss Ikon Baby Ikonta, Germany.   Zeiss Ikon Ikonta, Germany.

Film Formats in Early Showa.

Camera manufacturers design new products around widely available film formats, for reasons made clear by the problems of the early Rolleiflex. The largest photographic companies, makers of both cameras and film, have been able to produce and market new films and cameras interdependently, among them the first Kodak camera, which was sold loaded with its own film and sent back to the factory to be re-loaded; Polaroid films, which self-develop when activated by mechanical elements in Polaroid cameras; and Kodak's ill-fated Disc cameras and film discs, a system many thought was designed for the convenience of the photofinishing industry.

While 120 and 127 remained the principal roll formats, from the 1895 introduction of the first Kodak roll film in Japan (the 1890 #1 Kodak camera was factory loaded) to the beginning of the Taisho Era in 1912, there were a total of 30 types of film marketed in Japan. Kodak marketed a substantial progression of film and camera formats.

Zeiss Ikon Super-Ikonta, Germany.

Carl Zeiss (1816-1888), ca. 1865.

Year	Film	Name	Format Size in inches
1895	101	#2 Bullet Camera	3.5 Dia.
1895	102	Pocket Kodak Camera	1.5 x 2
1898	105	#1 Folding Pocket Kodak	2.25 x 3.25
1899	116	#1A Folding Pocket Kodak	2.5 x 4.25
1900	117	#1 Brownie Camera	2.25 x 2.25
1900	118	#3 Folding Pocket Kodak	3.25 x 4.25
1901	120	#2 Brownie Camera	2.25 x 3.25
1903	122	#3A Folding Pocket Kodak	3.25 x 5.5
1904	123	#4 Screen Focus Kodak	4 x 5
1912	127	Vest Pocket Kodak	1.625 x 2.5
1916	130	#2C Autographic Kodak Jr.	2.875 x 4.875

By contrast, European camera manufacturers, especially the Germans, were careful in designing cameras for new film sizes. The 1920 Contessa-Nettel Piccolette and Goerx Roll Tenax used 127 roll film. The 1924 Rolleidoscop used both 127 and 120, and the 1929 Rolleiflex, which used 117 film, was soon replaced with a 120 format model. Folding cameras followed, almost all designed for 127 and 120 roll films, which became and remained the most widely used in Japan.

Leitz Leica A, Germany.

Leitz Leica B, Germany.

The Leica Camera. 1925.

In 1925, Ernst Leitz, a German microscope manufacturer, introduced the Leica. The small camera, which used 35 mm. perforated motion picture film to make still photographs, would completely change the practice of documentary photography, and eventually, the world photographic industry. But the Leica was initially unpopular in Japan because of the small format negative; it was widely believed that only larger negatives could produce sufficient resolution, clarity and depth of tone for a satisfactory photograph. The Japanese at first rejected 35 mm., a format entirely dominated by Japanese manufacturers in subsequent decades, and a presumptive allegiance to larger formats persists today in some sectors of Japanese photography.

The first Japanese advertisement for Leica, placed by Schmidt and Company, a Tokyo camera distributor, in the July, 1926, issue of *Asahi Camera* magazine shows a Leica A with a Leitz Anastigmat Elmax f/3.5 lens.

Super Olympic.

Successive Leicas were introduced as the model B, the model C and the 1932 model D with a coupled rangefinder. The Leica D began to take on what are now the recognizable characteristics of the high performance 35 mm. camera. In the same year, Zeiss introduced the Contax I to compete with the Leica D, and Krauss introduced the Peggy, which, unlike the focal-plane shutter Leica and Contax, was equipped with a shutter between the lens elements.

The first Japanese 35 mm. camera was the between-the-lens shutter Super Olympic, introduced in May of 1935 by its distributor, Asahi Bussan Co. In September of that year, Seiki Kogaku Kenkyusho, now Canon, introduced the Hansa Canon. The focal-plane shutter Hansa Canon, an improved version of the Kwanon prototype, was advertised at the time as the world's best camera.

Hansa Canon.   *Kwanon.*

The Japanese Photographic Industry. 1924 to 1931.

I n 1924, tariff rates on imported photographic products were doubled, to 100 percent. The Japanese photographic industry, at that time still largely importing and marketing foreign products, suffered significantly. Today, that policy is considered to have helped guide Japanese enterprise from the import of foreign goods to the manufacture of domestic products.

Japan's 1927 financial panic was caused by the amount of debt issued to finance recovery from the 1923 Tokyo earthquake. Japan's depression was compounded two years later by the world depression following the U. S. stock market crash. The Hamaguchi government's disastrous decision to remove the gold embargo, intended as a demonstration of confidence, further deepened the economic crisis. The Japanese photographic industry entered a prolonged period of poor sales and falling prices. It was not until fighting broke out in Manchuria in the autumn of 1931, when Japan increased military spending, again imposed a gold embargo and devalued the yen, that exports began to rise and the Japanese economy slowly began to grow again.

Advertisement for Kwanon Camera.

As the economy revived, amateur photography began to increase. Photography evolved from a hobby and a craft to a professionally practiced commercial art, used in news illustration, scientific, industrial and military applications. The expanding applications for professional and technical photography paralleled the modernization and industrialization of Japan.

Films were improved, with increased spectral sensitivity and increased film speed. New printing papers were designed to be easier to handle and process, and the use of dry plates was rapidly giving way to roll film. Growing public interest in photography enlarged the market for imported equipment, but in new segments: imports of high performance 35 mm. and roll-film cameras increased, especially among models of Leica, Contax, Peggy, Retina and Baldina. At the same time, less expensive European and American cameras were being replaced by domestic products. The principal imported film was 35 mm., but imports of packaged sensitized products declined as the components for manufacturing sensitized materials, including gelatin, film base and paper, were imported in greater quantities.

High tariff rates and the devaluation of the yen made imported photographic equipment expensive, and government and civil drives to encourage the purchase of Japanese goods resulted in tighter trade restrictions. The combination of tariffs and trade restrictions is credited in Japan with having stimulated the development of Japanese photographic manufacturing.

Tougo Cameras.

The Tougo Camera. 1930.

The Tougo was a yen camera, one of a group of one- and two-yen cameras sold to build public interest in photography. The Tougo, widely used in 1930, had a newly devised, paper frame negative holder with which the photographer could process the film in daylight by dipping the exposed negative, with the paper frame, into a red-colored developer. The Tougo became popular because of a series of public demonstrations conducted on the streets, and the yen cameras in general, sold between 1929 and 1933, were highly influential in introducing photography to young people.

The Touga was available in models A, B and C, selling for one, two and three yen respectively. Among many other one- to five-yen cameras sold between 1929 and 1933 were the Katei (Home), Asahi, Light, Lion and Baby Sports. The 1931 Sakura, Konishiroku Honten's yen camera, was a box camera sold in both the Vest and Brownie formats. Olympic Camera introduced the popular Olympic Baby and Olympic Junior cameras, and Kodak's low cost box cameras were prominent in the Japanese market.

Sakura Camera.

Dai Meishi Cameras of the Early Showa Era.

The 6.5 x 9 cm. Dai Meishi format hand camera flourished during the early Showa Era. From 1926 to 1931, it developed from a wooden to an all-metal body, and became smaller in size. Hand cameras of the time, fairly uniform in design, had double extension bellows on rack and pinion mechanisms and front rise and fall movements. Better domestic models also had horizontal movement, but only the better quality imported cameras offered

Olympic Junior.

shifts or swings. Basic Japanese hand cameras had no movements, and single extension bellows. Accessories were generally limited to three metal, single-sided plate holders and a film pack holder. A number of Japanese hand cameras were copies of German models such as the Tessco, Glunz, Sonnar and Bergheil.

The Mikumi (Empire) Camera, made by Kuribayashi Seisakusho, now Petri, was one of the leading Japanese double-extension hand cameras of the 1920s. It was sold as a camera body only, or with German lenses and shutters, a Meyer f/4.5 or f/6.3, Welka f/4.5, Amigo f/4.5, or Tessar f/4.5 mounted in a Prontor, Ibsor or Compur.

Sone Shunsuido introduced the Lloyd and Apollo hand cameras. The Lloyd, with double extension bellows, was offered with a Modelar f/4.5 or f/6.3 mounted in an Ibsor or Compur. The Apollo was a deluxe model with a Modelar or Welka f/4.5 or f/6.3 mounted in an Ibsor or Compur. The Lloyd with an f/6.3 cost 64 yen, the Apollo with the same lens sold for 70 yen.

Sone Shunsuido also introduced the Monarch, an Atom format camera virtually identical to the Duchessa.

The Kyureido Palma camera was a double extension camera offered with a Welka, Meyer Helioplan, Anticomar or Unifocal lens, mounted in an Ibsor or Compur shutter. It had a folding finder at the upper left side of the camera, reminiscent of the Burgheil camera, and was available in Dai Meishi, Atom and Tefuda formats. The Atom and Dai Meishi Palmas were virtually identical.

Apollo. *First.*

The Minagawa Shoten First was a modestly priced camera with single extension bellows which was offered as a No. 1 for 34 yen, or a No. 2, with a frame finder, for 38 yen. First cameras had wooden bodies, were fitted with Trinar f/6.3 lenses in Vario shutters, and strongly revealed the influence of contemporary German cameras.

The 1929 Fuyodo Rubies was a double extension camera with either a Meyer f/4.5 or f/6.3 mounted in a Vario, Ibsor or Compur shutter. The German Deckel Compur shutter in the 1929 Rubies was the new rim set model, a design that was apparently replacing the dial set shutter about that time in Japan.

As the depression deepened, photographic equipment was repeatedly discounted; manufacturers of the Mikuni, Palma and Rubies cameras were forced to lower wholesale prices by as much as 15 percent.

Nichidoku introduced the Nifca-Klapp camera in 1930 in five different models, with a Welka f/4.5 or f/6.3 lens and a Compur or Vario shutter. Two more were soon introduced, the more expensive Nifca Sports, and the low cost Nifca-Dox.

The Nifca-Dox was named in reference to the Dornier-Dox 10X, one of Germany's largest airplanes. It was the first Japanese camera to use a front element focusing system, and had both a horizontal-folding configuration unusual for a Japanese design, and a characteristic hexagonal shutter cover. The 29 yen Nifca-Dox was sold with a Nifca f/6.8 mounted in a Koilos shutter, which had speeds of T, B, and $^1/_{25}$ to $^1/_{100}$.

The first Idea cameras, introduced by Konishiroku Honten in the Taisho Era, were similar to the Premo and Kodak cameras of the time. The later, 1930 Idea resembled the Voigtlander Vag, with single extension bellows and a metal body larger than older Idea models. The new Idea was sold with a Delta f/6.8 or Trinar f/6.3 in a Grammax, Prontor or Ibsor shutter.

Dai Meishi format remained popular with Japanese amateur photographers, in spite of the growing affinity for roll film, because the cameras were portable and the negative was large enough to produce a contact which could be used as a print.

Nifca-Dox.   Idea.

Completely Japanese Cameras. 1931.

Domestic lens manufacturing capability was a goal of both the photographic industry and the Japanese military. Under official auspices, a number of firms were engaged in optical research, including Nippon Kogaku Kogyo Kabushiki Kaisha; Konishiroku Honten/Rokuosha; Oriental Shashin Kogyo; Takachihi Kogaku Kikai Seisakusho, now Olympus; Tokyo Kogaku Kikai K. K.; Molta Goshi Kaisha, originally Nichidoku Shashinki Shoten, now Minolta; Tomioka Kogaku Kenkyusho; Asahi Kogaku Goshi Kaisha; Inoue Kogaku and Yamazaki-Shuzando. The first lenses were shown with the first Japanese between-the-lens shutters.

In 1931, Konishiroku Honten/Rokuosha produced, with German glass, what is generally considered the first Japanese photographic lens, the Hexar 105 mm. f/4.5, a four element lens in the configuration of the Tessar. In the same year, Nippon Kogaku completed a 120 mm. Anitar lens for the 6.5 x 9 cm. format which was never commercially produced. That year Asahi Optical completed a three element triplet, the Coronar 105 mm. f/4.5, which was sold by Molta Goshi Kaisha with its Eaton and Happy Hand cameras. Asahi Optical had

Nippon Kogaku, 1917.

begun in 1929 to prepare for photographic lens production; by 1934 it had become a specialized lens producer, and is believed to have made the lens for the Pearlette, the first camera of completely Japanese manufacture.

Tomioka Optical produced an f/4.5 lens called the Lauser, which was sold on the Dai Meishi format Proud DC hand camera in 1934, and Tokyo Kogaku made a lens called the State. Because of high costs in the new optical industry, domestic lenses did not lower the prices of Japanese cameras: the Proud DC was sold with a German Corygon f/4.5 in a Compur shutter for 85 yen; with a Japanese Lauser f/4.5 in the Compur, for 86 yen.

Domestic Shutters. 1931.

In 1931, Nichidoku introduced the first Japanese between-the-lens shutter. The Lidex, a two blade - 0 with speeds of T, B, 1, and 1/2 to 1/200; was sold in the Arcadia camera introduced that year. Molta then made two Crown shutters: the A had speeds of T, B, and 1/5 to 1/200; the S had an additional, built-in self timer. The Crown S shutter first appeared on the Molta Happy camera.

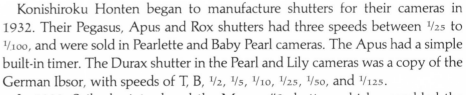

| Apus. | Crown. |

Konishiroku Honten began to manufacture shutters for their cameras in 1932. Their Pegasus, Apus and Rox shutters had three speeds between 1/25 to 1/100, and were sold in Pearlette and Baby Pearl cameras. The Apus had a simple built-in timer. The Durax shutter in the Pearl and Lily cameras was a copy of the German Ibsor, with speeds of T, B, 1/2, 1/5, 1/10, 1/25, 1/50, and 1/125.

In 1933, Seikosha introduced the Magna #0 shutter, which resembled the Vario and was supplied on the First camera. In 1935, Seikosha produced a copy of the S Compur called the Seiko, and there are indications that Fujimoto Seisakusho in Osaka began to manufacture shutters in 1935.

Rulex shutters were developed by Neumann and Heilemann, two Germans living in the Kansai area of western Japan. There were a group of models, including the Rulex A, with T, B, and 1 to 1/200; the B, which had T, B, and 1/5 to 1/150; and the D, with T, B, and 1/25 to 1/150. Even the inexpensive D had a speed setting ring around the outside of the shutter, in the style of the Compur. Through 1935, a number of other manufacturers produced similar shutters, including the Elka and Genila.

Seiko-Magna.

Japanese Dai Meishi Cameras. 1931 to 1933.

Kinka.

I n 1931, two Dai Meishi format hand cameras were introduced by Yama-moto Camera Manufacturing. The Kinka had a Meyer f/4.5 or f/6.3 lens mounted in a Vario, New-Vario, Auto-Prontor, Ibsor or Compur shutter. The Eliott camera had a Meyer f/4.5 or Trinar f/4.5 mounted in the new Prontor, Ibsor or the new rim-set Compur shutter.

The same year, Konishiroku Honten began to market the Tropical Lily. An advertisement said: "The camera body is of teak with a lacquer finish, the metal sections have brushed plating, the bellows have double extensions, and all parts are made of carefully selected materials. The camera is an outstanding example of the essence of Japanese made cameras, superior in quality to the principal cameras from abroad." With an exotic teak body and dark orange leather bellows, the Tropical Lily was fitted with a Hexar f/4.5, a four element lens in the Tessar style developed in the same year as the first Japanese lens, mounted in a rim-set Compur S.

Tropical Lily.

Happy.

Molta Goshi Kaisha introduced the Eaton and Happy hand cameras in 1931, and the Arcadia, which was fitted with the Lidex shutter.

In 1932, Minagawa Shoten introduced the New First and the New Kokka cameras. Initially, they were offered with Xenar or Trinar f/4.5 lenses in the rim-set Compur-S, Ibsor, Auto-Prontor or Vario shutters; in 1933, a domestic lens and shutter combination was added: the Tokyo Kogaku State lens in the Seikosha Magnar shutter. The domestic Japanese products were more expensive than their German competitors.

In 1932, Konishiroku Honten introduced the Idea Spring, a press camera in Dai Meishi and Tefuda formats; and the Idea Flex, a large format single lens reflex in the same formats. These two high quality cameras were fitted with a focal plane shutter with speeds from $1/8$ to $1/1000$, and offered with a Heliar or Tessar f/4.5.

In 1933, the eighth year of Showa, Konishiroku Honten introduced the Idea 8th Year Type. Available in dark green, gray and black, the double extension camera was equipped with domestic lenses, a Zion f/4.5 or f/6.3, in domestic shutters, an Apus or a Zeus, later renamed the Durax. The 1933 Proud was originally sold with an f/4.5 Schneider Radionar in a Verio shutter; it was later supplied with a Lauser f/4.5 in a Rulex or Compur-S, or a Corygon f/4.5 in a Compur.

Idea 8th Year Type.

In 1934, the first Minolta camera was made by Molta Goshi Kaisha, and marketed by Asanuma & Co. The first Minolta was a folding Dai Meishi press camera with a die cast body, and a moving, focusing lensboard on spring-opening struts, similar to, but sturdier than the 1931 Nifca-Dox.

Minolta.

Japanese Hand Cameras. 1933, 1934.

In 1933 and 1934, a number of lesser known Dai Meishi format hand cameras appeared on the market, including the Romax, New Peter, Kinka, Super Venus and Hope. They were quite similar to each other, and supplied with various combinations of Triplanat, Trionar, Minioplan, Heeder, Hope and Radionar lenses in Genira, Elka, Minion and Rulex shutters.

As the popularity of dry-plate hand cameras declined in the face of roll film, price competition followed. In 1934, Konishiroku Honten, the largest manufacturer, reduced the prices of Idea cameras by five yen, insisting that the reduction was intended as a service to its customers. The following year it began giving away a four section tripod to purchasers of its dry plate cameras, which were rapidly becoming obsolete.

Peerless.

Patent Etui, Germany.

In 1934, Minagawa Shoten introduced a copy of the Patent Etui called the First Etui, a high quality, 160-yen camera with an f/4.5 Zeiss Tessar. The Fukada Shokai Price Peerless, fitted with a thick leather base cover, reminiscent of the Curt Bentzin Primar, folded as compactly as the Patent Etui. The Price Peerless was offered with either an f/4.5 Tessar in an S-Compur, or an f/4.5 Schneider Radionar in a Perfect shutter. The First Etui and the Price Peerless far excelled previous Japanese hand cameras in design and performance; but they had been introduced at the end of the product cycle for dry-plate hand cameras.

Roll Film Cameras. 1920 to 1933.

The Pearlette, introduced by Konishiroku Honten in 1925, evolved through a number of minor modifications, including a 1929 frame finder with an auxiliary closeup lens, to become, with the 1932 addition of the Hexar 75 mm. f/6.3 in a Pegasus shutter, an entirely Japanese product.

The Color Pearlette, an elegant camera with red bellows and a bronze crepe finish, sold for 17 yen with a meniscus achromat, and 28 yen with a Hexar f/6.3, the same price as the Pearlette. The Color Pearlette was inspired by the Vanity Kodak which was available in brown, blue or gray.

The 1933 Pearlette was modified from side to rear film loading, had a 16-exposure adapter, and was sold with an Optor f/6.3. In 1936, an inexpensive, 9.5-yen Pearlette B was introduced, and in 1937, a higher quality Pearlette was sold with an Optor or Hexar f/4.5 lens with front element focusing.

Pearlette Special, 1929.   *Color Pearlette, 1932.*

The 1929 Special was completely unlike other Pearlettes. It was a copy of the Vest format Roll Tenax, with double extension bellows and a Trinar f/6.3, or f/4.5, or a Eurynar f/6.3 mounted in an Ibsor, Compur or Prontor shutter, sold at prices from 48 to 70 yen. The Special Pearlette was only coincidentally similar to the Nifcalette, the first camera made and sold by Nichidoku. The Nifcalette, which sold for 18 to 75 yen, resembled the German Krauss Rollette and had German lenses and shutters.

The Nifcalette also had a light leak. It was built in Mukogawa in a a two-story wooden building where even screws were turned out one by one on a lathe. Willy Neumann, a German engineer who had worked for Krauss in Paris, was operations supervisor at Nichidoku. He was a craftsman capable of all aspects of camera making, from lens polishing to machining body parts. Unable to determine the source of the leak, Neumann completely reworked the entire camera, which went on to enjoy a modest success.

Seiki Kogaku Kenkyusho, now Canon, Inc., was established in 1933. It began on the rented third floor of a wooden apartment house in Roppongi, Tokyo, where the straw mats were removed from the living room, a lathe was set up, and manufacturing began. The origins of many Japanese camera manufacturers were similarly modest.

Nifcalette.

Pearl 8th Year, 1933.

Konishiroku introduced the 1931 Pearl with a metal body smaller than the wooden one it replaced. Supplied with a Deltas or Trinar lens in a Gammax, Prontor or Ibsor shutter, the Pearl 1931 made eight 6 x 9 cm. exposures on 120 film, and accepted a frame adapter for sixteen 6 x 4.5 cm. exposures, the first dual format camera of its kind made in Japan.

Minagawa Shoten introduced the First Roll in 1933. The all metal, folding camera, similar to the English Butcher and the German Rietzschel, sold for 30 yen with a Trinar f/6.3 in a Vario shutter, 45 yen with a Trinar f/4.5 in a Vario. Later models had a State f/6.3 or f/4.5 mounted in a Magna or Rulex shutter, all made in Japan, and the last First was a model called the First Center.

Pearl, 1933.   *Minolta Vest.*

Japanese Automatic Folding Cameras. 1933.

The Pearl 8th Year was introduced in 1933 by Konishiroku Honten. A modified version of the earlier Pearl, it had a larger octagonal body and a spring action folding system, both copied from the 1929 Zeiss Ikonta. The 1933 Pearl had helicoid focusing, rare in folding cameras, as did the Semi Pearl and later post-war Pearl cameras. The Pearl 8th Year sold for 43 yen with a Zion f/6.3 lens in an Apus shutter; and 58 yen with a Zion f/4.5 in a Zeus, the same price as the Zeiss Ikon Ikonta with a Novar f/6.3 in a Derval. Later Pearl cameras were fitted with uncoupled rangefinders or Albada finders, with Hexar or similar f/4.5 lenses in Seikosha Leo shutters.

The 1934 Minolta Vest was made of Bakelite, and was the first camera designed with the lens mounted on a collapsing, three-element, Bakelite rigid bellows developed because of a shortage of soft leather in the wake of Japan's military expedition to Manchuria. Bakelite had been used in the bodies and the lens barrels of several cameras, but the Minolta Vest was the first to have bakelite bellows.

The Minolta Vest could also use the 16-exposure Baby format with a half frame adapter. The camera was supplied with a fixed focus, meniscus achromat or a Coronar f/4.5 or f/5.6, mounted in a Molta Marble shutter, which had speeds of T, B, and $^1/_{25}$ to $^1/_{1000}$. The camera with meniscus lens cost 19.50 yen, competitive with the 20 yen Pearlette with a similar lens.

Baby Pearl.   *Zeiss Ikon Baby Ikonta, Germany.*

The Baby Pearl, also introduced in 1934, was only 10 x 6.5 x 3.5 cm., and weighed only 350 grams. A copy of the 1934 Zeiss Baby Ikonta, it was the first Japanese Baby format, spring action folding camera. While the Zeiss sold for 42 yen with a Novar f/6.3, and 51 yen with a Novar f/4.5, the Baby Pearl was 25 yen with an Optor f/6.3, and 32 yen with an Optor f/4.5. The Pearl proved to be the equal of the Zeiss in performance, at only slightly more than half the cost.

The Baby Pearl sold well and led to two subsequent models, a color version, the Lady's Pearl, and a model with a fast f/3.8 Hexar lens. The camera line survived the war; the last version had coated optics and a shutter release on the body.

In 1934 the baby format Picny, with a collapsible lens mount, was introduced by Miyagawa Seisakusho; the First Speed Pocket, a spring-loaded folding camera for Vest and Baby formats, was introduced by Kuribayashi Shoten; and Proud introduced the Rosen 4, which made twelve exposures on 127 film.

Picny.

Rosen 4.   *First Speed Pocket.*

Chapter Six

Modern Cameras

from an article by Masao Tanaka and Hajimu Miyabe

Creative Japanese Cameras.

Leitz Leica III, Germany.

I n 1934 and 1935, Japan continued to import cameras and photographic equipment in what one writer called "the explosive growth of imports of German cameras...which crowded the shelves of Japanese camera stores." Among the principal imports were the Leica III, which sold for 580 yen; the Ikonta cameras group, of which the Super Semi Ikonta cost 335 yen; the 220 yen Rolleicord; and the 195 yen Kodak Retina. At the turn of the year, customs revenues from Zeiss products alone were more than 200,000 yen.

Cartridge-loaded 35 mm. film, which Kodak, du Pont and Agfa introduced in 1934, was soon imported into Japan. In 1936, Eastman Kodak introduced Kodachrome; two year old Fuji Photo Film began to produce a Japanese 35 mm. film, and Konishiroku introduced Sakura 16 mm. cine film and Sakura Infrared. Konishiroku marketed the first Japanese color film, Sakura Natural Color, in 1940.

Most Japanese cameras were copies of foreign products until 1934, when fairly novel and original designs began to appear among the newer Japanese folding, roll film cameras, Japanese Semi Format and 35 mm. Cameras.

Semi Minolta Model I and Model II.

In 1935 Asanuma & Co. marketed the Semi Minolta I, Molta Goshi Kaisha's copy of the 1933 Zeiss Ikonta. Semi format, 16 exposures, 4.5 x 6 cm. on 120 film, was also called Semi Brownie, as 120 was frequently labelled Brownie film. The Zeiss Semi Ikonta and Super Semi Ikonta (called Super Ikomat A in the U. S. until 1937, then Super Ikonta A) were introduced in 1934. These coupled rangefinder cameras were highly influential, and a number of Japanese semi format, folding cameras appeared the next year.

The Semi Minolta I had a die cast aluminum body, an accessory shoe and a shutter release button on the body. That year Molta also introduced the Baby

Minolta, a bakelite Vest format, collapsing-front box camera, and the Auto Minolta, a folding Dai Meishi press camera with a coupled rangefinder.

There were a number of other contemporary semi format cameras, including the Semi Prince, made by Fujimoto Manufacturing, the Semi First, made by Minigawa Shoten, the Semi Proud, made by Proud, the Sun Stereo Camera by Yamashita Shoten and the Semi Olympus, made by Takachiho Seisakusho, now Olympus Optical.

Auto Minolta.

Semi First.

Sun Stereo Camera.

Three 6 x 6 cm. format folding cameras were introduced in 1935: the Mulber Six, made by Kuwata Shokai; the Minagawa Shoten First Six; and the Molta Minolta Six. The Minolta Six was equipped with rigid bakelite bellows similar to those of the Minolta Vest.

The 35 mm. Exakta, introduced by Ihagee in Germany in 1935, was sold in Japan by J. Osawa & Co.. The camera was an improved version of the Exakta B, a Vest format single lens reflex introduced in 1933. The Exakta was the first 35 mm. single lens reflex imported into Japan.

In 1935, Fuji began to market roll film, and Konishiroku, which had reorganized from a limited company to a joint stock corporation, introduced the Pearl 6 x 9 cm. camera with a built-in, uncoupled rangefinder.

Minolta Six.

Hansa Canon.

In 1935 Seiki Kogaku Kenkusho, now Canon, completed the Hansa Canon, Japan's first 35 mm. camera, which it marketed through Omiya Photo Supply. The Hansa Canon was a focal-plane shutter, coupled rangefinder 35 mm. camera, the first of its kind in Japan. Soon afterward, Asahi Bussan marketed the Super Olympic, a Japanese 35 mm. camera with a between-the-lens shutter, and in 1936, Mizuno Shoten introduced a 6 x 4.5 cm. focal-plane shutter camera, the Nippon.

Super Olympic.

A Japanese 6 x 6 cm. Twin Lens Reflex. 1937.

The Marco Polo Bridge Incident on July 7, 1937, was the outbreak of widespread combat in China, and the Japanese economy shifted to a wartime schedule. Emergency export and import controls were enacted, and cameras soon became scarce. While the government encouraged Japanese camera manufacturers to increase production, amateur photographers found picture taking restricted for security purposes.

In 1937, Molta Goshi Kaishia became Chiyoda Kogaku Seiko (Optical Precision). Asahi Bussan was established in a section of a Riken Sensitized Paper Co. plant, and the company was renamed Riken Kogaku Kogyo (Optical Industries) in 1938.

Chiyoda Kogaku Seiko, now Minolta, introduced an improved Semi Minolta, the II, and two other cameras. The Auto Semi Minolta was a copy of the German Weltur, with a coupled rangefinder and an automatic film advance stop, and the Auto Press Minolta was a Dai Meishi press camera with automatic parallax correction and built-in flash synchronization.

Japanese 6 x 6 cm. twin-lens reflex cameras introduced in 1937 included the Minolta Flex I, a composite copy of the Rolleicord and the Ikoflex; the Fukada Shoten Prince Flex; and the Minagawa Shoten First Flex.

Auto Semi Minolta.

Clover Baby Reflex.

Minolta Flex I.

Auto Press Minolta.

Weha Chrome Six.

In 1936, Omiya had marketed a semi format twin lens reflex, the Hansa Rollette. In 1937, Ohashi Koki introduced the Roll Light, a helicoid focusing twin lens reflex, and Hagi Kogyo introduced the Clover Baby, a 3 x 4 cm., 127 roll-film twin lens reflex.

In 1937, Konishiroku introduced the New Lily, a hand camera with an Albada bright frame viewfinder; the Semi Pearl, a semi format folding camera; and the Sakura, a 4 x 5 cm. camera made of phenolic resin. The Weha Chrome Six, a 6 x 6 cm. format camera with a Drehkeil rotating wedge coupled rangefinder, was introduced by Yamamoto Camera. The Meisupi camera for 3 x 4 cm. sheet film was made by Togodo, and Misuzu Shokai made the 14 x 14 mm. format Midget camera. The Midget was the first Japanese subminiature camera, a size which would become popular immediately after World War II.

Japanese camera production rose substantially in the several years preceding 1937, causing a general concern the market would be flooded with crudely made, cheap models.

Midget.   Super Semi Proud.

In 1937, an unusually large number of folding cameras similar to the Super Semi Proud were introduced: four 6 x 6 cm. format and at least five semi format models. While they differed in external design and appearance, they were much alike in construction and mechanism.

Minion.

Baby Super Flex.

Shortages in the Wartime Economy. 1938 and 1939.

I n April 1938, as part of the growing government control on business and industrial activity, a National Mobilization Act was invoked to convert civilian enterprises to military production. As the war enlarged, the results of existing research and design programs in the photographic industry were continuing to come to market.

In 1938, a number of Vest format cameras were introduced. Tokyo Kogaku made the Minion, a 4 x 5 cm. folding camera marketed by Hattori Tokeiten (watch store). Kikodo introduced a 4 x 4 cm. single lens reflex, the Baby Super Flex, and Tachibana Shokai imported the Pilot Reflex, a 3 x 4 cm. format twin lens reflex. Riken Kogaku introduced the Riken Camera, a 3 x 4 cm. format focal plane shutter design reminiscent of the Leica, and other Japanese manufacturers introduced a total of seven new semi format, one 6 x 6 cm. format and four baby (3 x 4 cm.) format folding camera models.

Yamashita Shoten introduced the Boltax, a 24 x 24 mm. format camera using 35 mm. paper-backed film, a Japanese version of the Photavit made by Bolta in Germany.

Subminiature cameras were popularized by the Guzzi 18 x 18 mm., made by Earth Kogaku. Maruso Kogaku made the Hamond B, a camera built into a pair of binoculars, and a subminiature called the Micro I enjoyed substantial sales. The success of miniature cameras during the war is frequently attributed to a

Riken Camera.

Boltax.

patriotic response to materials shortages, and to an inventive response to the increasingly broad official restrictions on picture taking.

By 1939, stocks of imported cameras had dwindled, but a supply route had been developed in Manchuria, through which small quantities of imports continued. Severe materials shortages had reduced Japanese camera production substantially; only a few new models were introduced in 1939.

Chiuoda Kogaku completed the Minolta Automat, which had a self-cocking system similar to that of the Rolleiflex. Optochrome introduced the Tsubasa Super Semi, and Fuji Kogaku introduced the Lyrax, which had an uncoupled rangefinder. A total of ten folding cameras were introduced, none with novel or innovative features.

Minolta Automat.

Mamiya Six. 1940.

1940 was the 2600th year in the traditional Imperial Japanese Calendar, and a number of official events were staged to stimulate nationalism, even as living conditions continued to decline. government regulations were introduced to control the manufacture and sale of luxury items, and plans were announced for the establishment of a New Economic Structure. Production of civilian goods was largely brought under government control, and controls were placed on the distribution and consumption of consumer products. Retail prices of photographic equipment were regulated, and official prices were set on domestically made cameras.

Camera	1940 Regulated Price
Baby Pearl I	28 yen
Baby Pearl II	48 yen
Pearlette	33 yen
Semi Leotax	155 yen
Waltax	160 yen
Mamiya Six	252 yen
Canon	480 yen

Under hardship and restriction, innovation continued in photographic technology. In 1940, Rokuosha completed and introduced Sakura Tennenshoku (Natural Color) Film, the first color film manufactured in Japan; and Mamiya introduced the Mamiya Six I, an unusual 6 x 6 cm. folding camera with a coupled rangefinder.

The Mamiya Six I was manufactured by Mamiya Koki, jointly established by Seiichi Mamiya, designer of the Mamiya Six, and Tsunejiro Sugawara. The rangefinder focusing system, rather than moving all or part of the taking lens, moved the film plane. Two cam shafts, located on either side of and parallel to the frame, established the film plane, which was moved by a knurled focusing knob located high on the back of the camera. In 1941, a modified version was introduced with built-in flash synchronization, and a series of subsequent, upgraded models stayed in production through the war, after which the Mamiya Six was still regarded as one of the best folding cameras.

Mamiya Six I.

In 1940, Yamashita Shoten introduced the Shinkoflex, a 6 x 6 cm. single lens reflex with interchangeable, helicoid focusing lenses. The Misuzu Shokai Leotax was the second Japanese focal plane shutter 35 mm. camera, but unlike the Hansa Canon, the Leotax rangefinder was not coupled to the focusing system.

The BB Semi First, marketed by the First Camera Works, was a folding camera with a built-in extinction exposure meter. The Togodo Meikai was substantially an improved version of the three year old Meisupi. The Meikai used paper backed 35 mm. film, rather than sheet film, and upgraded the fixed focus lens into a focusing system. Five other semi format folding cameras were introduced in 1940.

Shinkoflex.

Leotax.

Meikai.

Wartime Camera Production. 1941 to 1945.

The legislative and administrative ordinances of the New Economic Structure took effect in early 1941. Production of cameras, prohibited in principle, was permitted using materials already in stock, enabling camera manufacturers to remain in limited production. Photography was prohibited in a steadily increasing proportion of the country. Pictures with a sweeping view, taken from places higher than 20 meters, were totally forbidden, even in the cities. Photographers, anxious not to be seen carrying cameras over their shoulders, prudently concealed them in brief cases or furoshiki (Japanese wrapping cloths), or carried the increasingly popular miniature models.

A number of new cameras were introduced in 1941, including two twin lens reflexes with helical focusing, the 6 x 6 Ricohflex B and the Auto Keef, a 4 x 4 cm. camera with a coupled rangefiner made by Kokusaku Seiko and distributed by Hattori Tokeiten. There were also three 6 x 6 folding cameras, including the Mamiya Six III, eight cameras in semi format, and three baby format models introduced that year.

Japanese camera production reached its peak in the years 1939 through 1941, and dropped precipitously from 1942, when the Industrial Conversion Ordinance gave complete priority to military production. Manufacturing in the photographic industry for other than military purposes was largely prohibited. While some new cameras were introduced in 1942, there are no figures for camera production for the remaining years of the war.

Ricohflex B.

Taxes on Cameras.

Auto Keef.

Mamiya Six III.

Excise taxes dominated price determination in the Japanese photographic industry for almost a decade. Bogged down in the bitter and unending war in China since 1937, Japan regularly increased emergency taxes to pay for the enormous growth in military expenditures. Excise taxes applied to items such as pearls, precious metals, products made of coral, phonographs and musical instruments, cameras, except for aeronautical and microscopic photography, photographic enlargers, projectors, parts and accessories, and dry plates, film and sensitized paper, except for aeronautical and X-ray photography. The taxes included all related equipment.

The excise rate was 20 percent of the price at the factory. Imported goods were assessed an additional 20 percent, but they already carried 100 percent duties imposed earlier. Goods for export were exempt from tax.

The recorded retail prices for imported and domestic cameras in Japan during this period reflect the vendors' prices, based as usual on costs and market factors, skewed dramatically by these extraordinary taxes. Excise rates were 20 percent in August, 1937, when they were first established; 15 percent in March, 1938; 20 percent in March, 1940; 50 percent in November, 1941; 80 percent in January, 1943, and 120 percent in February, 1944.

After the war, excise rates were reduced on photographic items to 100 percent in September, 1946; 80 percent in April, 1947 (on film and printing paper only); 80 percent in September 1948, including a turnover tax, but only 50 percent on sensitized materials; 60 percent in January, 1950 when the turnover tax was eliminated; 40 percent in January, 1951, now 30 percent for sensitized materials; 30 percent in June, 1953; 20 percent in March, 1963, sensitized materials at a 10 percent rate for film, dry plates and printing papers, 20 percent for color film; and 15 percent in January, 1966, on both cameras and sensitized materials.

Chapter Seven

The Sound of Clicking Shutters Heard Again In Postwar Japan

from an article by Tatsuo Shirai

The Japanese Photographic Industry. 1945.

At the end of World War II, which the Japanese called the Pacific War, the facilities of the photographic industry had either been destroyed or converted to wartime production. Asahi Optical's main plants in the Sugamo and Mukohara districts of Tokyo were burned in March, 1945. Asahi's Oyama plant in Itabashi, Tokyo, and its Ogawa plant in neighboring Saitama Prefecture had escaped destruction, but were closed for some time because of transportation and construction problems. In May, 1945, Olympus, then Takachihi Optical, lost both offices manufacturing facilities in Hatagaya, Tokyo, but retained plants at Suwa and Ina in Nagano Prefecture.

Rokushoa, renamed Konishiroku Photo in 1943, remained in operation; only the Yodobashi, Tokyo, plant and an optical research institute in Nakano were damaged.

During the war, Nippon Kogaku had become the largest entity in the optical industry, with 24 plants and 25,000 employees. Damage to Nippon Kogaku was minimal: only a single warehouse, in Ohi, Tokyo, burned down in December, 1944. By October, 1945, Nippon Kogaku had reduced its work force by three quarters, and shut down all but the Ohi plant.

In March, 1945, Mamiya's offices and facilities at Hongo, Tokyo, were destroyed, and the Petri Camera facility in Shitaya, Tokyo was destroyed, and Petri relocated to Saitama Prefecture.

In May, 1945, the main offices of Minolta, then Chiyoda Kogaku Seiko, were destroyed in Osaka, as were Minolta plants in Bukogawa, Komatsu and Amaga-saki. The Sakai facility survived, as did machinery and equipment Minolta had evacuated to facilities in Kameoka, Kyoto, and Mt. Ikomo, Nara. Okada Optical, Kigawa Optical and Bikodo suffered varying degrees of war damage.

Allied Occupation Forces in Japan evidenced an interest in the photographic industry, and a number of firms applied for permits to resume peacetime production. Between October, 1945 and early 1946, the General Headquarters of the Occupation authorized virtually every camera manufacturer to resume production. Some manufacturers were able to begin again with materials already in stock, Mamiya had to begin by buying a building in Tokyo, and rebuilding the entire company. The first postwar cameras were assembled from existing parts, materials and designs, and were sold entirely to Allied Forces personnel, not to the Japanese public.

Konishiroku made three folding cameras in 1945, the Pearlette, which made 8 or 16 exposures on 127 film; the Semi Pearl, which made 16 semi format exposures on 120 film, and the Baby Pearl, which made 16 exposures on 127. The other camera made in Japan in 1945 was the Seiki Kogaku Kogyo Canon J, a simple focal-plane shutter 35 mm. camera, with no rangefinder, which had been manufactured before the war. The Canon J had shutter speeds of B, and 1/20 to 1/500, and was originally fitted with a Nikkor 50mm. f/3.5 lens, later replaced with a Serenar made by Seki.

Canon J.

Folding Cameras. 1946.

On January 22, 1946, at the Marunouchi Industrial Club, an Optical Instruments Conference was held to improve cooperation among the manufacturers engaged in rebuilding the Japanese optical industry. The 17 companies attending the conference formed the Optical and Precision Products Industry Association. They included Nippon Kogaku, which was elected president, Konishiroku, Tokyo Kogaku, Chiyoda Kogaku, Mamiya Camera, Fuji Photo Optical, Seiki Kogaku, Elmo, Toshiba, Takachiho Optical, Tomioka Kogaku, Toa Koki, Ehira Koki, and Iwaki Glass Works. Konishiroku headed the camera division, which held its first meeting in November, 1946 on matters of standardization.

The first products of the postwar Japanese camera industry were almost entirely prewar designs of folding cameras. In February, 1946, the Olympus Six returned to the market. It had been introduced in 1939, discontinued in 1943, and the first cameras were assembled from parts Olympus had evacuated to safety during the war. Production was severely limited: 77 units in January, 89 in February, 202 in March, 198 in April, 160 in May, 250 in June and 129 in July.

Minolta Semi IIIA.

In 1946 Konishiroku reintroduced the Pearl, Mamiya Camera marketed the Mamiya Six III, Chiyoka Kogaku showed the Minolta Semi IIIA and Tokyo Kogaku introduced the Minion II. The Elmoflex I, a twin lens reflex, and the Dan 35 I, a 24 x 24 mm. format camera using Bolta film, were marketed by Yamato Koki.

Camera manufacturers faced an immediate shortage of shutters, but the greater, more fundamental shortage they faced was the capital necessary to finance new dies and machinery.

While virtually all postwar cameras were sold to the Allied Forces, older imported cameras, and prewar Japanese cameras, were in great demand on the domestic market. Many camera stores in larger cities had burned during air raids, and immediately after the war were doing business from small temporary shacks, often in black market areas.

In July, 1946, the first officially fixed retail prices were set for 13 cameras from four manufacturers. The Pearlette with a single element lens was sold for 635 yen; the Baby Pearl with a Hexar for 960 yen; the Semi Pearl B, 3,050 yen; the Pearl, 2,320 yen; the Minion II, 1,100 yen; the Olympus Six, 2,350 yen; and the Mamiya Six III, 5,250 yen.

Minolta 35.

Bolty.

35 mm. and Midget Cameras. 1947.

Agroup of better quality Japanese 35 mm. cameras were marketed during 1947, beginning in November, 1946 with the Canon SII. With a coupled rangefinder and a focal plane shutter with speeds of 1 to 1/ 500, T and B, the SII was offered with a Leica-thread Serenar 50 mm. f/3.5 or f/2. Two other rangefinder coupled lenses were available, a 135 mm. f/4 and an 85 mm. f/2. The Canon SII was the design from which subsequent Canon 35 mm. cameras were developed.

In May, 1947, Chiyoda Kogaku introduced the Minolta 35, the first Japanese camera with a self timer for a focal plane shutter. The Minolta 35, designed to address handling issues in Leica cameras, was fitted with a single eyepiece for a combined rangefinder/viewfinder, and a hinged rear cover. The camera used the new 24 x 32 mm. format.

The 1947 Chiyoda Bolty was a midget folding camera, the first of its kind in Japan to use paper-backed Bolta film. The Steky, made by Riken Kogaku Kogko, was a high quality subminiature offered with interchangeable lenses. It made a 10 x 14 mm. format image on 16 mm. film in a double magazine.

Steky.

Nippon Camera introduced the Nippon, later renamed Nicca, and Showa Kogaku reintroduced the prewar Leotax DIII. Both were exact copies of the Leica II.

In 1947, Mamiya introduced an improved Mamiya Six model IV; Minolta introduced Minolta Semi IIIB, a revised Semi IIIA with an added shutter release, and the prewar Okada Kogaku Waltax II was reintroduced, for export only. The Mamiya Six IV was produced unchanged for seven years, until October, 1953. While most folding cameras of this type were annually modified, at least in appearance, the Mamiya proved to be a sound, trouble-free and comparatively low priced camera of unusual longevity.

In July, 1947, the Occupation forces, through the Japan Chamber of Commerce and Industry, instructed the three sensitized material manufacturers, Fuji, Konishiroku and Oriental, to stop manufacturing roll films. Until the supply of X-ray film was sufficient for medical and public health needs, photographic materials were suspended. Brownie 120 and Vest 127 films were discontinued, and only a limited amount of 35 mm. film remained available on the consumer market.

Shutters remained scarce. Mamiya, unable to buy a sufficient quantity from Chiyoda, began to manufacture shutters, and both Seikosha and Toyo Watch, now Citizen, increased their production as much as possible.

As the economy inflated in the first years after the war, the Occupation Forces repeatedly changed regulated prices. By September, 1947, the Baby Pearl with a Hexar lens sold for 2,440 yen, the Elmoflex for 10,710 yen and the Canon SII for 20,940 yen.

Between 1947 and 1948, two 16 mm. subminiature cameras were introduced: the New Midget, made by Misuzu Shokai, and the Mycro, made by Miwa Shokai. They sold for 800 yen, and became popular souvenirs among the Occupation forces. Monthly production of the Mycro reached 2,000 units, unusually high volume for a Japanese camera at the time.

The Japanese Camera Industry. 1948.

By 1948 factories were rebuilt and labor problems which had begun during the massive layoffs of 1945 were gradually subsiding. It was the year the 35 mm. camera was introduced in the domestic market, and a number of other interesting new cameras were made, and 1948 came to be thought of as the real beginning of the postwar Japanese camera industry.

In October, 1945, Nippon Kogaku had set up a research unit to develop a camera which would be called the Nikolette. Blueprints for the new camera, renamed the Nikon, were completed in September, 1946. It resembled the Contax, with a shutter mechanism similar to that of the Leica. From the first, the Nikon had a single shutter speed dial, from B and 1 to 1/500, while Leica retained dual dials until the 1954 M3.

Nikon I.

The 1948 Nikon I was the first camera made by Nippon Kogaku. It used the 24 x 32 mm. format, which Nippon Kogaku called Nikon format, and Hajimu Miyabe, the chief designer of the Minolta 35, called Nippon format. Miyabe advocated the format because the aspect ratio closely fit printing papers, and 40 frames fit on a 36-exposure roll. After the Minolta and the Nikon I, the format was used in the Olympus 35 I and Minion 35.

Allied occupation forces had designated Japanese photographic manufacturing a critical export industry. Export of cameras using this new format was banned because it was not an accepted standard elsewhere, perhaps in response to a protest from Eastman Kodak about compatibility with standard slide mounts. Manufacturers of these cameras asked occupation authorities to approve domestic sale, and eventually received permission to market 24 x 32 format cameras within Japan. An improved Minolta 35 introduced in March, 1949, made 36 exposures, 24 x 32.5 mm., on a standard 36-exposure roll, and Nippon Kogaku changed to 24 x 34 mm. in the 1949 Nikon M.

Konica I.

Early 35 mm. Cameras. 1948.

The first leaf shutter 35 mm. cameras were introduced in 1948. In March, the Konica I was marketed by Konishiroku. Modified from the Rubicon, an indirect radiography camera, the Konica I was clearly the precursor of the many popular Konica cameras, notably the C35 series, that were to follow. The I was sold originally in occupation post exchanges, and appeared on the domestic market only in the late autumn.

Takachiho Kogaku, renamed Olympus Optical in October, 1948, had introduced the Olympus 35 I in May of that year. At the same time, Tokyo Kogaku introduced the Minion 35. The cameras were quite similar, and clearly predecessors to subsequent decades of compact 35 mm. cameras. Both were introduced in the 24 x 32 mm. format and later converted to the standard size, the Minion with the introduction of the model C in March, 1949.

Hansa Jupiter 35.

Eiichi Sakurai, manager of Olympus Optical's Suwa plant, recalls: "These early 35 mm. cameras were high quality, expensive, and small in production quantities. Imports of cameras were prohibited at the time and the general public could not get high quality foreign cameras. We thus worked to persuade the camera public to buy and use domestically made 35 mm. cameras. It was my firm belief at that time that the future in cameras lay with the 35 mm."

Although the Minion 35 was designed to accept interchangeable lenses, none was made for it. Interchangeable lenses were not available until the introduction, five years later, of the the Topcon 35.

Other 35 mm. cameras introduced in 1948 included the Hansa Jupiter 35, marketed by Omiya Photo Supply; the Super Dan and the Dan II, made by Yamato Koki, and the Shinano Koki Pigeon 35 I. The Pigeon was an inexpensive camera, precursor to the popular 35 mm. cameras that appeared five years later.

Minion 35.

Olympus 35I.

Subminiature Cameras. 1948.

T he 1948 Fujica Six IA was the first camera made by the Fuji Photo Optical subsidiary of Fuji Photo Film. Advertised extensively in a nationwide sales campaign, it was rushed into production as the film ban was being lifted, and early units had mechanical problems. Modified and reintroduced as the Fujica Six IBS in August, 1949, it was the first Japanese leaf shutter camera with a two-pin flash contact.

Other folding, self-locking cameras were the Olympus Chrome Six II, which had a die cast body and a new f/2.8 Zuiko lens; the Minolta Semi IIIC, an improved IIIB with an automatic film advance stop lever; and the Petri I, II and III cameras, the first folding cameras made by Kuribayashi Camera Works, later renamed Petri Camera. All were exported.

Fujica Six IBS.

There were few Japanese twin lens reflex cameras. The Mamiyaflex Junior, introduced in August, had a fine silver finish on the front and the first rotating-gear focusing mechanism on a Japanese twin lens reflex. At about the same time, Elmo introduced the Elmoflex Junior IA and IS.

Petal.

Mamiyaflex Junior.

In addition to the products of major camera manufacturers, Bikodo Works introduced the Bikoflex, later the Superflex, an inexpensive twin lens reflex which sold well. The Bikodo plant moved in July of that year from Hongo to Kami-Negishi, and daily production increased to 50 units.

Sales of Mycro midget cameras were quite good. In 1948, 35,000 subminiature cameras were exported, and monthly output reached 15,000 units. In March, Miwa Shokai held the first public photography contest after the war, offering a 3,000 yen first prize for pictures taken with its Mycro cameras. In November, the company staged an exhibition of Mycro photographs by four professional photographers at the Mitsukoshi Department Store in Nihonbashi, Tokyo.

The Mizuno Camera Store in Ueno introduced Petal Optical's subminiature Petal Camera. This unusual camera made six circular exposures, each 5 mm. in diameter, within a 24 mm. circle on 35 mm. film. The name refers to the resemblance of the pattern of small images to the petals of a flower.

The Photographic Industry. 1948.

By 1948, the Japanese photographic industry had started to again manufacture accessories. In particularly strong demand were tripods, flashbulbs, photographic lamps and filters. Darkroom equipment was also returning to the market: Fuji Photo Film introduced an enlarger and Nippon Kogaku introduced an El-Nikkor 50 mm. f/3.5 enlarging lens.

Fuji Natural Color Film, the first color film made in Japan, was introduced in April, 1948, and in October, Konishiroku introduced Sakura Natural Color Film.

Shutters remained in such short supply that manufacturers such as Nippon Seiko, maker of NKS, were unable to meet demand. Some camera manufacturers began to make their own: Chiyoda Kogaku produced the Konan Fliker, Kuribayashi Camera Works built the Carperu for their Petri camera, and the Stamina shutter was built at Mamiya's Setagaya works, later Setagaya Koki. Mamiya also bought lenses from Olympus Optical, to whom they sold Koho shutters which, curiously, Olympus had made and sold to Mamiya before the war.

Kobayashi Seiki was reestablished as Copal Koki Seisakusho in January, 1948, and incorporated in May, 1949. The Copal shutter, introduced by the company in 1948, soon became world famous.

In the second half of 1948, the industry confronted rumors that occupation headquarters would again ban camera production. There was a fairly active black market in sales of Japanese cameras to the Allied Forces, while General Headquarters policy required that camera production be exported to pay for food imports. Facing a threatened ban, industry representatives negotiated an agreement with General Headquarters that cameras in stock could be marketed in Japan until the end of September. In October, 80 percent of total production would be exported, 20 percent could be marketed domestically.

The German photographic industry was also rebuilding, and Carl Zeiss, East Germany, introduced the world's first 35 mm. pentaprism single lens reflex, the Contax S, in 1948.

Mamiya 35.

Minolta Memo.

Minolta Memo. 1949.

A number of new and reissued Japanese cameras appeared in 1949. The Canon SII, Minolta 35, Leotax, and Nicca were among the new, high performance 35 mm. cameras, while folding cameras such as the Minolta-Semi, Semi Pearl and Mamiya Six appeared or reappeared on the market in 1949. The ban on sales of roll films was lifted in October, 1949, stimulating sales of folding and twin-lens reflex cameras. The new Fuji and Konishiroku color films were widely marketed in 1949: in June, a 20-exposure roll of 35 mm. Sakura Natural Color Film cost 600 yen, a roll of 120 sold for 900 yen.

In September, Chiyoda Kogaku introduced the Minolta Memo, which had a film wind lever in the base five years before a lever wind mechanism appeared on the Leica M3, which is frequently thought of as the first such camera. The shutter button of the Minolta remained lowered after release to indicate the shutter had been tripped, and the lens cap could be used as a lens shade. The camera body, including the finder cover, was designed in black plastic with rounded corners, in something of an advanced style. But the film wind lever was also plastic, and its tendency to break off damaged irreparably the reputation and sales of the interesting and innovative Minolta Memo.

The Mamiya 35 was announced in October, 1948 and marketed in January, 1949. The first Japanese camera to automatically cock a leaf shutter as the film was wound, it had a shutter-ready indicator and the finder cover and rear

Look.   *Cooky 35.*

focusing system of the Mamiya Six. But the Mamiya 35 had problems with film flatness, and the rear focusing design was abandonded.

The Look camera, which resembled a Leica, used a double magazine system similar to that of the Contax, in which the film was transported between two magazines housed in the camera. The camera had no rewind mechanism, a film cutter was built into the back. The Look had been designed to accept interchangeable lenses which coupled to a rangefinder, the most sophisticated mechanism in such a camera at the time. But the interchangeable lenses were never made, the complex mechanism frequently broke, and the Look soon disappeared from the market.

Several other cameras with leaf shutters were introduced during 1949, including the Cooky 35, made by Kashiwa Seiko; the Dan 35II and 35IV, manufactured by Daiwa Koki; and the Shinano Koki Pigeon 35II.

Canon IIB.

High Performance Cameras. 1949.

The 1949 Canon IIB had an unusual variable magnification finder. The predecessor Canon SII had a single eyepiece, while the Leica had two, one for viewing, one for focusing. A single eyepiece was easier to use, but because its rangefinder could not have the magnification possible in a dual system, it was less accurate. The Canon IIB had variable finder magnification from .67 X for the 50 mm. lens, to 1:1 for a 100 mm. lens, to 1.5 X for a 135 mm. lens. The 56 mm. baseline of the rangefinder was quite sufficient for critical focusing. The variable magnification finder and die cast body of the IIB remained on a number of later Canon cameras.

The Nippon camera, a copy of the Leica, was first introduced about 1940. It reappeared in 1947, substantially unchanged, and was renamed the Nicca I in July, 1949. In October, the Nicca III was introduced. An exact copy of the Leica F, which was called the Leica D III in Japan, the Nicca accepted almost all Leica accessories. Both the Nicca I and III had Nikkor 50 mm. f/2.0 standard lenses. There is no record of a Nicca II.

Leotax cameras had also been introduced before the war, and their copy of the Leica DIII, called the Leotax DIII, was introduced in April, 1947. In August, 1949, the manufacturer, Showa Kogaku Kikai, was renamed Leotax Camera Company, and the DIII was named the Leotax T. It was fitted with a Tokyo Kogaku Simlar 50 mm. f/1.5.

Nicca III.

Mamiyaflex Automat A.

Automatic Film Advance. 1949.

There were a number of twin-lens reflex cameras available in 1949, and by 1951 there would be a virtual boom. In 1949, Elmo introduced the Elmoflex IA, IS, II and IIIB. The Mamiyaflex Automat A, introduced in April, was the first Japanese twin lens reflex with automatic film advance. Well received, it became quite successful, went through a number of evolutionary developments, and Mamiya continues to make highly regarded twin-lens reflex cameras, with interchangeable lenses, more than forty years later.

Other Japanese twin lens reflexes were equipped with safety windows through which frame numbers on the film's paper backing could be read. Film was either manually advanced to each successive frame, or in semi-automatic systems, the first frame was visually aligned and subsequent frames were automatically stopped in position.

The Mamiyaflex Automat ran film automatically up to the first frame, and through all the subsequent frames on the roll, and the film counter reset when the back cover was opened. Apertures and shutter speeds were set with small dials on the camera front, as on the Rolleiflex.

In 1949, a number of folding cameras were introduced, including Konishiro-ku's Pearl I; the Karoron, made by Kuribayashi Photo Industry, now Petri Camera; Ehira Koki Seisakusho's Ehira Six IIIA; and the Tosei Koki Frank Six II.

The Pearl I, marketed in January of 1949, was a modified Semi Pearl with an added rangefinder. It was supplied with a Hexar 75 mm. f/4.5 quite popular for its sharpness, and the became the first in a long line of Pearl cameras. The Karoron, a popular version of the Petri I, II, and III, was fitted with a reverse Galilean finder. The Frank Six I was a basic camera with a similar finder, and the Ehira Six IIIA, introduced in October, resembled the Zeiss Super Ikonta B, including its Drehkeil —rotating wedge— rangefinder coupled to the front lens element.

Subminiature Cameras. 1949.

Gemflex.

1949 was the peak of the subminiature camera's popularity. The Mamiya 16, the Gemflex and the Konishiroku Snappy were well made, sound examples of the type, while the Tone, Vesta, Tacker, Rubix, Hit, Blondy and Mighty were dubious products of small, back street workshops.

The Gemflex, manufactured by Showa Kogaku, maker of the Leotax, was a fixed focus, miniature twin lens reflex for paper-backed 16 mm. film. The Mamiya 16, designed by Seiichi Mamiya, was an innovative, sophisticated subminiature camera far superior to most others. All the controls, the aperture setting device, shutter button, film wind and film counter, were positioned on top of the matchbox-sized camera, which opened by pulling out the frame finder.

The principal subminiature formats were the Mycro, on 16 mm. film, and the 16 mm. format on 16 mm. cine film. There were more than 30 different subminiature camera types on the market, and the tiny picture formats presented problems for photofinishers. Originally made as souvenirs for Allied Forces personnel, and at one time ranked first in camera exports, the subminiature cameras were of such poor quality they began to disappear from the market.

In July, 1949, Miwa Shokai, manufacturer of the Mycro camera, established the Miwa Photographic Science Institute. Initially funded with one million yen for study and research in all fields of photographic science, the institute was as short lived as the public interest in subminiature cameras, and by the end of 1949 Miwa Shokai, already in financial trouble, withdrew funding.

Snappy.

In July, the police in Okayama Prefecture bought Dan 35 cameras for criminal investigations, one of the first uses of the miniature format cameras in a professional application beyond snapshooting.

In September, at the Mitsukoshi Department Store in downtown Tokyo, Fuji Photo Film staged the first large exhibition of color photographs in Japan, part of an advertising and public relations campaign to demonstrate domestic color film in the Japanese market.

Chapter Eight

From Back Street Workshops To Industrial Parks

from an article by Tatsuo Shirai

The Photographic Industry. 1950.

In the December 10 *New York Times, Life* magazine photographer David Douglas Duncan described favorably the Nikon 35 mm. camera and Nikkor lenses, which he had tested in professional applications. At the time, editorial and documentary photography were still practiced with larger roll and cut film formats. The article endorsed the much smaller 35 mm. format for professional use because of the quality of Nikon cameras and lenses.

The Korean war, which began in June, would eventually lead to substantial deployment of United Nations forces in Korea and Japan, among whom Japanese cameras became quite popular. Because of Korea, Allied Occupation concerns shifted from the regulation of Japan's economy to its defense from Communist threat. Occupation economic controls were relaxed, trade developed in textiles and metals, and more jobs at higher wages revived consumer spending, particularly for leisure goods.

On March 19, 1950, the Harukaze camera train took amateur photographers from Tokyo to photograph a plum blossom festival in Mito. The trip, sponsored by the Tokyo Photo Dealers Cooperative Association and the Tokyo Railway Bureau, was quite successful. On May 20, a second camera train, the Shinryoku, took photographers to the highland resort of Karuizawa, and later, the Nagisa went to the Miura Peninsula west of Tokyo.

A Photographic Culture Exhibition sponsored by Asahi Newspapers, at the Matsuzakaya Department Store in Ueno, Tokyo, drew more than half a million visitors during the eight days from May 16 to 24. In addition to cameras, there were displays of photographic literature, and exhibits of Japanese films, printing papers and accessories. In June, 1950, Fuji Photo Film announced prizes of one million yen in a contest which drew 7,000 entries from 1,500 photographers, one of a number of contests held that year.

In March, official prices for cameras, film, and paper were removed. A number of groups concerned with photography immediately formed an association to try to lower the 60% tax on cameras, and the 50% tax on film and sensitized paper.

The Ricohflex III proved to be an inexpensive camera which operated well, and became the first popular camera in postwar Japan.

The Twin Lens Reflex. 1950.

Ricohflex III.

I n March, the first and most important of the 1950 twin-lens reflex cameras was introduced. The Ricohflex III had been under development at the optical division of Riken Kogaku Kogyo, now Ricoh, since 1947. It was a simple mechanism, made entirely of fabricated sheet metal, designed to be produced inexpensively. The few moving parts, including a rotating gear drive similar to the Mamiyaflex Junior, were made with great precision. The Ricohflex was designed to be inexpensive while rising above the Japanese reputation for inferior goods. Principles of manufacturing design not found in earlier Japanese cameras were introduced in the Ricohflex, and when most twin lens reflexes cost more than 20,000 yen, it sold for 5,800 yen, only four times the price of its case.

The Ricohflex III was fitted with a coated Ricoh Anastigmat triplet 80 mm. f/3.5, which was quite sharp for an inexpensive camera. The shutter was a Riken 00, with four speeds, B, $^1/_{25}$, $^1/_{50}$ and $^1/_{100}$, and a flash terminal in the manner of the Kodak, the first in a Japanese camera. Film was loaded first onto a frame, which was then inserted into the camera.

The Ricohflex III was almost an overnight sensation. It was soon in short supply, and customers were willing to pay up to half again retail for it. Each morning, there were lines waiting to purchase the camera in front of Sani, the distributor, on the corner of the Ginza 4-chrome intersection in downtown Tokyo.

The first 35 mm. twin lens reflex made in Japan was the Yallu, a copy of the expensive 1935 Zeiss Contaflex. The Yallu was an unusual design: there were no projections from the rounded body, the film advance lever was located in the

Zeiss Ikon Contaflex.

Yallu.

base, and overall it had something of a resemblance to a square, upright stove. The Yallu was supplied with a Hexar 50 mm. f/3.5 in a Seikosha Rapid shutter, both considered high quality at the time, but after only limited production, the camera was discontinued. By August, Yallu Optical had changed its name to Aires Camera Works, and it later became a successful manufacturer of twin lens reflexes and inexpensive 35 mm. cameras.

Among the other twin lens reflexes introduced in 1950 were the Beauty Flex, made by Taiyodo Koki; the Primoflex I and IA made by Tokyo Optical; the Nippon Koken Nikkenflex I; the Super Flex B, a product of Bikodo Seisakusho; Oriental Photo's Oriflex; Rokuwa Shoji's Minorflex I and II, and the Taisei Koki Welmy Flex. The Elmoflex went through a succession of model changes during 1950, appearing as the IIB, IIIC and IIID.

Tanyflex.

Nikon M.

The Tanyflex was introduced in September, 1950 by Taniyana Camera Industries, a view camera manufacturer in Osaka. A 6 x 6 single lens reflex, the Tanyflex was in effect a reflex version of a view camera. It had a large wooden body, and used 105 mm. to 210 mm. lenses from hand cameras on a conventional lensboard mount.

The Tanyflex was the first Japanese camera with a built-in flashbulb socket. Six AA batteries were housed in the camera base, and the flashbulb was inserted onto the end of an arm in front of the focusing hood, which could be fitted with a reflector. The Tanyflex had a focal plane shutter with speeds to $^1/_{300}$.

While no 35 mm. cameras with leaf shutters were introduced in 1950 in Japan, among the many new focal plane cameras was the January introduction of the Leotax DIV, an improved DIII with an additional shutter speed, $^1/_{30}$, and a large protective ring around the shutter button. In March, Nikon introduced the M, with a new 24 x 34 mm. format; 2 mm. longer than the format of the Nikon I.

Japanese Cameras and U. S. Photographers. 1950.

David Douglas Duncan, a *Life* magazine photographer, used Nikkor lenses in his coverage of the Korean War. Jun Miki, a Japanese photographer with the Time-Life bureau in Tokyo, provides this account in the book, A History of Postwar Japanese Cameras.

"Mr. Duncan was photographing ancient Japanese art in late March 1950, after an assignment in India. I was an assistant to Mr. Duncan. One day Ryuichi Murai, carrying a Nicca camera with a Nikkor 85 mm. lens, called on Takamsas Inamura, who was working for East-West Press Agency near the Time-Life Tokyo Bureau Office. I happened to be visiting Mr. Inamura and I borrowed the Nikkor 85 mm. lens from Mr. Murai and mounted the lens on a Leica IIIf, showed it to Mr. Duncan and took a portrait of him. The next day when I showed him an 8 x 10 enlargement of the negative, he was surprised and impressed by the sharpness of the lens and asked me if we could visit the plant manufacturing the lens. I got in touch with Dr. Masao Nagaoka, then president of Nippon Kogaku and made the arrangements for the visit. Mr. Duncan and I visited the plant in Ohi, Tokyo. Mr. Duncan, of course, always used the best in cameras and lenses, such as Leicas and Rolleiflexes, and his interest in the Nikkor lens was a surprise to me.

"At the plant, Mr. Duncan and I met with Dr. Nagaoka, Hiroshi Shirahama, Sanetoshi Kuratsuji and Ryoichi Watanabe, the chief inspector of lenses. We borrowed a Nikkor 50 mm. f/1.5, an 85 mm. f/2.0 and a 135 mm. f/3.5 for test shots. A week later, at 5 A.M. on June 25, the Korean War broke out. Mr. Duncan was informed that American troops would land in Korea on June 30. Carrying two Leica IIIf cameras mounted with the Nikkor 50 mm. f/1.5 and the 135 mm. f/3.5 lenses, he accompanied General MacArthur and his forces to Korea.

"When his first photographs were transmitted to New York, Life staff members asked us by cable whether the photographs had been taken with a 4 x 5 camera. Their sharpness was outstanding. Later Carl Mydans and Hank Walker came through Japan to cover the Korean War and purchased cameras and lenses in Japan. Mr. Mydans bought a Nikkor 50 mm. f/1.4 lens for his Contax camera and Mr. Walker a Nikon M as he had with him only a Rolleiflex. Mr. Walker was the first foreign professional photographer to purchase the Nikon camera and Nikkor lenses. We then got orders for 150 Nikon cameras from New York which kept us busy for a while".

A December 10, 1950 *New York Times* column by Jacob Deschin describes a group of American photojournalists, including *Life* photographers, using Nikon cameras and lenses in Korea, and believing their performance superior to German products. It proved to be an extremely important endorsement because it resulted in other tests, investigations and comparisons, frequently with similar conclusions.

16mm. Design. 1950.

The Konan 16 Automat, an improved Mika Automat redesigned for volume production, was renamed the Minolta Automat 16 when Chiyoda Optical changed its name to Minolta Camera. Originally designed by Masanuki Nishimura, of the Konan Camera Research Institute, with Kanbe Hanaya, a professional photographer, the Mika Automat had been manufactured only in small volumes in the 1940s.

Widely considered the apotheosis of the style, the Minolta resembled nothing so much as a match box. The camera was opened, the shutter cocked and the film advanced by a push/pull action, the first time this system was used on a

Konan 16 Automat.

Japanese camera. It was also the first Japanese camera to use a double magazine with a central frame, and a two-blade, horizontal guillotine shutter.

The Mamiya 16 Super, also introduced in 1950, was the first Japanese camera with a built-in filter: a small lever on the side slid interchangeable filters into the optical path. The Minolta and Mamiya were important in establishing the reputation of Japanese subminiature cameras abroad.

A specialty 16 mm. camera was introduced by Toko Shashin in 1950. The Teleca consisted of a telephoto lens camera mounted over a small pair of 3x binoculars, which served as the viewfinder. The camera was fitted with a fixed 90 mm. lens, quite long for the 16 mm. format.

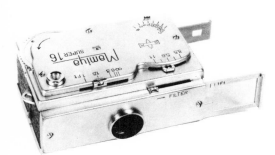

Mamiya Super 16.

Teleca.

The Photographic Industry. 1950.

Introductions of new folding cameras continued in 1950, among them the Olympus Chrome Six IIIA and IIIB, the Kigawa Optical Tsubasa Semi I, the Shoei Sangyo Ruvinal Six, the Million Proud I, Proud II and Semi Proud, the Yamato Minon Six II and the Semi Leotax.

The Million Proud I, inexpensive at 4,300, was advertised as a camera for the millions. It proved to be a substantial success for its small manufacturer, Million Optical, later renamed Sumida Koki Manufacturing.

While subminiature cameras were much less popular by 1950, when only three new models were introduced, the industry as a whole had begun to prosper. Component makers, supplying retailers and manufacturers with parts, accessories and optics, prospered in the expanding photographic goods market.

In January, 1950, Leitz products were imported for the first time since the war. According to the Japan Optical and Precision Instruments Manufacturers Association, Japan exported 7,000 cameras in July, more than 10,000 in October. Monthly exports of 35 mm. cameras were valued over 4.5 million yen; twin lens reflexes and folding cameras, 20 million yen. Monthly exports of cameras using paper-backed 16 mm. film were one million yen; cameras using cine 16 mm. film, 400,000 yen. Monthly exports of interchangeable lenses were ten million yen.

In June, Michisaburo Hamano introduced the first high-speed lens for 35 mm. cameras, a 50 mm. f/1.2. A former engineering officer in the Imperial Japanese Navy, Hamano had worked for six years on the design.

Olympus Chrome Six III.

In August, Shochiku began making Japan's first color motion picture, "Struggle in the Alps". The Ministry of International Trade and Industry provided subsidies of 5.5 million yen to Fuji, and 4.5 million yen to Konishiroku, for research and development of color motion picture film.

In November, four scientists at Olympus Optical completed a camera for photographing accurately the interior of the gastro-intestinal system. It was the beginning of the Japanese photographic industry's significant presence in medical diagnostic markets.

New Cameras. 1951.

By 1951, prewar cameras had aged, and many of the immediate postwar models had proven mechanically defective. Domestic camera sales were strong, particularly among models for amateurs, and new cameras were frequently sold above retail in an economy expanding from the Korean War.

The table below, from the November, 1971 Camera Journal, compares list prices with actual trading prices among camera dealers at an April trading session. Some folding and twin-lens reflex models were higher than 35 mm. cameras in part because a number of new folding cameras were introduced in 1951, some with noteworthy new mechanisms.

Camera	Trading Price Among Dealers	Retail Price
Mamiya Six IV,f/3.5	30,000 yen	15,350 yen
Pearl II,f/4.5	33,500 yen	26,650 yen
Ricohflex IIIb	10,300 yen	7,300 yen
Minoltaflex II	39,000 yen	31,900 yen
Rolleicord II	51,000 yen	—-
Olympus 35, f/3.5	16,600 yen	—-
Canon IIB,f/1.9	57,500 yen	60,000 yen

Tomic.

The Olympus Chrome Six IIIA and IIIB, introduced in 1950, were modified in 1951 to improve sharpness. Initially, the pressure plate bulged the 120 film forward into the open frame, out of the rather narrow field of back focus. In 1951, Olympus added springs to the film spool cavities and a roller to each side of the film gate. Together, they exerted sufficient tension at the frame that the film remained flat. Olympus also fitted a better lens, a D-Zuiko 75 mm. f/2.8. The improvement was substantial, and the somewhat bulky Olympus Chrome Six suddenly became quite popular, with production eventually reaching 5,000 cameras a month.

The Toko Shashin Tomic appeared to resemble the Zeiss Super Ikonta B, although it contained two novel mechanisms. The coupled rangefinder, which was similar in design to the Zeiss unit, was actually an optical system based on a Japanese patent. The camera used both 6 x 6 cm. and 6 x 4.5 cm. formats.

The Tomic was fitted with a rotary sector shutter, the first in a Japanese camera. In operation, shutter sectors begin to open from the edges, begin to close at the center. Four rotary sectors were incorporated in a square shutter case, described in one Japanese text as "looking like maidenhair tree leaves". The design was based on the premise that conventional leaf shutters, which open at the center, tended to exacerbate lens fall off, a not inconsequential issue with the optics of the day. Unfortunately, the shutter frequently broke, the patented rangefinder was inaccurate, only a few Tomics were manufactured and even fewer were sold.

Quite a few new folding cameras were introduced in 1951. The Karoron S and SII semi format cameras were introduced by Kuribayashi; the Atom Six by Atom Koki; the Semi Blond by Endo Photo Products; the Royal Junior, a fixed focus camera for both 6 x 6 cm. and semi formats, by Sanshin Sangyo, and the Baby Suzuka, an exact copy of the Baby Pearl, by Sanwa Shokai.

Okada Kogaku, later Daiichi Optical, made the Waltax Senior, and the Zenobia CI, CII, PI and PII in 1951, while Togodo, the well-known distributor of Togo cameras, introduced the Shinko Rapid II. Tosei Koki introduced the Frank Six II and Semi Frank; Tokiwa Seiki introduced the First Six VA; Mizuho Koki made the Mizuho Six, and Leotax introduced the Semi Leotax DL.

Binox.

The Binox was introduced in October 1951 by Binoca. A semi format box camera with a brilliant finder, it was fitted with a revolving back and a fixed focus, 70 mm. f/8 lens with speeds of B and $^{1}/_{25}$ to $^{1}/_{100}$. The Binox was made of black plastic, and the camera came with a flashgun, unusual standard equipment for an inexpensive camera.

The Twin Lens Reflex. 1951.

The Mamiyaflex I was an improved Mamiyaflex Junior. The front plate was done in a bright silver finish, the film advance lever also cocked the shutter, and a focusing lever was fitted to the front lens ring. A Sekor lens in a Merit shutter replaced the Stamina mounted Necon of the Mamiyaflex Junior, and the I proved to be a modestly popular, inexpensive version of the Mamiyaflex Automat.

The Japanese camera industry produced a significant number of new twin lens reflexes in 1951. Taiyodo Koki introduced the Beautyflex II and III, and Tokyo Kogaku made the Primoflex II. Among the many inexpensive models were the Erika Koki Erikaflex I; the Masumyflex II, made by Takagawa Koki, and the Tsubasaflex and Graceflex, manufactured by Kigawa Kogaku. Like the Ricohflex, these cameras had pressed plate bodies and front focusing systems. Some had engraved decorations and gloss plating on the lens board, which manufacturers of inexpensive cameras at the time considered elegant.

35 mm. Cameras. 1951.

All of Japan's major manufacturers introduced improved single lens reflexes in 1951. In January, Nippon Kogaku introduced the Nikon S. The format had been enlarged to 24 x 34 mm., and a two pin flash terminal was added. Foreign news photographers passing through Japan on the way to Korea frequently bought Nikons, presumably because of favorable publicity in the New York Times and other U.S. publications.

In March, Canon announced the Canon III, an improved IIB with two new speeds, T and $^{1}/_{1000}$. The Model IV, announced in May, had a built-in flash terminal; and in December, the III was replaced with the IIIA, which had a film type indicator.

Nippon Camera, manufacturer of the Nicca, changed its name to Nicca Camera in December and announced the Nicca IIIA and IIIB. The IIIA was fitted with a Nikkor standard lens which could focus to 50 cm., much closer than the coupled rangefinder could indicate. The IIIB had a synchronization terminal for FP flashbulbs, which was not uncommon: by 1951, most upmarket 35 mm. focal-plane shutter cameras were fitted with flash synchronization, and sales of flashbulbs were rising.

The Minolta 35E, an improved Minolta 35, was designed to use the standard 24 x 36 mm. format, and had a focusing eyepiece. The 1951 Tanyflex II had a higher shutter speed, $^1/_{200}$, than the earlier Tanyflex.

There were two new 35 mm. cameras with leaf shutters in 1951. The Konica II had a new Hexanon 50 mm. f/2.8 lens and a decorative front plate; the Shinano Koki Pigeon 35 III and IIA had top film wind levers. The Pigeon 35III was a sleek design, unusual for the time, with a front shutter release, a Trilausar 45 mm. f/3.5, and a TSK shutter with speeds to $^1/_{250}$.

Pigeon 35III.

The Photographic Industry. 1951, 1952.

Japan's first color movie was completed in 1951, and on March 21, a preview was held of the Shochiku production originally called "Struggle in the Alps", now entitled "Carmen Returns Home", which had been made on Fuji color film.

A Day of Photography was held in the Matsuzakaya Department Store hall in Ueno, Tokyo, on June 1st, attended by photographic industry and trade association representatives, by officials from the Ministries of International Trade and Industry, Education and Welfare, and diplomatic representatives of France and the U.K. The Award Screening Committee of the Day of Photography Commission went on to become the Photographic Society of Japan.

A number of unusual and prototype cameras were announced in 1951. Suzuki Kigaku introduced the Echo 8, a cigarette lighter combined with a camera. The Echo made 6 x 6 mm. images on split 16 cine film. Unpopular when it was introduced, the Echo was a prop in the Hollywood movie Roman Holiday, and has since developed a value among collectors of photographic ephemera. The Zumanflex was a prototype single lens reflex made by Zuman Koki. It made 14 exposures, 50 x 55 mm., on 120 film, had a self-cocking, metal focal plane shutter with speeds to $^1/_{600}$, automatic-stop film advance and a preset aperture. The plastic Start 35 used Bolta film, and soon became popular with young people.

Echo 8.

Konishiroku held an amateur photo contest, and the All Japan Portrait contest for professionals, to promote the 20th anniversary of Sakura film. Fuji Photo Film held a second one million yen photo contest. On March 17, the Photo Material Dealers League in Tokyo, in cooperation with Japanese National Railways and the Japan Travel Bureau, arranged another camera train, the Hagoromo, to take photographers on an excommunicated to Shizuoka.

The photographic industry grew steadily until the end of the Korean conflict in 1953. The Japanese economy as a whole was expanding, and demand far exceeded supply in camera stores. As major manufacturers increased production, small firms and individual entrepreneurs, many operating tiny back street workshops, marketed inexpensive twin lens reflex and folding cameras of questionable quality.

At the time, when many camera components for major manufacturers were made by small enterprises, a three element, 75 mm. f/3.5 lens could be supplied for as little as 300 yen. The names of the various off-brand shutters —NKS, NSK, NKK, KOC, TKK, TSK, UKS, Lotus, Rectus, SKK, MSK, MKS— reflect their obscure origins: most of the initials were for unheard of, or nonexistent names, most of the shutters were of questionable quality.

Dubious parts were usually purchased by small firms which assembled, rather than manufactured, cameras: they bought die cast bodies from other small manufacturers, frequently made from molds discarded by large companies. Along with pressed parts and low-bid lenses, the components were assembled into something resembling a camera and rushed to market.

An article describes the situation at the time:

"A camera firm in Sumida, Tokyo, that I visited was nothing more than a private residence. I entered the front door by crossing a covered ditch. An elderly man and his son were assembling twin-lens reflex cameras in a tiny room by the entrance. There were literally hundreds of such cheaply made cameras on the market. All letters from A to Z had been used for the first letter of these camera brand names." Camera retailers had so little stock, they spent more time buying cameras from manufacturers and distributors than selling them to customers. Small manufacturers bid aggressively for whatever parts they could buy, and parts brokerages became lucrative businesses.

This vast production of poor quality cameras lead to the eventual establishment of the Japan Camera Inspection Institute, JCII, the publisher of this book. On May 1, 1973, surveying instruments and biological microscopes were added to its inspection responsibilities, and it was renamed Japan Camera and Optical Instruments Inspection and Testing Institute, although the abbreviation JCII remained unchanged.

Asahiflex I.

The First Japanese 35 mm. Single Lens Reflex. 1952.

The Asahiflex I, introduced in May, 1952, was the first Japanese 35 mm. single lens reflex. It was fitted with a 50 mm. f/3.5 Takumar lens of the Tessar design, with a Praktica-thread lens mount. It had a cloth focal plane shutter with B, and $1/20$ to $1/500$, was little larger than a rangefinder camera and weighed only 647 grams. It had both a reflex screen and a reverse Galilean finder in the camera body.

The Asahiflex was equipped with a mirror which returned to the optical path when pressure was removed from the shutter button, a direct predecessor to the instant return. At the time, mirrors returned when the film was wound.

Hajime Miyabe at Mamiya produced a prototype single lens reflex in 1952. It was called the Mamiya Prismflex, and designed with the pentaprism finder the name suggests. It was never manufactured.

35 mm. and Folding Cameras. 1952.

Nicca IIIS.

I n 1952, a number of new focal plane cameras were introduced with coupled rangefinders. The Canon IVF, subsequently the IVS, was a synchronized flash version of the IIIA. The IID was a less expensive IVS, fitted with a Serenar 50 mm. f/3.5 lens, from which ¹/₁₀₀₀ speed and flash synchronization had been removed. At 45,000 yen, it was 32,000 yen less than the IVS. The IID, Canon's first effort in the lower price ranges, was one of the best selling rangefinder cameras of its time.

The Nicca IIIS and IIIA, which replaced the IIIA and IIIB respectively, were also introduced in 1952. The Nicca IIIS was the first Japanese camera of its kind with a German flash synchronization socket on the front of the camera. It was fitted with a Nikkor 50 mm. f/2, rather than the f/3.5 Nikkor of the IIIA, and a cloth focal plane shutter with speeds to ¹/₅₀₀. At 37,500 yen, it competed directly with the Canon IID.

The Minolta 35, criticized for rangefinder inaccuracy, was replaced with the 35F, on which finder magnification was increased from .33x to .7x, while the effective base line of the rangefinder was lengthened from 13 mm. to 28 mm.

The 1952 Arco 35, the first Japanese 35 mm. camera with folding bellows, was fitted with a 50 mm. f/2.8 in a Seikosha shutter which could focus to 14 inches. The Arco 35 had a descending frame counter at a time when the industry had not yet standardized on ascending counters, and sold for 27,700 yen, quite expensive for a leaf shutter camera.

Arco 35.

Most of the other 35 mm. cameras introduced in 1952 were made for export. The Elega 35, made by Nitto Photo Products, closely resembled a Leica, but had a double film magazine with a film cutter. The Pax 35, made by Yamamoto Optical, was a miniaturized Leica IIIA.

The Samoca 35 was made by Sanei Industry, which later changed its name to Samoca Camera. It had a squat plastic body, and although the rear cover detached, the film pressure plate was fixed in the camera body. Two buttons on the front cocked and released the shutter. The inexpensive, 6,800 yen Samoca enjoyed some popularity because of its price, as did the Shinano Koki Pigeon 35J, and together they contributed to the growth of the domestic 35 mm. camera market.

A number of folding cameras were introduced in 1952. The Minolta Semi P sold with a case for 13,600 yen, extremely low for a camera from a major manufacturer. It sold quite well amidst complaints from the trade that it would force manufacturers to compete with each other on prices. The Semi P had a slim, light, die-cast body, a three element Promar lens, and a simple Konan Flicker shutter with speeds to ¹/₂₀₀. To lower the price, designers avoided a mechanical film system and used the antiquated red window, and offered the rangefinder as an accessory. The Minolta Semi P was the first example of this design and marketing method in the Japanese camera industry.

In 1952, Rich-Ray Shokai introduced the Rich-Ray 6, an unusual 6 x 6 cm. camera with variable picture format and Z-shaped optical axis. The Fujica Six II CS had a die-cast body, a new Fujinar 75 mm. f/3.5 in a Seikosha shutter, and a distinctive round finder cover.

Other folding cameras were the Karoron RF and Petri Super RF from Kuribayashi Camera Works, the Atom Six II from Atom Optical, the Middle 120-A from Otowa Koki, the Planet from Toko Photo, the Frank Six III from Tosei Koki, the First Six from Tokiwa Seiki, the Mizuho Six IIIB from Mizuho Camera, the Baron Six from Baron Camera, the Semi Masumy IIIA and IIIB from Takagawa Koki, the Mihama Six and Six II from Suruga Seiki, the Semi Oscon from Yamagata Kikai, and the Wagen Six and Six J from Yamato Optical.

All had similar specifications, with compatible 6 x 6 and 6 x 4.5 cm. formats, a 75 or 80 mm. f/3.5 lens, and shutters with speeds to $^1/_{200}$. The Karoron RF and Petri Super RF were coupled rangefinder cameras. Yamagata Kikai, affiliated with Nippon Kogaku, made the body of the Semi Oscon and bought the Toko lens from Tokyo Kogaku. The Semi Oscon was a popular, practical camera, with a number of small mechanisms that made it better than it had to be, including a film winding stop, but Yamagata Kikai soon went out of business.

Rich-Ray 6

The Twin Lens Reflex. 1952.

The Olympusflex was completed in prototype form in January, 1952, and marketed at year's end to compete with the Rolleiflex. The six element, 75 mm. f/2.8 Zuiko was not self cocking, as was the Rollei, but did have a multiple exposure device, which the German camera did not. The Olympusflex had an excellent four element finder, and at 48,000 yen was the most expensive Japanese twin lens reflex.

The Koniflex was plain, as traditional Konishiroku designs were, but technically quite sophisticated. It had a particularly bright viewfinder, and was fitted with an 85 mm. f/2.8 Hexanon lens which retracted into the body to make the closed camera more compact. At 47,000 yen, competed directly with the Olympusflex.

While the original Minoltaflex was a popular prewar twin lens reflex, the 1952 Minoltaflex IIB was a substantially new design. It had the semi-automat film loading system introduced on the 1950 Rolleicord II: when an arrow on the

Koniflex.

Minoltaflex IIB.

film's paper backing was aligned with a mark and the camera back closed, the film advanced a mechanically determined distance to the first frame. The Minoltaflex also had a focusing magnifier, a small convex lens which flipped up from the front of the focusing hood, which became common on twin and single lens reflex roll film cameras. Minolta called the magnifier a Focus Eye. Advanced amateurs and some professional photographers not satisfied with the Ricohflex, and evidently unwilling to buy the more expensive cameras, created a steady market for the Minoltaflex IIB.

As Japanese manufacturers began to introduce twin lens reflexes almost weekly, two distinct groups appeared. Cameras which sold for less than 10,000 yen were typically fitted with gear rotation focusing, in the manner of the Ricohflex. Those selling for 20,000 yen or more, midmarket models, typically had semi-automat film loading and were frequently reminiscent of the Rolleicord.

The Airesflex Z was a semi-automat design fitted with a Nikkor lens. The Elmoflex IIIE was a semi-automat version of the IIID. Taiyodo Koki made the Beautyflex IIA, IV and V; and the all-black Beautyflex S, a semi-automat which sold for less than 20,000 yen; and the much higher priced Beautyflex U. The best selling Ricohflex was modified and sold as models IIIB and IV. Alfa Camera Works introduced the Alfaflex I, II and Cosmoflex I; Isokawa Koki made the Isocaflex; Hachiyo Kogaku made the Alpenflex I; and Nippon Koken made the Nikkenflex II. Walz, a well-known manufacturer of filters and other photographic accessories, introduced the Wagoflex, and Togodo the Hobbyflex. Aries introduced the Airesflex YIII, U and US; Koyo Seiki made the Elizaflex; Musashino Seisakusho made the Malcaflex; Kojima Kogaku, the Mikonoflex C and P; Miwa Shokai, the Dorimaflex A, and Shoei Industry, the Ruvinaflex.

Airesflex Z.

The Photographic Industry. 1952.

In February, a rare earth optical glass, F15, was produced at Fuji's Odawara factory. It had been developed by a technical group established by the five Japanese optical glass manufacturers, with financial assistance from the Industrial Technology Agency at the Ministry of International Trade and Industry.

On March 8, 1952, four Japanese Industry Standards specifications were established: JIS-7101 for camera accessory shoes, JIS-7102 for flash synchronization sockets and plugs, JIS-7103 for tripod connections, and JIS-7106 for aper-

Tomy.

Panon.

ture scales. In April, Fuji Photo Film introduced the first Japanese ASA 100 black and white film, Neopan SS, and Fine Technic Products became a Japanese distributor for Zeiss Ikon.

The 1952 Ars Seiki Tomy was a 6 x 4.5 roll film camera made unusually thin by a Z-shaped optical axis like that of the Rich-Ray 6. The first medium format Japanese panoramic camera was introduced in 1952. The 120 roll film Panon, designed by Shozo Nakayama for Panon Camera, held the film fixed in a curved plane while the lens was cocked by moving the optical housing to one side, and the exposure was made as the lens swung back. The panon made a 140 degree panoramic image 43 x 115 mm.

Ricohflex VII.   Laurelflex.

The Twin Lens Reflex. 1953.

The May, 1953, Rolleiflex 2.8C had two new features which were quickly incorporated into Japanese cameras: an optional multiple exposure device, and internal anti-reflection frames. The new Rolleiflex five element Xenotar f/2.8 "astonished" Japanese optical engineers, who also found the less expensive Rolleicord IV made to surprisingly high standards.

The 1953 Riken Ricohflex VII was the first Japanese twin lens reflex with a contour viewfinder. Better twin lens reflexes had direct viewing frames, or sportsfinders, created by folding the front plate of the focusing hood down onto the screen. Considered too costly for inexpensive cameras, they were replaced on the Ricohflex by slits in the front of the hood. When the photographer looked at the slits with one eye, the subject with the other, frame lines appeared superimposed around the subject. The 6 x 6 Ricohflex, which used 35 mm. film with an adapter called the Ricohkin, had a contour finder for both formats.

The Laurelflex, made by Tokyo Optical and distributed by Hattori Tokeiten, a watch store, was the first Japanese twin lens reflex with a plastic fresnel lens fitted below the focusing screen, a design copied from the Kodak Reflex II. The 32,000 yen Laurelflex was equipped with a Seikosha Rapid shutter, and closely resembled Tokyo Kogaku's other camera, the Primoflex, which was also soon fitted with a fresnel lens.

Hattori Tokeiten also marketed the The Zenobiaflex I, a twin lens reflex manufactured Daiichi Optical, which it introduced with a lavish public relations campaign.

In 1953, Yashima Seiki introduced the Yashimaflex, which was immediately renamed the Yashicaflex, then renamed Yashimaflex in February, 1954. It was the first of the Yashicaflex cameras, which continued in production four decades later.

The Ofunaflex was a high quality twin lens reflex made by Ofuna Optical and Mechanical Works, a World War II subsidiary of Nippon Kogaku. Fitted with a Seikosha shutter, well made and quite similar to the Rolleiflex, it suffered from being an unknown brand marketed with little advertising. It was expensive at 30,000 yen, and sold poorly. An improved Ofunaflex II was introduced in May, at 27,000 yen, and in October an upmarket Ofunaflex Automat was introduced with a self-cocking shutter. None sold well, and the company went out of business in 1954.

Among the many inauspicious twin lens reflexes which continued to appear on the market were the Elmoflex IIIF, the Nikkenflex III, made by Nippon Koken, and the Toyo Seiki Princeflex, a revived prewar design. The Tokyo Kogaku Primoflex IB had a Simlar lens in a Koni Rapid S shutter; the IC had a direct viewfinder. The Alpenflex III and IV, and the 6,000 yen Hobbyflex III and 8,500 yen Hobbyflex IV, were twin lens reflexes for novice photographers. A small manufacturer, Tokiwa Seiki, built X synchronization into the Firstflex PI and PII before the larger firms offered it. Two Toyo cameras were introduced, the Larkflex and the upgraded Elegaflex, Alpha made the Cosmoflex II, Otowa the Middleflex, and Kuribayashi Camera made only one twin lens reflex, the Petriflex. Nippon Koki, in Osaka, known for such popular enlargers as the Lucky Silver, copied the Ricohflex IV for the Silverflex S. Konto Kogaku made the Amiflex; Ginrei Koki the Vesterflex, a plastic box with a fixed focus lens which sold for 3,750 yen; and Cristar Kogaku made the popular Cristarflex.

Firstflex PI.

Press Van.

Folding Cameras. 1953.

The most outstanding folding camera of 1953 was the Press Van, made by Suzuki Optical. A 6 x 6 roll film camera which could use 35 mm. film by inserting several components and a mask, it was the first dual format camera of its kind in Japan, and one of the few in the world. It was fitted with an Asahi Takumar 75 mm. f/3.5 in a Seikosha Rapid shutter.

Among the other folding cameras introduced in 1953 were the Mamiya Six V, an improved IV with both 6 x 6 and 6 x 4.5 formats; the Zenobia RI, RII and RIII, 6 x 4.5 format cameras; the Ofuna Six, a copy of the Mamiya Six; the Endo

Photo Products Pigeon Six; the Middle 120 A2; the Flora Six, made by Kyowa; the Semi Cristar and the Ruvinal Six A and B.

Taisei Koki, a manufacturer of camera components, lenses and shutters, introduced the Welmy Six ES and the surprisingly inexpensive model L, a 4,800 yen camera designed with a minimum of mechanical parts. Other new introductions included the Beauty Six from Taiyoko Koki; the Daido Six and Daido Semi from Takane Kogaku; the Takai Photo Products Angel Six; the Tosei Koki Frank Six V; the Tokiwa Seiki First Six V; the Nishida Wester Chrome Six R; the Nippon Silver Six I; the Renown Six IA from Fujiwara Seisakusho; the Million Proud IV coupled rangefinder camera from Sumida Koki, and the Union Semi from Union Kogaku, a microscope manufacturer. Most relied on distance estimates for focusing, rangefinders were separate accessories.

Topcon 35.

Lord 35I.

Konilette I.

35 mm. Cameras. 1953.

The Tokyo Optical Topcon 35 was the first 35 mm. camera in Japan with a leaf shutter and interchangeable lenses. Because the shutter was located behind the lens mount, an 80 mm. f/5.6 lens lens with an accessory viewfinder could be mounted in place of the standard 40 mm. lens. The Topcon 35 was based on the design of the 1948 Minion 35.

The Okaya Kogaku Lord 35 Model 1 was a compact, coupled rangefinder camera on which a modest advance was introduced: the Lord was the first camera on which it was not necessary to hold the release button while rewinding the entire roll of film. The Lord also had a blade built into the camera for cutting film in mid-roll, although the exposed film had to be removed from the camera in a darkroom. The first Japanese camera with such a cutter was the Jansa Jupiter 35, introduced in September, 1948, by Omiya Photo Supply.

A number of leaf shutter 35 mm. cameras were introduced in 1953, including the Olympus 35IVA, Dolca 35, Purple 35, Monte 35A, Arba 35I, Windsor and Samoca 35II. Some back street workshops began to make mechanically substandard and optically inferior leaf shutter cameras, and the public was soon cautious of, and resisted, off-brand models.

In January, 1953, Konishiroku introduced a very inexpensive compact folding camera and a new film format. The Konilette Model 1 used unperforated 35 mm. film in a special cartridge to make 12 exposures, 30 x 36 mm. The compact

Mammy.

Richlet.

plastic camera was finished in two-tone grey and brownish black, had a 50 mm. f/4.5 lens, shutter speeds to $1/200$, and sold for only 5,500 yen. Although the empty film cartridge could be reloaded with regular 35 mm. film, and the camera included a mask for the conventional format, sales of the Konilette, like the first Rolleiflex, depended on the availability of a film which was never widely distributed.

Two cameras using paper-backed 35 mm. film were introduced in 1953. The Mamiya Mammy had a color-coded focusing scale in the viewfinder, and the Rich-Ray Richlet had a compartment for a spare roll of film.

The Canon IV Sb, introduced in June, was the first Japanese camera of its kind with X shutter synchronization for electronic flash. The camera was offered with a range of interchangeable lenses and a long list of accessories.

The 23,800 yen Tanack 35 1, and the 25,000 yen Chiyoca 35 were exact copies of the Leica. Another Chiyoca, the 35 IF, had no rangefinder, and at 17,300 yen was cheaper by half than other focal-plane shutter cameras, and sold well in the domestic Japanese market.

The Asahiflex, the first Japanese 35 mm. single lens reflex, was modified into the Asahiflex IA, with M and X flash terminals, and three new interchangeable lenses were available, an 83 mm. f/1.9, a 135 mm. f/3.5 and a 500 mm. f/5.

Canon IVSb.

Asahiflex IA.

The Photographic Industry. 1953.

In January, Oriental Photo Industry introduced a color coupler film, and in March, Konishiroku introduced Konipan, an ASA 100 black and white film. Fuji Photo Film built a 1,150 million yen facility adjacent to its Ashigara plant to make non-flammable film, and Aires Camera ran a highly popular a one million yen photography contest.

An f/1.1 lens, the 50 mm. Zunow, designed by Suzuki and Hamano of Teikoku Optical, stimulated the interest of both the public and the industry, and Japanese optical engineers began to compute wide aperture lens designs.

A shortage of leaf shutters in 1953 caused more camera makers to design their own, and to seek new sources of supply. Citizen Watch, in coöperation with several camera firms, introduced the Citizen MXV, designed after the Prontor, which was incorporated into the Minolta Autocord. Daiichi produced the Rapid, a copy of the #00 Compur with a self timer, for its own cameras.

Total camera production in Japan rose sharply 1953, to 700,000, 600,000 by members of the Japan Optical Industry Association, the rest by other manufacturers.

The Photographic Industry. 1954.

By 1954, the twin lens reflex was the most popular camera in Japan. Domestically, photographic products and supplies were significantly overproduced in, at best, a mild market. Cameras, and camera manufacturers, proliferated in Japan, and as sales declined an industry which abhors competition began lowering prices. Chiyoda Optical reduced the Minolta Semi P by 1,800 yen, to 11,800 yen, the Olympusflex was discounted by 9,000 yen, and other prices followed. Some cottage industry camera makers switched from twin lens reflexes to inexpensive 35 mm. cameras, others went out of business. There were 80 camera manufacturers in Japan in 1953; by the end of 1954 there were 50.

In order to avert further competition within the industry, and to allow it to engage world markets as a cohesive whole, four organizations were established in 1954. Two would provide the context and the structure for the extraordinary growth of the Japanese camera industry, in both domestic and export markets, during the coming decades: the Japan Camera Industry Association, and the publisher of this book, the Japan Camera Inspection Institute.

The Japan Camera Industry Association was organized in April with Dr. Takeshi Mitarai, president of Canon, Inc., the first president. The Japan Camera Inspection Institute was founded in June to assure strict quality standards in cameras for export markets. The president and driving force behind the growth and effectiveness of JCII was the Honorable Kinji Moriyama, to whom this book is dedicated. The Conference of Camera Manufacturers, Wholesalers and Retailers was founded in July, and in August the Society of Camera Wholesalers was established.

Two new photographic magazines were published in 1954. Sankei Newspapers began *Sankei Camera* in April, and Mainichi Newspapers began *Camera Mainichi* magazine in May.

At the fourth Photokina, in April, Leitz introduced the revolutionary Leica M3, which proved to be orders of magnitude ahead of any other 35 mm. camera. Overnight, it became the catalyst for a complete reappraisal of rangefinder camera design, and it profoundly effected the Japanese camera industry. The M3 had a life-size, bright frame range and viewfinder with automatic parallax correction. The focal-plane shutter dial was stationary; film was advanced with a lever rather than a knob, and counted on a self-resetting frame counter; and an exposure meter slid into the accessory shoe and coupled to the shutter control.

A number of new German cameras incorporated a new Compur shutter with a light value scale, and M/X flash synchronization, that was substantially more advanced than competitive Japanese shutters.

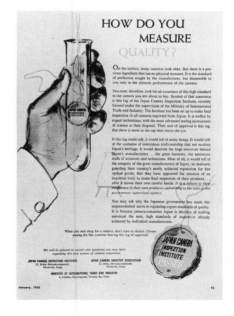

Japan Camera Inspection Institute advertisement in an overseas photography publication.

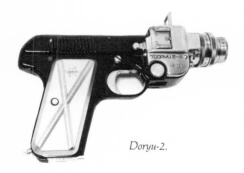

Doryu-2.

The Doryu 2-16 was a subminiature camera which made 10 x 10 mm. exposures on 16 mm. film. It was shaped quite like a semi-automatic handgun. With a C lens mount, the Doryu could fit standard 16 mm. cine optics, and was supplied with an f/2.5 17 mm. lens with helicoid focusing by estimating distance. The shutter had B, and $^1/_{50}$ to $^1/_{200}$. Perhaps the most unusual feature of this uncommon novelty camera was its ability to chamber flash bullets. The handgrip housed objects that closely resembled revolver cartridges, which contained flash powder and an igniting chemical. When chambered, a striker fired the flash powder. It was considered advisable to keep the camera at arm's length when using the flash, to avoid severe facial burns.

The 1954 Escaflex was the first Japanese 6 x 6 cm., leaf-shutter single lens reflex. Made by Eska Optical, it had a fixed lens and an NKS shutter with speeds to $^1/_{300}$. Designed for the general photographic public and priced accordingly at 12,500 yen, it was soon discontinued, then later revived by Rolly Optical as the Rollyflex, with an instant return mirror and semi-automatic diaphragm.

The Stereo Alpen was the first 35 mm. stereo camera made in Japan. Manufactured by Hachiyo Optical, it made an image pair in the Stereo Realist format, 23 x 24 mm.

Taiyodo Camera introduced the Reflex Beauty in 1954, an exact copy of the Reflex Korelle, and the first electronic flash unit made in Japan, the Evertron ATIII, was manufactured by Kawasaki Electric, and marketed by Hattori. Fuji introduced two large aperture Fujinon lenses, a 50 mm. f/1.2 and a 35 mm. f/2.

Escaflex.

Stereo Alpen.

Folding Cameras. 1954.

Aram Six.

The Aram Six, designed by Kennosuke Nakagawa with a cam driven lensboard coupled to a rangefinder of superior accuracy, won an Invention Award from the Ministry of International Trade and Industry. Nakagawa established the Aram Optical Research Institute in April, and began to sell the camera in July, but it was poorly marketed, and soon discontinued.

Other folding cameras introduced in 1954 were the Mamiya Six K; Petri Super V; Cristar 15; Baby Suzuka II; Press Van 120; Mine Six; Elbow Six 1A and IIIA; Semi Doris P and II; Wester Chrome Six 2; Mizuho Six V and Super T; Plato Six P; Tenor Six; Luck and Walcon Semi.

Fujicaflex Automat.

Minoltacord.

The Twin Lens Reflex. 1954.

The surprising popularity of inexpensive twin lens reflexes made by small camera makers led major manufacturers to produce sophisticated, technically advanced models. The market was soon saturated with models at every conceivable level of quality, and at a wide range of prices.

In May, Fuji introduced the Fujicaflex Automat, at 65,000 yen the most expensive Japanese twin lens reflex. A single knob on the right side of the camera focused the lens, and when pulled out a notch, advanced the film and cocked the shutter. A close focusing range was controlled by a gear on the front. The film path extended vertically from top to bottom, and the film was not bent until after passing the exposure gate. The aluminum alloy body was lighter than it appeared, and the shutter release could be positioned either left or right. The Fujinar 83 mm. f/2.8 was mounted in a Seikosha #0 shutter. Certainly the best twin lens reflex of its time, the Fujicaflex Automat sold poorly in a market created by cameras a fifth its price, and there were no later versions.

In April, Chiyoda Optical introduced the Minoltacord, which focused when a lever in the front operated a helicoid behind the lensboard. The focusing lever was operated with the left hand, the film was wound with the right, and the reasonably priced Minoltacord became popular as the most rapidly operated twin lens reflex.

The inexpensive 15,000 yen Yashimaflex was renamed the Yashicaflex in 1954. The Yashicaflex S, introduced in October, was the first Japanese twin lens reflex with a built in, but not coupled, selenium cell exposure meter. With semi-automat film loading and a self-resetting frame counter, the S was sold inexpensively at 20,000 yen, while the Yashicaflex AI, with a Copal YB shutter, was only 9,500 yen. Yashica continued to introduce a steady series of inexpensive twin lens reflexes, some quite comparable to more expensive cameras, in a strategy which soon provided the company a significant world market.

The Koniflex Model II was the first Japanese twin lens reflex with some capacity for interchangeable lenses: the front element could be exchanged to convert the lens to a medium telephoto.

Among the many other twin lens reflexes introduced in 1954 were the first Kowa camera, the Kalloflex Automat I; the Elmoflex V; Olympusflex BII; Primoflex IVA; Mamiyaflex Automat B; Minoltaflex III; Nikkenflex IB & IID;

Koniflex II.

Yashicaflex S.

Princeflex II; Alpenflex IIS; Toyokaflex I; Airesflex Automat; Cosmoflex III; Eilaflex; Dorisflex; Marioflex; Vestaflex II; Cristarflex IIA; Cristar 45; Veriflex; Dorimaflex ALL, AL and B; Pigeonflex; Queenflex J and Zenobiaflex II.

35 mm. 1954.

Nikon S2.

Asahiflex IIB.

Riken 35.

In December, Nippon Kogaku introduced the Nikon S2, widely regarded as one of the best focal plane shutter, rangefinder cameras ever marketed. Designed to compete with the Leica M3, which it did successfully, the S2 was introduced with a shutter calibrated, as are contemporary shutters, in a linear progression. The rewind knob had a small, folding crank, also in the contemporary idiom, the film was advanced with a lever rather than a knurled knob, and the 1:1 finder showed 90 percent of the picture area. The Nikon S2 became a standard in its field.

A number of other cameras with focal plane shutters were introduced in 1954, including the Nicca 3S, the Leotax F, and the Tanack 35 IIC, IIIC, IIF, IIIF and IIIS. Orion Seiki showed a prototype 35 mm. pentaprism single lens reflex called Phoenix, which was marketed a year later as the Miranda T. Nobuyuki Yoshida, an engineer at Asahi Optical Company, designed the first instant return mirror for a single lens reflex, which was incorporated into the 1954 Asahiflex IIB. In the fall, at a convention of the Japan National Federation of Photo Dealer Unions in Kyushu, Asahi also showed a prototype Asahiflex with a pentaprism finder.

Tokiwa introduced the Firstflex, a 35 mm. single lens reflex which resembled the German Exakta. The leaf shutter, with speeds to $1/200$, was located behind the bayonet-mount lens, permitting the camera to use interchangeable lenses. The Olympus 35 1 Va was a compact, fixed lens camera with a glass pressure plate, the first of its kind in Japan. At the time, improving film flatness was an important concern; the glass plate provided a flat film plane, but in Japan's high humidity, the film tended to partially adhere to the plate, inhibiting winding, or worse, to simply stick firmly. In other conditions, (a glass plate was in use in a German camera as well), friction between the film and the glass generated static electricity arcs which exposed the film. Olympus made a modified plate with a surface of tiny convex mounds, but it proved impractical, and the notion of glass was discarded.

In April, the Riken 35 was introduced with two film advance controls, a rapid advance lever on the bottom and a conventional knurled knob on the top. The Windsor, a modestly priced, fixed lens 35 mm. introduced in October, was the first Japanese camera with a 1:1 coupled rangefinder. The Aires 35II was the first Japanese camera with a bright frame viewfinder. The Riken Ricohlette was an inexpensive 35 mm. camera for the general public, in the manner of the Ricohflex. It was ambitiously designed, with a self-cocking mechanism and double exposure prevention, and cost only 6,800 yen. While the Ricohlette did not enjoy the popularity of the Ricohflex, it was the beginning of a long line of successful Ricoh 35 mm. cameras. Petri introduced the Petri 35, the first of many 35 mm. models, and other manufacturers introduced the Lacon 35, Novo 35, Pigeon 35III, C and JII, and the Welmy 35. The Neoca 35 had a rangefinder coupled to a focusing front lens element by a linkage through the lens barrel.

Chapter Nine

The Era of Originality

from an article by Kakugoro Saeki

The Pentaprism Single Lens Reflex.

The 1949 Zeiss Contax S is widely regarded as the first 35 mm. single lens reflex with a pentaprism viewfinder. But the Contax closely resembled the Czech Duflex System Reflex S, a prototype camera with a prism finder, a few hundred of which were built about 1943. An article in the April, 1970 issue of the Hungarian magazine Foto suggests that about 1943, Dr. Nandor Barany, a technical advisor to the Gamma Works in Budapest, urged Gamma to make cameras with a viewfinder having "correct image prisms", which were then being used in telescopes. One was designed by Jozsef Nemeth, and tested by Janos Barabas, the chief optical engineer. Over the still-mysterious objections of Jeno Dulovits, Gamma's chief camera designer and inventor of both the Duto soft-focus attachment lens and the Duflex, a porro-mirror single lens reflex, several hundred Duflex System Reflex S cameras were built.

There is a rumor that co-workers of Dulovits illegally sold the Duflex System design in the Eastern Zone. Striking similarities between the Duflex and the Contax S, particularly in the pentaprism housing and the apron section around the lens mount, have kept the rumor alive.

Contax S, D.D.R.

Duflex System Reflex S, Hungary.

The Japanese Pentaprism Single Lens Reflex. 1955.

In August, 1955, Orion Camera introduced the first Japanese pentaprism single lens reflex, the Miranda T. Known as a manufacturer of bellows units and pentaprism finders for 35 mm. rangefinder cameras, Orion had shown a prototype, the Phoenix, in June, 1954. Because there was already a German camera called Phoenix, they chose the name Miranda, believing it suggested a reflex camera with a mirror, and that it had a soft, feminine sound.

The company said, "The camera body is like the Exakta —not too bulky— easy to handle like a Leica, with dimensions similar to those of the Pentacon. Its flange focus distance is a short 41.5 mm., the lens mount is larger than earlier cameras of other makes taking the Mirax [a single-lens reflex housing they made for Leica and Contax rangefinder cameras], its focal plane shutter, differing from that of the Leica, releases the front and rear curtains simultaneously in the slower shutter speed range; a speed governor has a longer operating time to give more accurate exposure control."

Phoenix.   *Miranda T.*

Kine-Exakta, Germany.

35 mm. single-lens reflex cameras of the time were equipped with waist level finders, through which they provided the typically reversed image. Because it was inconvenient to make photographs in the vertical orientation, the rectangular 35 mm. format proved ill suited to this design, which remains standard for the square format on roll film. The Miranda pentaprism was located above the focusing screen in what is now the traditional configuration. The Miranda, like other early single lens reflexes, was fitted with a mirror which returned to the viewing position only when the film was wound.

There had been few single-lens reflex cameras in the past: the first 35 mm. format was the 1936 Kine Exakta; the first in Japan was the 1952 Asahiflex, a photographic unit for an astronomical telescope.

The Miranda T was strongly influenced by the 1951 Exakta V. It had a shutter release on the front, presumably to couple with an anticipated automatic aperture control. Both cameras had shutter releases on the top for an accessory cable, countdown frame counters and detachable pentaprisms.

The Miranda T had large viewfinder magnification, a geometric progression shutter speed scale, and a standard lens which focused down to 35 cm. It accepted Exakta, Leica and Contax mount lenses with adapters, although the latter two could not focus at infinity. The Miranda was a versatile camera which suggested the range of possibilities single lens reflexes would eventually encompass.

Four months before the Miranda T was introduced, Tokiwa Seiki briefly marketed the Pentaflex, a leaf shutter design which was the first Japanese porromirror single lens reflex.

The Minolta A, a rangefinder camera with a leaf shutter, was introduced by Chiyoda Kogaku in April, 1955. It was the first Japanese camera with a linear, equally spaced aperture scale. The shutter dial was next to the accessory shoe, in the manner of the Leica, in anticipation of the 1957 Super A, which was offered with a coupled meter.

Pentaflex.

Minolta A.

Olympus Wide.

Other Cameras. 1955.

The 1955 Olympus Wide was the first simple snapshot camera with a fixed 35 mm. lens, a configuration which became extremely popular on the autofocus and fixed focus "point-and-shoot" cameras of the 1980s. Although the Olympus had estimated, scale focusing, a limited range of shutter speeds, and film was advanced by a knob rather than a lever, the camera sold well. Several similar cameras soon appeared on the market, and over the next decades the subgroup was refined into a highly important segment of the amateur camera market.

Teraoka Seikosho, a manufacturer of platform scales, introduced a camera called the Auto Terra, which had a spring-driven film wind adapted from the spring mechanism of scales. A single full turn of the film wind knob provided sufficient tension to advance six exposures. The Auto Terra II, introduced in February, 1957, had 12-frame automatic advance and a self-cocking shutter. The Auto Terra IIB, October, 1957, could make multiple exposures, and the November, 1968, IIL had a built-in exposure meter.

The November, 1959 Auto Terra Super, the final model in the series, had 20-frame wind, and both 35 mm. and 80 mm. conversion lenses. The camera, with case, sold for 15,800 yen, half the 29,500 yen price of the original Auto Terra.

The Neoca 35 Model IS was an inexpensive fixed lens 35 mm. rangefinder camera designed, for reasons of economy, to focus by moving only the front lens element. It was the only camera ever made with the front element coupled to an optical rangefinder system.

Auto Terra.

Neoca 35IS.

The Walz 35 was the first Japanese camera which accommodated all three flash systems of the time: electronic, filament, and gas-filled bulb. The compact Lord 35 IV B camera had a rewind knob that opened into a small crank, a standard design on all subsequent 35 mm. cameras.

Minolta Autocord L.

Roll Film Cameras. 1955.

After the Leica M3, coupled exposure meters began to appear on both upper and midmarket Japanese cameras. The Minolta Autocord L was introduced with an exposure meter calibrated in light values, each a combined shutter speed and aperture. The Minolta meter was not coupled, readings were manually set, and the design premise was to transfer only a single number from the meter to a single camera control. The scale on the Minolta had a rather narrow range, LV5 to LV18, because of the limitations of the selenium cell meter. When the meter was removed, the Autocord, with a helicoid focusing lever, resembled the Czech Flexaret, which evidently was a design influence.

Mamiya Six Automat.

The original Mamiya Six Automat was introduced in 1940. Through successive models during the following 15 years, it developed into a folding camera competitive with the 35 mm. cameras of the day. Originally designed to back focus, with a movable film plane and stationary lens, it had what was then an unusual mechanism to cock the shutter when the film was advanced. By July, 1958, when the Mamiya Six Automat Model 2 was introduced, fitted with a bright frame finder, the Zuiko lens was replaced with a Mamiya Sekor, and the price had been reduced by 5,500 yen to 24,000, with case.

The Pearl IIB, unlike most Japanese cameras of the day, was fitted with a flash synchronization terminal of the German rather than the Kodak type. The rather typical semi format, 6 x 4.5 cm. folding camera was made considerably more attractive by the recessed, rather than protruding, pin terminal.

The Primoflex VA was a 6 x 6 cm. twin lens reflex with a diaphragm in the viewing lens coupled to the taking lens, providing depth of field preview in the viewfinder. The design was later used in a Mamiya Sekor 205 mm. f/3.5 DS lens for the Mamiya C330.

Stereo Hit.

Stereo Rocca.

Two stereo cameras were introduced in 1955. In February, the Stereo Rocca was introduced. It made a stereo pair 23 x 24 mm. on 120 film, while the Stereo Hit, introduced in March, made a pair 30 x 40 mm. on 120. They were inexpensive, but because their photographs required stereo viewers or projectors, they were not well received, and were soon removed from the market.

The Hofman, a Tefuda format predecessor to the Horseman technical camera, was designed to compete with the Speed Graphic, the leading press camera of the time.

The Mamiyaflex. 1956.

The Mamiyaflex C Professional was introduced in October, 1956, when twin-lens reflex cameras were in gradual decline. Based on the Rolleiflex, the design had successfully replaced the cut film press camera in photojournalism, and was popular for fashion, portrait and commercial photography as well. Until the Mamiyaflex, however, no twin lens reflex had been equipped to use interchangeable lenses; only conversion lenses and front element interchanging systems had been available.

Each interchangeable optic for the Mamiyaflex was actually a pair of lenses on a retaining flange. A spring rod could secure the flange to a lensboard at the end of a rack-and-pinion driven bellows. The length of the bellows was sufficient to provide reasonably close focus with longer lenses, and unusually close focus with normal and, eventually, wide angle lenses. When lenses were to be changed, the retaining rod could open only when the bellows were fully retracted, and a light capping plate could be positioned to protect the film.

Mamiyaflex C Professional.

The camera was introduced with two sets of lenses, the normal focal length Mamiya Sekor 80 mm. f/2.8, and a 135 mm. f/4.5. Among the first accessories were a paramender, a parallax correction device which attached between the camera and a tripod and elevated the camera exactly the interaxis distance of the lenses; and a porroflex, a porro-mirror finder made in part by Nippon Kogaku.

To create a flat film plane, the lower spool was located directly beneath the frame, unlike the Rolleiflex, which bent the film beyond the frame. This resulted in a protrusion at the back of the camera, requiring two small posts in the front to level the camera, which could not fit on certain tripod heads.

In June, 1958, the modified C2 was introduced. It had focusing knobs on each side of the camera, a distance scale, and it accepted masks for the sportsfinder to frame the coverage of the 105 mm. and 135 mm. lenses.

The 3 series were parallel rather than replacement models to the C2 cameras. The C3 had a large film wind crank, and from 1965, the C33 had a lever which cocked the shutter as the film was wound. The C33 accepted 220 film, and had a bar in the viewing screen to indicate the top of the picture as parallax was introduced at closer focuses. The C22 was introduced in 1966, the C220 in 1968, and the C330 in 1969. The cameras remained in production in 1990 as the C220 Professional-f and the C330 Professional-s.

Ricohflex Dia.

The 1965 Ricohflex Dia had an unusual set of focusing levers on either side of the camera, which were moved up or down to shift the lens. The design provided rapid focusing and offered a firm grip on the camera, but the levers often moved when one hand had to be taken off the camera to trip the shutter, a design flaw from which sales never recovered.

The Leica Influence. 1956, 1957.

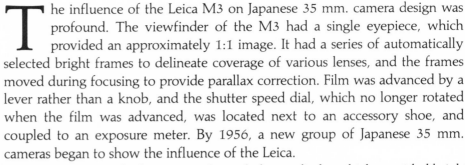

Topcon 35S.

The influence of the Leica M3 on Japanese 35 mm. camera design was profound. The viewfinder of the M3 had a single eyepiece, which provided an approximately 1:1 image. It had a series of automatically selected bright frames to delineate coverage of various lenses, and the frames moved during focusing to provide parallax correction. Film was advanced by a lever rather than a knob, and the shutter speed dial, which no longer rotated when the film was advanced, was located next to an accessory shoe, and coupled to an exposure meter. By 1956, a new group of Japanese 35 mm. cameras began to show the influence of the Leica.

The Topcon 35S had an optional coupled rangefinder which provided bright frames over a 1:1 image which covered 82 percent of the picture area. While the two stroke, ratcheted film wind lever was designed after that of the Leica M3, the automatically elevated rewind knob was carried over from the earlier Topcon Super DM.

Production of Japanese 35 mm. cameras with focal plane shutters reached a peak in 1957, when Nikon introduced the SP, the top of the Nikon S series. The SP had viewfinder brightframes for lenses from 28 mm. to 135 mm. A white frame in the main finder showed the coverage of the 50 mm. lens, and a selector in the hub of the rewind crank added, sequentially, another white frame for an 85 mm. lens, then a yellow frame for a 105 mm., then a red frame for a 135 mm. lens, by which time it was a very busy looking finder. Slightly to the side was a second finder, at .33x for a 28 mm. lens, with a black frame for a 35 mm. lens.

The Nikon SP was the first Japanese camera with a single pivot shutter speed dial that turned only to select a value. In the idiom of the Leica, an exposure meter coupled over it.

The Nikon SP, Nippon Kogaku's best rangefinder camera, remained in production substantially unchanged. The 1958 S3 was a less expensive version of the SP, and the 1959 S4 was a simplified S3. Nikon continued to make rangefinder cameras until 1965.

The Konica IIA had M flash synchronization with adjustable delay. The Koni-Rapid shutter synchronized at all speeds by varying the flash sync with the shutter speed. The Konica III had a film advance lever on the front of the camera, in the manner of the German Tenax.

The 1956 Rittreck was a 6 x 9 cm. single lens reflex, reminiscent of the boxy shape of the Graflex reflexes, with a front cover which functioned as a lens shade. Designed as a portrait camera, the manufacturer originally provided no lenses, only a lensboard, as with view cameras.

Konica IIA.

Konica III.

Nikon SP.

Mamiya Magazine 35.

Japanese Midmarket Cameras. 1957.

After its introduction, sales of the Leica M3 soon eclipsed those of competitive 35 mm. cameras. By 1957, the Nikon SP and the Topcon had begun to compete with the Leica, and midmarket products had begun to display the maturing Japanese camera industry's recent inventiveness and originality.

The Mamiya Magazine 35 had a life-size viewfinder and lever film wind. Reminiscent of the 1941 Kodak Ektra, the camera, including the lens and rangefinder, could be detached from the light-tight film chamber. A large knob in the camera base released the couplings, and the camera separated into two parts after a metal shutter covered the film. Designed to permit photographers to switch films in mid roll, the interchangeable film magazines, which were virtually separate camera bodies, were color coded green and red. The camera was bulky and heavy, and actually less convenient than changing bodies with more conventional cameras. It was a commercial failure, evidently to Mamiya's surprise, and was soon removed from the market.

In February and March, three cameras were introduced with quite different built-in exposure meters. The Mamiya Elca had an electrically coupled match-needle meter in which aperture, shutter and film speeds were connected by resistors, and the needle was aligned against a fixed pointer. The Minolta Auto Wide had a mechanically coupled pursuit-needle system in which aperture, shutter and film speeds were adjusted to align the needles. The exposure meter of the Minolta Super A fitted the accessory shoe, coupled to the shutter dial, and displayed the correct aperture, as on the Leica M3. All three were selenium cell meters.

Minolta Auto-Wide.

Minolta Super A.

The Minolta Auto Wide, like the Olympus Wide, was fitted with a fixed 35 mm. lens. The 1957 Fujica 35M focused by a knob on the camera back which turned a distance scale on the top as it focused the lens. It was fitted with a Copal Special MXV shutter, as was the Mamiya Elca, but the Fujica had a geometric progression shutter scale, the first on a leaf shutter.

Sky Camera.

The Photographic Industry. 1957.

O nly one new single lens reflex was introduced in 1957, the Topcon R. Japan's third, after the Miranda and Pentax, it had the only split-image rangefinder. Strongly influenced by the Exata, the Topcon R had a semi-automatic diaphragm, an Exakta lens mount, and a front shutter release.

A number of 120 cameras were introduced in 1957. The Amano 66 was a 6 x 6 cm. single lens reflex made by Amano Special Machinery. The reflex mirror movement served as the shutter mechanism, so by definition it became the first large format reflex with rapid mirror return.

Fujipet.

The Nippon Kogaku Sky camera, also called the Nikon Fish Eye, was an improved commercial version of a meteorological camera made for the Defense Academy. Pointed straight up, the 16 mm. lens recorded the entire celestial hemisphere, making a 180 degree image in a 2 inch circle on 120 film. When combined with automatic timing devices, the camera could photograph at intervals of 5 to 180 minutes.

The 1957 Fuji Fujipet was an inexpensive 6 x 6 with a single speed ($^1/_{60}$) leaf shutter. Film advance relied on the outdated red window, the single element lens was sharp largely at the center, but the camera was much more successful than Fuji anticipated. With an unusual built-in lens shade, somewhat characteristic appearance and a reputation as a sound basic camera, the Fujipet became a popular first camera for school children and remained marketable for decades.

Minolta 16.

In 1957, the Minolta 16 was redesigned to slightly lift the pressure plate as the film was advanced, to prevent film scratching. The variable pressure plate and the push/pull film wind carried over from the 1950 Konan 16 Automat became distinguishing features of Minolta 16 series cameras.

Automatic Diaphragm Systems. 1958.

Zunow.

In April, Zunow Optical Industry introduced a version of what would become the standard automatic diaphragm mechanism for some decades: a coupling pin inside the lens which stopped down the diaphragm to a pre-selected aperture as the shutter was released. The Zunow camera was particularly small, a size not again seen until the 1973 Olympus OM cameras. The Zunow had a depth of field preview, and shutter speeds to $^1/_{1000}$. On the large dial at the base of the film wind lever, intermediate speeds could also be set.

Zunow Optical had been a pioneer maker of large aperture lenses, introducing f/1.1 and f/1.3 Leica mount lenses in 1953, when f/1.5 was widely thought the largest practical aperture. But the advanced Zunow camera was marketed less than three years when the company was decimated by the bankruptcy of Arco in January, 1961.

Miranda B.

Minolta SR-2.

The Miranda B, like the Exakta, had an external automatic diaphragm system. An appendage on the lens barrel was positioned over the shutter release; when it was pressed into the release the aperture stopped down, further pressure operated the shutter. A lever on the lens then had to be cocked each time to open the aperture. The Prominar Auto 50 mm. f/1.9 lens fitted with this system could also be used on earlier Miranda bodies: the Miranda T, the first Japanese 35 mm. single lens reflex with a pentaprism; the T II, and two export models, the A and AII.

The film wind lever of the Minolta SR-2 tensioned a spring which stopped down the aperture when the shutter was released. Because the Miranda and Minolta semi-automatic systems were called automatic, when actual automatic apertures were introduced later, they were called fully automatic.

The Pentax K was announced in 1958, one year after Asahi's first pentaprism single lens reflex, the Pentax. The K was fitted with the first microprism focusing screen, an important optical advance which would soon become standard on single lens reflexes. At this writing, more than three decades later, microprism screens remain standard and Asahi continues to market a K series camera.

Asahi Pentax K.

The 1958 Pentax K, which won a gold medal at the World Exposition at Brussels that year, had a $^1/_{1000}$ shutter and semi-automatic diaphragm. Asahi made a group of new lenses for the second Pentax, including two 35 mm. optics, an f/2.3 and an f/4.; a 105 mm. f/2.8; a 300 mm. f/4 and a 1,000 mm. f/8; and continued to offer the earlier 83 mm. f/1.9; 100 mm. f/3.5; 135 mm. f/3.5 and 500 mm. f/5.

4 x 4 Format. 1958.

As 35 mm. single lens reflexes were becoming popular, a small format for twin lens reflexes was being re-introduced. The 4 x 4 cm. image on 127 film had first been made in the pre-war Baby Rollei, which was produced again in 1957. Fitted with a Xenar 60 mm. f/3.5 taking lens and a Heidosmat 60 mm. f/2.8 viewing lens, it had a Synchro-Compur LVS shutter calibrated in Light Values. The Rollei made 12 exposures, 41 mm. square, on 127 film which was advanced with automatic frame stops. The compact camera was thought to have a particular appeal to women because of its size, and attractive grey leather housing.

Rolleiflex 4 x 4, B.R.D.

Primo JR.

Yashica 44.

The Baby Rollei was quite popular, in part because it introduced the Super Slide format, a 4 x 4 cm. transparency mounted in an otherwise standard 2 x 2 inch slide mount. With an overall image area almost twice that of a 35 mm. slide in effectively the same mount, it was at once compatible with existing projection and storage systems, and a somewhat more imposing projected image.

The first Japanese 4 x 4 cm. twin lens reflex was the Yashica 44. Supplied in seven different "symphonic colors" of charcoal grey, silver grey, pastel blue, lavender, golden brown, rosy brown and burgundy, the 44 had an f/3.5 lens, semi-automatic film advance and a manually cocked Copal shutter.

Immediately after Yashica announced the camera, at the Master Photo Dealers and Finishers Association show in Chicago in 1958, Franke & Heidecke AG publicly charged the Yashica was a copy of the Rolleiflex 4 x 4. The incident led to the creation of the Japan Machinery Design Center, which screened all cameras exported from Japan from November, 1959.

In the same month, Tokyo Optical introduced the Primo Jr., a camera similar to the Yashica with a faster, f/2.8 lens in a Seikosha shutter. It had semi-automatic film advance, parallax correction marks in the finder, and close focus to 0.6 meter.

The Yashica 44 and Primo Jr. were followed by the Ricoh Super 44 and Ricohmatic 44, the Minolta Miniflex, the Waltz Automat 44, and a second Yashica, the 44LM Deluxe. Olympus showed a prototype automatic exposure

Olympus Eye 44.

camera, the Olympus Eye 44, with a shutter priority system not used in a production model until the Olympus Auto Eye, a 1960 35 mm. camera. Interest in the 4 x 4 format in the United States was brief, and the cameras were soon withdrawn from the market, widely believed to have failed because the general public couldn't accept using reversed image finders with uncorrected parallax.

Konica IIIA.

Aires 35V.

The Photographic Industry. 1958.

The Konica III-A had a sophisticated rangefinder/viewfinder system which provided unusually accurate parallax correction. Rather than simply moving the bright frames within the finder, the Konica, which had significant close focus, recorded the actual shift with great accuracy in all dimensions. It was the only example of this very expensive system in a production camera. The two-stroke film advance lever on the left front, similar to the German Tenax, was continued from the Konica III.

Canon VL.

The October, 1958, Aries 35V was fitted with a leaf shutter and an f/1.5 lens. The Aries was one of a group of cameras supplied with fast lenses, and the large apertures were causing an odd problem with cloth focal plane shutters: sunlight could focus through the lens and burn holes in the shutter curtains. Canon introduced an .018 mm. stainless steel shutter curtain in the Canon VL, while Nikon installed a titanium curtain in the SP.

The Panorax Z1-A was the only panoramic camera in the world to use a rotating mirror optical system. An external mirror at the beginning of the optical system directed light into the lens, an internal mirror directed the focused image onto the film. The film was positioned in a circle within the body, and the optical system rotated on a clockwork mechanism in an arc variable from 45 to 342 degrees. The Panorax used standard 35 mm. film cartridges, on which a 45 degree image occupied a film area equivalent to a standard 24 x 36 mm. frame. The take-up spool and film cartridge made a full 360 degree field impossible, the space was used for a tall stalk, with the reflex finder at the base. Nippon Tokushukoki made only a few of these unusual instruments, which were very expensive at 450,000 yen.

The unusual viewfinder of The
Panorax Z1-A.

Panorax Z1-A.

Nikon S4.   *Canon P.*

By 1959, rangefinder cameras were competing principally on price, and most new 35 mm. cameras were single lens reflexes. The two major new rangefinder models introduced in 1959, the Canon P and the Nikon S4, were less expensive versions of current models, the Canon VIL and Nikon S3.

Unable to convert to single lens reflexes, the makers of Leotax and Honor cameras were forced out of business, and Yashica absorbed Nicca, whose technology was evident in the 1960 Yashica Pentamatic single lens reflex.

Canonflex.   *Nikon F.*

The first Canon single lens reflex was the May, 1959 Canonflex; the Nikon F was introduced a month later. The Canonflex was innovative: it had a split image rangefinder with a microprism, and an exposure meter coupled to the shutter control. But it was also curious: the film advance lever was fitted into the base of the camera, where it would encounter tripod heads, and while there were five telephoto lenses, there were no wide angle lenses. It was discontinued after only three months in production.

On the other hand, the Nikon F had the longest production run in the history of the postwar Japanese camera industry. It remained in production until 1973, and was followed by successive F models in subsequent decades. The Nikon F was introduced with six interchangeable lenses, a 21 mm. which could be fitted only with the mirror locked up; a 28 mm.; a standard 50 mm.; 105 mm. and 135 mm. telephotos, and an 85-250 mm. f/4.0-f/4.5 zoom. With adapters, the Nikon F could mount five lenses from the Nikon S rangefinder cameras, all 100 mm. or longer.

The Nikon F was the first Japanese camera with interchangeable focusing screens, and a locked up position for the reflex mirror, designed to accomodate the back elements of the 21 mm. lens.

In a continuing effort to keep up with the lenses offered for single lens reflexes, Kowa made three rangefinder cameras with fixed lenses of various focal lengths, creating special purpose cameras rather than hybrid front-element interchanging systems. The 1958 Kallo Wide F had a 35 mm. f/2.8 lens and a built-in meter. The two 1959 telephoto cameras, the Kallo T85 and T100, had 1:1 bright frame finders which were difficult to use, the cameras were awkward, and they were soon discontinued.

Kallo 140.

The Kallo 140 took the other design position: a leaf shutter was designed into the body behind the lens mount, and the camera was offered with interchangeable lenses.

The Kallo 180 was notable largely for an unusual film rewind system in which three claws clamped onto the cartridge stem, held it during rewind, then retracted.

Half Frame. 1959.

The Konica III-M was the first Japanese camera, and one of the few in the world, to use both full and half frame formats. Introduced in March, the III-A was converted to half frame by a mask which was fitted over the film gate. The gate also engaged a device above the take-up sprocket, causing the the two-stroke film advance for full frame 35 mm. to become a single wind for half frame.

Konica IIIM.

The Mamiya Sketch was also introduced in March. It was the first camera made in Japan for the pre-war, German Robot format. A compact rangefinder camera finished in grey leather, the unusual 24 mm. square image it made on 35 mm. film, although larger than half frame, never became popular on domestic or export markets.

In September, the Olympus Pen was introduced. It was the first, and the best known Japanese half frame camera. It was also the first Japanese camera to use a thumb wheel to advance the film.

The Olympus Pen was small, about 4 x 2½ x 1¾ inches, and the 28 mm. f/3.5 lens was quite sharp for a simple camera which cost only 6,800 yen with a case. The camera remained inexpensive: almost 25 years later, in 1983, the Pen EE-3 sold for only 14,800 yen. Because of their size, half frame cameras became latter-day detective cameras (see Chapter 2, page 11). A Japanese magazine photographer became infamous for having concealed an Olympus in a pocket, and through a hole cut in his clothing, photographed the Sanya slum district in Tokyo.

Mamiya Sketch.

Olympus Pen.

Within a year or two, there were a number of half frame cameras, some single lens reflexes, some with interchangeable lenses. One of the evident advantages of the format, that it made twice as many frames on a roll as the conventional format, proved soon to be a disadvantage to amateurs. Color photofinishing was expensive, and the longer rolls of film seemed endless to snapshooters. Half frame cameras were infamously called "calendar cameras", because a single roll might encompass a year's photos. The 1963 126 cartridge cameras, the 1972 110 cartridge cameras, and the compact 35 mm. cameras of the 1970s and 1980s all overshadowed half frame cameras, although Olympus and Ricoh continued to produce them into the 1980s, and eventually Olympus made and sold more than ten million Pen cameras.

Zenza Bronica.

The Bronica. 1959.

The Zenza Bronica was the first Japanese 6 x 6 single lens reflex with fully interchangeable lenses and film backs. Introduced in April, it had been designed and built over a period of several years by Zenzaburo Yoshino, president of a company which manufactured cosmetic compacts and smoking articles. He also owned a camera store in the Nihonbashi district of Tokyo, and when he first saw and admired a Hasselblad, Yoshino perceived it as a challenge. He made a prototype, originally called the Yoshinoflex, of a camera he thought would be even better than the Hasselblad, and after several years, he introduced the first Zenza Bronica.

The Bronica was originally supplied with automatic diaphragm Nikkor lenses. In addition to the standard 75 mm. f/2.8 lens, the first two additional optics were a 50 mm. f/3.5 and 135 mm. f/3.5. Later lenses included an 85 mm. f/1.8, 180 mm. f/2.5, 250 mm. f/4, 350 mm. f/4.5, 500 mm. f/5 and 1000 mm. f/5.6. An accessory pentaprism finder was also available.

The Zenza Bronica had a focal plane shutter with speeds to $^1/_{250}$, and used the self timer to make exposures from one to ten seconds. A single knob on the right side of the camera functioned as shutter dial, film advance and focusing knob. The reflex mirror dropped down, rather than flipping up, to clear the protruding back elements of wide angle lenses. Interchangeable film magazines were equipped with dark slides and an exposure lock, and were also available in 4 x 4 and 35 mm. formats.

Despite its high price, the Zenza Bronica was popular, and sold well. It did not always work well, however, and it was not until subsequent models that Bronica became the reliable professional camera it has remained for more than three decades. Hasselblad litigated, accusing Bronica of plagiarism, but the quality of the camera, especially the backs, was a greater concern. The next models had fixed film backs, with interchangeable inserts, and various mechanisms were simplified. Interchangeable backs, and a wide range of Zenzanon lenses, were offered in the following years as the camera became increasingly competitive in professional markets.

Yashica Y16.

Ramera.

The Photographic Industry. 1959.

The Yashica Y-16, introduced in March, used 16 mm. film in a pre-loaded cartridge, the direct precursor of 110 cartridge film. It was a relatively early example of a well-made Japanese subminiature, and had a certain novelty value: the film could be advanced by holding a large knob on top and swinging the camera body around an arc in the air.

The Kowa Ramera combined, as its name suggests, a 16 mm. subminiature camera with a six transistor portable radio. It can charitably be said that the Ramera, primarily made for export, was more radio than camera. The Okamoto Koki Septon Pen was a 16 mm. subminiature camera combined with a mechanical pencil, and the pencil operated well.

The film speed dial of the 1959 Ricohmatic 44 was also the shutter speed control: each film speed was a different shutter speed. The aperture was set by matching a needle visible from above, and a plastic front cover replaced a camera case.

Panon Camera, maker of the Panolux, introduced the Widelux in 1959. The Widelux made a 140 degree panorama on 35 mm. film by rotating the lens horizontally as a vertical slit, synchronized with the lens, moved across the film. It was the first 35 mm. panoramic camera with a fixed film plane and moving lens ever made for general sale. The Widelux remained in production for decades.

Septon Pen.

Widelux.

Ricohmatic 44.

Chapter Ten

New Materials

from an article by Kakugoro Saeki

The First Japan Camera Show. 1960.

By 1955, Japanese camera models had begun to change frequently, in part because many of the rapid changing technologies of the day were being incorporated into camera design. By 1960, the increasingly intense competition made possible by shorter product cycles, price-based marketing strategies and more efficient production, was considered in the Japanese business culture to be "getting out of hand".

The industry asserted that aggressive competition among manufacturers "brought more trouble than benefits for the consumer". A series of rationales were advanced why it would be in the consumer's interest for competition to be regulated. One held that in the highly competitive state of rapid technological development, product life cycles had become so short a consumer might find a new camera obsolete the day after it was purchased. Another asserted that competition lowered rather than raised quality levels: there was a growing public perception that cameras were frequently mechanically defective, and in fact, many cameras were marketed hurriedly, without thorough testing. Another concern was that endemic price cutting created public doubt as to the real worth of any camera, that prices were increasingly perceived as entirely market, rather than value based.

Most seriously for the industry, the endless proliferation of new models and price cutting had led to bankruptcies among camera manufacturers and distributors. A relatively complex rationale was put forward that this was as bad for the consumer as for the industry, on the premise that bankruptcies left customers without warranty service.

Nippon Koki went bankrupt in July, 1957; Taiyodo Koki in September, 1957; Nishida Kogaku in January, 1958; Nicca Camera in May 1958, when it was taken over in receivership by Yashica; Leotax in October, 1959; Arco and Zunow in December, 1959; Neoca in January, 1960; Bell and Koon and Aires in July, 1960, and Waltz in April, 1961.

Although far from bankrupt, film and sensitized paper manufacturers such as Fuji, Konishiroku, Oriental and Mitsubishi had begun a similar cycle of competition in 1957, when they reduced retail prices by 10 to 20 percent.

In October, 1959, to alleviate what they called "a situation of damaging competition", the 44 member companies of the Japan Camera Industry Association agreed to limit new product introductions to twice a year. The agreement, which would not have been possible in some of the other photographic manufacturing countries, led to the formation of the Japan Camera Show as the format and site for introducing and exhibiting new products.

The first Japan Camera Show, held at the Takashimaya Department Store in Nihonbashi, Tokyo, March 1 to 6, 1960, was seen as "an important step towards more orderly competition in the camera industry". More than 300 representatives of the government, the industry and the press gathered for an opening ceremony attended by Princess Takamatsu, and total attendance during the six day period reached 130,000. The 44 member firms exhibited 300 cameras, including 30 new models, and 200,000 copies were distributed of a 60-page catalog of products from 32 manufacturers.

Olympus Auto Eye.

The First Japanese Automatic Exposure Camera. 1960.

The Olympus Auto Eye was the first production model of a Japanese automatic exposure camera. It was a shutter priority 35 mm. camera based on the Olympus Eye 44, a 1958 prototype automatic 4 x 4 cm. twin lens reflex. Film speed was entered, the shutter speed was selected manually, and when the shutter was released, the aperture stopped down to a value determined by a galvanometer. The Auto Eye was marketed for only two years, largely due to competition from the 1961 Canon Canonet.

In 1960, nineteen 35 mm. single lens reflexes were introduced in Japan, the largest number to date in a single year. Seven medium priced cameras were fitted with leaf shutters: the Topcon PRII, Aires Penta 35, Kowaflex, Topcon Wink Mirror, Aires Ever, Nikkorex 35 and Kowa E.

The Nikkorex 35 used porro mirrors, allowing the top of the camera to remain flat; the reflex mirror was not instant return, and there was a selenium cell on the camera front. Only two interchangeable lenses were offered: a 35 mm. f/5.6 and a 90 mm. f/5.6 in a front converter attachment system, along with adapters for telescopes, microscopes and binoculars. The camera was not popular, and in 1962, a Seikosha SLV shutter was added and the price was lowered by 2,500 yen; in 1963, the camera was reduced to 11,500 yen, almost half the original price. Apparently because they contradicted the public image of Nikon cameras, none of Nippon Kogaku's leaf-shutter single lens reflexes sold well. The Nikkorex 35, the related Nikkorex Zoom 35 and the Nikon Auto 35 were soon discontinued. The focal plane shutter Nikkorex F sold well, and was later redesigned into the extremely popular Nikkomat.

Nikkorex 35.

Miranda Automex.

Konica F.

New Shutter Mechanisms. 1960.

T he Konica F was a production model of the Konicaflex, a prototype shown at the International Trade Fair at Harumi, Tokyo, in 1959. The Konicaflex prototype was the first 35 mm. single lens reflex with a built-in exposure meter.

The Konica F was quite thin: the lens mounting flange was only 41.5 mm. in front of the focal plane. To accommodate the rear lens element, the reflex mirror moved back as it flipped up. Because of the short flange, the camera could accept adapters and lenses from other models. The shutter, what is now called the Copal Square type — four metal blades traveling vertically — had a $1/2000$ speed, the fastest focal plane shutter of the day. The vertical travel of the shutter blades made possible M flash synchronization at all shutter speeds, and X flash synchronization up to $1/125$, one stop faster than the common horizontal cloth shutters. Konishiroku called it the High Synchro Shutter.

The Miranda Automex had a coupled, match-needle system, similar to the Konica F, and a selenium cell on the pentaprism housing.

Topcon Wink Mirror.

The first instant return mirror in a leaf-shutter single lens reflex was incorporated into the compact Topcon Wink Mirror. The following year, an exposure meter was added in the E model, which was modified into the subsequent Wink Mirror LS, and finally, in 1964, into the Topcon Uni.

In February, 1960, Minolta announced a programmed leaf shutter developed jointly with Citizen Watch Co. A single set of five blades functioned as both shutter and aperture, creating aperture values by opening to various diameters, shutter values by doing so for various times. Minolta called this the Optiper Uni-Citizen Special Luminance Shutter, and called the camera the Uniomat. The concept originated in the States on a turn of the century Bausch & Lomb shutter, and while the Minolta was the only 35 mm. example, a not dissimilar shutter was used in the Polaroid SX-70. The Uniomat was controlled by matching meter and pursuit needles in the viewfinder, which set combined aperture/shutter values on a scale from EV 6, f/2.8 at $1/8$, to EV 18, f/16 at $1/1000$.

Minolta Uniomat.

Two other Minolta cameras were introduced with high speed Optiper HS Citizen leaf shutters. The Optiper M-10 in the 1958 V2, $1/2000$, and the M-13 in the 1960 V3, $1/3000$, were the fastest leaf shutters supplied in cameras at the time. Drawing on the premise of the Uniomat, the fastest shutter speeds were

Minolta V2.

Minolta V3.

achieved by not opening the shutter blades fully: the M-10 produced $^1/_{1000}$ at f/4 and smaller, $^1/_{2000}$ only at f/8 or smaller. The M-13 could produce $^1/_{2000}$ at f/4, $^1/_{3000}$ no larger than f/8.

There was no meter in the V2, and the selenium meter in the more sophisticated V3 was not coupled to the controls. Because of the aggressive competition of the day, the V3 was introduced at the same price as the V2, its case was 300 yen less than the V2 case.

Lord Martian.

Aires Radar-Eye.

The Photographic Industry. 1960.

In 1960, Okaya Kogaku introduced the Lord Martian camera, which had photocells for the selenium exposure meter positioned around the front lens element, the first such arrangement in a Japanese camera. Filters covered both the metering cells and the lens, producing direct exposure compensation, and the large lens barrel was perceived as an attractive design. The 1961 Canonet used the same design.

The Aires Viscount M2.8 had an exposure meter needle visible in the finder, as did the Aries Radar-Eye, introduced in April. The name Radar-Eye was intended to imply that all the required data for picture taking was displayed in the viewfinder. Distance was determined with the coupled rangefinder, exposure was determined by matching meter and pursuit needles at the edge of the finder, and composition was done within parallax compensating bright frames.

Aries Camera Works closed in July, bankrupt after an unsuccessful venture in leaf-shutter single lens reflexes.

By 1960, postwar austerity in Japan was giving way to consumerism, and in an expanding market, capital investment in the camera industry began to increase. Japanese camera manufacturers exhibited more actively that year at Photokina, where the most significant introduction was the Canon 7, with an f/0.95 lens, a considerable advance over the currently fastest Nikon and Zunow f/1.1 lenses. While technical advances were not unusual in new Japanese products, high prices were, and the $800 retail price of the Canon 7 did not go unnoticed in the industry.

Canon 7.

A Japanese Polaroid Camera. 1960.

I n April, 1960, Polaroid Corporation in the U.S. contracted to have Yashica manufacture the Polaroid Model 120 Land Camera, the first Polaroid camera made in Japan.

The first Polaroid Land camera, the Model 95, was introduced in the United States in November, 1948. Dr. Edwin H. Land, the inventor of the Polaroid camera, had founded Polaroid in 1937 to market his invention of sheet polarizing material. That material became the basis for a number of stereo photography systems, and led to further photographic research from which Polaroid One Step photography emerged.

Polaroid Land Camera Model 120.

The Japanese-made Polaroid Model 120 Land camera, marketed in May, 1961, was an international-market version of the 1957 Model 110A, equipped with an f/4.7 127 mm. Yashinon lens in a Seikosha SLV shutter. The aperture stopped down to f/90, the shutter had speeds to 1/500, and the camera had an exposure range of EV 5 to EV 22. A small fill flash was available, as was an accessory exposure meter, scaled in EV. In Japan, because Polaroid Land film, including an extremely high speed ASA 3000 material, was imported from the States, the price of one roll was 980 yen. While Polaroid products were prohibitively expensive on the Japanese domestic market, a number of other international-market Polaroid cameras were made in Japan in subsequent years. The 1962 Model 160 Land camera was a version of the earlier U.S. Model 150, a coupled-rangefinder camera with a parallax correcting viewfinder; and the 1965 Model 180 was a sophisticated, manually-controlled pack-film camera for professional photography.

Canonet.

Automation in Midmarket Cameras. 1961.

I n February, 1961, the Canon Canonet was introduced. It had been announced in August of the previous year, to bitter objections from rival camera manufacturers: the announcement had disregarded the industry agreement of publicly showing new models only in the spring and the fall of each year. Worse, competitors considered the Canonet's price too low for its performance. There had been only one automatic exposure camera before the Canonet, the Olympus Auto Eye, and at the time, cameras with coupled exposure meters sold for more than 20,000 yen.

The medium-priced Canonet, with an f/1.9 lens, coupled rangefinder, automatic parallax correction and automatic exposure warning mark, was perceived as offering too much value for its price. It caused considerable controversy among the members of an industry which had agreed not to compete. Rival camera manufacturers insisted that the low price of the Canonet was in violation of the manufacturers' agreement to fix prices industry wide. Under industry pressure, Canon delayed the 1960 introduction until the spring of 1961.

The Canonet had an automatic shutter-locking device which engaged when the light level was outside the automatic exposure range. When the shutter locked, the photographer could select another shutter speed. The system radically changed the novice photographer's notions of camera mechanisms: the Canonet appeared to refuse to make an incorrect exposure.

The Canonet was highly influential. In addition to changing public expectations in matters of camera price and performance, it exerted pressure on other manufacturers to begin to produce automatic exposure systems.

The Fujipet EE was the automatic exposure version of the 1957 Fujipet camera. The single aperture blade of the EE had an eliptical opening which varied the effective aperture as it moved across an arc. But the entire exposure range was only three stops: at the sole shutter speed of $^1/_{60}$, the only apertures were f/11, 16 and 22. Automated or not, the effective range was so restricted the Fujipet proved of no practical use.

Fujipet EE.

Automatic Exposure 35 mm. Cameras. 1961.

The Ricoh Auto 35 was introduced in April, 1961. The aperture was regulated by a selenium cell exposure meter against a single shutter speed for each film speed: the shutter operated only at $^1/_{25}$ for ASA 10 films, $^1/_{32}$ for ASA 50 films, $^1/_{100}$ for ASA 100, $^1/_{200}$ for ASA 200. The grey and silver camera was typical of the fashion in camera design of the time.

The Ricoh Auto 35 V, a zone-focusing version of the fixed-focus Auto 35, was introduced in October. The lens barrel and viewfinder displayed three symbols for focusing distances: a hill for infinity, a full figure for 3.2 meters, and a half figure for 1.5 meters. The automatic exposure mechanism was unchanged, but the faster f/2.8 lens increased the coupled exposure range with ASA 100 film from EV 10.7 - 15.7, to EV 8 - EV 17. The two-tone finish was chrome and black.

The Fujica 35 Auto M, with a shutter called the Copal Magic, had an unusual meter coupling mechanism. When the shutter priority system could not find a proper aperture for the selected speed, the camera began to change shutter speeds until an exposure became possible. If no combination was found, the shutter locked.

Automatic exposure was not offered on higher priced rangefinder or single-lens reflex cameras with focal plane shutters. It was generally believed that automatic exposure mechanisms were too fragile, that galvanometers were not sufficiently shock resistant, and that built-in exposure meters were unreliable. Hajimu Miyabe, a leading camera designer of the time, had declared that automatic exposure devices were too risky a proposition for the better cameras.

Fujica 35 Auto M.   *Ricoh Auto 35 V.*

Asahi Pentax S3.

The Photographic Industry. 1961.

The more costly single lens reflexes soon had detachable CdS exposure meters, in the manner of the Leica M3. While the first detachable meter to appear on a Japanese camera was the selenium cell unit on the 1957 Minolta Super A, the first such CdS meter was for the 1961 Asahi Pentax S3. The Pentax meter had a duplicate shutter dial which sat over, and coupled to, the dial on the camera. When a speed was selected, the meter needle indicated an aperture value. The meter had two ranges, and overall covered EV 1.7 to EV 18 at ASA 100.

The Mamiya Automatic 35 EEF, exported as the Tower 39, was the first camera manufactured in Japan to use the then-new AG-1 flashbulb. It had a flash reflector completely integrated into the camera body, and semi-automatic exposure control. The camera shutter had four speeds: FL, for flash, which was ¹/₄₀; BL, for backlight, which was ¹/₁₀₀; and ¹/₆₀ and ¹/₂₅₀. It also had four apertures: f/3.8, f/8, f/11 and f/22. The shutter priority system added 2.5 stops when the shutter was set to BL.

Tower 39.

Graphic 35 Jet.

Yashica Rapide.

The Graphic 35 Jet was made for export only by Kowa, under license from Graflex Inc., U. S. It was the first and only camera to use gas pressure to advance the film and cock the shutter. A cartridge of carbonic gas, the type used in soda siphon bottles, drove a motor mechanism in the camera, and a manual winding lever was provided in case the gas ran out. Pushing dual levers below the finder window focused the camera, which had a built-in, match-needle exposure meter, and a shutter release was located on the front, where self timers are usually found.

The Yashica Rapide was an unusual half frame 35 mm. camera with a two-tone body and a leather strap at the camera base to advance the film and cock the shutter. It had a built-in meter which was not coupled to the controls, and the bright frame finder was not clear. The camera was discontinued after a year.

The Viscawide-16, a 16 mm. panoramic camera in the idiom of the Widelux, was introduced in March. It made a 140 degree panoram on a 10 x 52 mm. format. Because it used 16 mm film, it was more popular abroad than in Japan.

Fuji Photo Film marketed an ASA 100 color reversal film in July, and introduced an ASA 50 color negative film in October. Abroad, Eastman Kodak introduced an improved Kodachrome, Kodachrome II.

Viscawide-16.

The Photographic Industry. 1962.

In March, 1962, sales and production of photographic goods increased when excise taxes were reduced from 30 to 20 percent on cameras and from 20 to 10 percent on black-and-white sensitized goods. The industry produced 1,792,805 viewfinder 35 mm. cameras during 1962, a volume it would not again achieve until 1969. It was a record year for Japanese camera manufacturers: the Japan Camera Industry Association recorded 2,907,232 still cameras manufactured in 1962, 879,847 more than 1961. The total value of camera production was 28,900 million yen, up 9,500 million yen.

Minolta Hi-matic.

Interest in photography among amateurs continued to grow during the year, and more than 250,000 entries were received in the Fuji Amateur Photo Contest. The Minolta Hi-matic camera, introduced in December, 1961, became famous in 1962 when U. S. astronaut John Glenn used it to make photographs from space. During the year, a number of manufacturers changed their company names to their brand names, as Chiyoda Kogaku Seiko became Minolta Camera, Kuribayashi became Petri and Riken Kogaku was renamed Ricoh.

CdS Metering. 1962.

The CdS cell was much smaller than the earlier selenium cell, and because it was externally powered, could operate in much lower light.

In 1961, Asahi made detachable CdS exposure meters which coupled with the Pentax S2 and S3 cameras. The Taron Marquis, introduced in April, 1962, was the first camera with a built-in CdS exposure meter, and the first camera to couple a power switch to the film wind lever.

In July, the Minolta SR-7 was introduced. The CdS light meter was located on the left shoulder of the camera, and its somewhat unusual appearance became quite popular. But the meter switch was located in the camera base, and could not be turned on or off when the camera was in its case. It was not until the case for the later SRT-101 that an opening was made for the switch.

Taron Marquis.

Minolta SR-7.

Nikkorex Zoom 35.

In December, Yashica introduced the J3 with an equally inaccessible power switch. Film and shutter speeds were set into the CdS meter, which then displayed the appropriate aperture value.

In December, the Nikkorex Zoom 35 was introduced. It was the first 35 mm. camera ever fitted with a permanently mounted zoom lens. The 43 mm. to 86 mm. f/3.5 Zoom Nikkor was also offered as an interchangeable optic for Nikon cameras.

While it provided only modest wide-angle and telephoto perspectives, the Nikkorex Zoom was a clever, versatile camera. The drawback was not the limited focal lengths of the zoom, but the fact that the zoom was fixed, and interchangeable lenses could not be fitted. At more than 40,000 yen with case, the leaf shutter, fixed-zoom Nikkorex was almost as costly as a focal-plane shutter single lens reflex. The Nikkorex only coincidentally resembles the popular cameras of two and three decades later; it had no influence on single lens reflex design at the time.

Leaf shutters limited interchangeable optics, and required manufacturers to produce front converter attachments rather than proper interchangeable lenses. Wide angle units were generally about 35 mm., with f/4 or f/5.6 apertures, while telephoto attachments were 80 mm. to 90 mm., f/4 or f/5.6. Fuji's Fujicarex prototype, which was never marketed, had two interchangeable front elements, a 35 mm. f/4 and an 80 mm. f/2.8. The Mamiya Prismat PH, with a shutter behind the lens flange, had two fully interchangeable lenses: a 38 mm. and a 100 mm., both f/3.5.

The Konica FSW was essentially an FS with a data imprinting mechanism in the rear cover. Consisting of a miniature watch and calendar, a tiny electronic flash and a lens, it made 300 exposures with a nine volt battery. The four-second recycling flash was connected to the X synchronization terminal of the camera. The Konica FSW was initially made for law enforcement, and later sold publicly.

Konica FSW.

Half Frame. 1962.

The Olympus Pen EE had a single shutter speed, $^1/_{60}$, and an f/3.5 lens with automatic apertures controlled over a range of EV 9.5 to EV 15 at ASA 100. A safety locked the shutter outside the exposure range, and apertures were manually set for flash. In 1966, the Pen EE was modified with a two-speed shutter and simplified film loading. The 1968 Pen EE-2 had a hinged rear cover and an ascending frame counter. The EES had a two speed programmed shutter and automatic aperture, a system later used in the Olympus Trip 35.

Olympus Pen EES.

The Yashica Sequelle, a half-frame camera which resembled an 8 mm. cine camera, was essentially a popularized version of the 1960 Nikon S3M. It was the first camera manufactured in Japan with an electric motor to advance the film. Powered by three batteries housed in the camera, the Sequelle motor could wind each half-frame in .8 second or less, and the camera would continue, as the shutter button was continuously released, until the count-down frame counter reached a halt mark. The Sequelle sold poorly, and was soon withdrawn from the market.

Yashica Sequelle.

Metering Through the Lens. 1963.

Although Asahi had shown a prototype in 1960, the 1963 Topcon RE Super was the first production model of a Japanese single lens reflex which metered through the lens. The exposure meter was developed jointly by Tokyo Shibaura Electric, a leading electronics manufacturer, and Tokyo Optical, maker of Topcon. CdS cells on the back of the mirror, behind a series of .05 mm. slits, made averaged readings at full aperture from about seven percent of the total light. The film speed ring, shutter dial and aperture ring were mechanically coupled with three chains.

The Kowa H, introduced in March, was the first Japanese single lens reflex with a leaf shutter designed to meter through the lens. The selenium meter drove an automatic exposure system which locked the shutter outside the automatic range, and front converter lens attachments were available.

Topcon RE Super.

Kowa H.

Half Frame. 1963.

Production of half-frame cameras increased sharply in 1963, with the introduction of the Olympus Pen F, and the Canon Demi and Dial 35.

The Olympus Pen F was introduced at the Tokyo Camera Show in the spring of 1963. It was the central component in a half-frame single lens reflex system which included five interchangeable lenses. The camera, which made a vertical picture in normal orientation, was less than 3 x 5 inches, a size made possible by an ingenious optical path with a reflex mirror which swung sideways, and a porro prism. It had an unusual metal rotary shutter which synchronized at all speeds. The first interchangeable lenses included a 25 mm. f/4, 60 mm. f/1.5, 70 mm. f/2, 100 mm. f/3.5 and a 50-90 mm. f/3.5 zoom. There were two standard lenses, a 38 mm. f/1.8 and a 40 mm. f/1.4. Eventually, there were 14 lenses for the Pen cameras, including an 800 mm. catadioptric telephoto.

Olympus Pen F.

Canon Dial 35.

An improved Pen F was introduced in October, 1966. The Pen FT metered through the lens, while the Pen FV, an inexpensive version without a meter, was introduced in February, 1967, at 27,900 yen. The Pen half-frame single lens reflex was eventually to develop into the extremely successful Olympus OM-1, a compact, full-frame 35 mm. single lens reflex.

The Canon Demi, introduced in March, had a built-in, match needle exposure meter, and a Kepler finder similar to the accessory finder on Leicas. The 28 mm. f/2.8 lens was unusually small, and the camera and lens were only 37 mm. thick.

The Canon Dial 35 was introduced in October. The name referred to the circular placement of CdS meter cells around the front of the lens, which resembled a telephone dial. Unlike most half-frame cameras, the film transported vertically, so the camera provided a horizontal frame in normal orientation. Like the Ricoh Auto Half, the Dial had a clockwork film transport mechanism. The Dial had two other features: after the film was loaded it was automatically advanced to the first frame, and at the end of the roll, it was rewound under power. A full wind of the spring in the handgrip could advance more than 20 frames.

Nikonos.

The Photographic Industry. 1963.

In 1963, Nikon introduced the Nikonos, an underwater design which functioned at depths to 50 meters, and was frequently used as an inclement weather camera. Rubber O-rings in the body shell, and around the bayonet lens mount, were designed to seal more tightly under water pressure. Distance and aperture were set with large knobs on the sides of the lens. The single stroke film advance lever pulled out to wind the film, pushed in to release the shutter, and a contact was fitted to the base of the camera for an underwater flash.

Minolta Himatic 7.

The first Nikonos was based on a design by, and built under a licensing agreement from, the French company La Spirotechnique. In 1968, Nikon introduced the Nikonos II, with a hinged film pressure plate, a rewind button and crank, and indicators at the distance and aperture knobs on the lens barrel. The 1975 Nikonos III had an illuminated brightframe finder.

The Minolta Hi-matic 7 was marketed in December. It was the first Japanese camera with an automatic-exposure sensing cell mounted immediately adjacent to the lens. The meter of the otherwise standard 35 mm. rangefinder camera accepted an angle 14 degrees vertically and 23 degrees horizontally, narrower than the field of the lens.

Konica EE matic.

Canon AF.

The Flashmatic system in the Konica EE Matic provided semi-automatic flash exposure control and a reliable means of coupling a flash, bulb or electronic, to a camera. After the guide number was set, the aperture adjusted itself automatically when distance was set.

Some 500 firms from 18 countries took part in the 1963 Photokina, including 30 Japanese firms. Midmarket Japanese 35 mm. cameras substantially exceeded the number of German products, and there were a group of unusual Japanese prototypes, including the Canon AF, Yamato Koki's Artronic F and Konishiroku's Domirex.

In the States, at the Master Photo Dealers and Finishers Association exhibition on March 4th, 1963, in Atlantic City, Eastman Kodak introduced Instamatic cameras, films and photofinishing. The Instamatic system provided cartridge loading of paper-backed film in a series of simple cameras. Initially, three ASA 64 emulsions were available, color negative and transparency, and black-and-white negative. The Instamatic system was an effort to standardize snapshot films, of particular importance to the color photofinisher, who confronted a range of formats. The Kodak Instamatic system led Agfa to introduce the ill-fated rival Rapid system, using 35 mm. film in special cartridge. Japanese camera manufacturers, caught between the two systems, were forced into a period of trial and error to choose between them.

Konica Domirex.

Argus 260 Automatic.

The Instamatic and Rapid Systems. 1964.

Agfa Rapid film and cameras were marketed in July. Fourteen Japanese manufacturers had licensed the Rapid system, and with a similar number of German manufacturers entered into direct competition with the Kodak Instamatic system. But as the Instamatic format became more popular, some of the Japanese manufacturers took licenses from Kodak while retaining affiliation with Agfa. Eventually, the Japanese manufacturers who had formed the Rapid System Society failed in their efforts to compete with Instamatic, and when even Agfa finally found itself forced to manufacture Instamatic film and cameras, the Japanese market for the Rapid system collapsed.

There were many reasons for the failure of Rapid, foremost the public perception that there was nothing really new or different about it. The cameras were substantially early 35 mm. viewfinder models, the film was similar to Agfa Karat and Ansco Memo.

In 1964, there were a number of Japanese Instamatic and Rapid cameras. The Argus 260, 264 Automatic, made by Mamiya for Argus U. S., was a mid-range model, comparable to the Kodak Instamatic 300. In July, Ricoh introduced a half-frame automatic exposure camera, the Ricoh EE Rapid Half, and the Ricoh 35K Rapid, a full-frame 35 mm. Rapid model. The EE Rapid Half was a Ricoh Auto Half modified for Rapid film but otherwise little changed. First an export model, it was introduced domestically in June, 1965, and discontinued two months later. The 35K Rapid remained an export camera, distinguished by an exposure table on the top of the camera coupled to the Rapid cartridge to vary the film speed and aperture value.

Ricoh EE Rapid Half.

Ricoh 35K Rapid.

35 mm. Cameras. 1964.

I n July, Asahi introduced the Pentax SP, the production model of the 1960 Pentax Spotmatic prototype, which had been the first Japanese single lens reflex to meter through the lens. Asahi had tried various systems. First, a selenium cell was placed on the back of the reflex mirror, as on the Topcon RE Super. When the selenium cell proved too weak for metering through the lens, a retractable 3 mm. CdS cell was introduced over the focusing screen. The movable cell was ultimately replaced with a fixed unit on the focusing screen which measured a center spot, and the camera was called Spotmatic.

The production Pentax SP had two CdS cells, one on either side of the finder eyepiece, to measure the entire focusing screen area, providing averaged, overall readings stopped down. Asahi was promoting the accuracy of stopped-down metering because it measured light at the actual aperture. But the SP was eventually modified to the SPF, a full-aperture metering camera introduced in July, 1973. It is likely Asahi began with stopped-down metering, and continued it for nine years, because it allowed the continued use of screw-mount lenses from earlier Pentax cameras.

Also in July, Fuji introduced the the Fujicarex II, an export model leaf-shutter single lens reflex derived from a prototype shown at the Tokyo Camera Show in the spring of 1962. Like the Kodak Retina Reflex, the Fujicarex had interchangeable front elements: the standard 50 mm. f/1.9 could be converted to a 35 mm. f/4 or an 80 mm. f/2.8.

Pentax SP.

Topcon Uni.

Fujicarex II.

The Topcon Uni was the first leaf-shutter automatic exposure single lens reflex which metered through the lens. Introduced in November, 1964, the shutter priority automatic Uni was based on the Topcon Wink-Mirror S. Two interchangeable lenses were available, a UV-Topcor 35 mm. f/3.5 and a 100 mm. f/4. A 135 mm. f/4 was introduced later. The Uni stayed in production for five years, when it was modified into the Topcon Unirex in 1969.

The Olympus Pen W was the first wide angle half-frame camera. The 25 mm. lens covered 62 degrees, close to the field of a 35 mm. lens on full frame.

The Ricoh Auto Shot had a flashgun built into the lens cap, which was detached and mounted in the accessory shoe. The collapsible carrying case, made with the Textile Division of San-ai, a subsidiary of Ricoh, was constructed with an unusual method of seamless stitching.

Ricoh Auto Shot.

The Photographic Industry. 1964.

1964 was an extremely successful year for the Japanese photographic industry, which produced a record 4,597,346 cameras valued at 51,624 million yen, of which domestic sales of 3,029,795 cameras accounted for 34,384 million yen. The largest component category was the 1,824,757 half frame 35 mm. cameras, for which the strong demand in the first half of the year, before the 1964 Tokyo Olympics, dwindled substantially by the end of the year. Attendance at the fifth Tokyo Camera Show, on March 3, exceeded 210,000, a new record.

While variable focal length lenses for still cameras were relatively new, a number of new zoom lenses were introduced at the 1964 show, including Asahi Takumar, Olympus Zuiko, Canon, Nikkor, Minolta Rokkor and Tamron. Canon introduced a 19 mm. f/3.5, with a 96 degree angle of view, which required the reflex mirror be locked up before it could be fitted. Like many extreme wide angles, it was later redesigned as a retrofocus lens to permit normal mirror operation.

Kowa SW.

Nikon introduced four long lenses which had neither aperture nor focusing mechanism. Instead, the 400 mm., 600 mm., 800 mm. and 1,200 mm. lenses were designed to attach to a common, separate unit containing a focusing mount and automatic diaphragm. A number of leaf shutter cameras were introduced with fast lenses, including the f/1.5 Mamiya 35 Super Deluxe, the f/1.8 Yashica Half 17, the f/1.9 Konica Eye and the f/1.6 Kowa SE. The Kowa SW, marketed in July, was a compact, thin camera with a fixed 28 mm. f/3.2 lens which was frequently used as a backup by professional photographers.

The Photographic Industry. 1965.

For the Japanese camera industry, 1965 was a particularly innovative year. Seventeen new cameras were eventually designated historically important, the largest number in a single year since the war.

While cameras became more sophisticated, business conditions in the industry worsened, particularly in comparison to the previous Olympic year. Manufacturers affiliated with the Japan Camera Industry Association "were forced into concerted action to deal with the recession. In September, they asked for government approval of restraints to check excessive competition."

In October, the Fair Trade Commission restricted the use of giveaway promotions for camera sales. The industry staged a nationwide campaign between October 15, 1965, and January 15, 1966, promoting a sweepstakes which offered a chance to win a free trip to Hong Kong.

Overseas, Leica introduced the Leicaflex single lens reflex, and in the States, Sylvania introduced the flashcube.

Electronic Shutters. 1965.

Yashica Electro Half.

Olympus Pen EM.

Olympus 35 LE.

The first cameras with electronic shutters, the American Polaroid Model 100 Land Camera and the Japanese Artronic, were shown in 1963 at Photokina. A number of German shutters, including the Prontor Electronic 500 and 300, and the Compur Electronic 3 were introduced almost immediately afterwards.

By 1965, a number of new cameras had begun to incorporate electronics in control mechanisms and shutters. The Yashica Electro Half was the first camera to be equipped with both an electronically controlled shutter and programmed, fully-automatic exposure control. Based on the Yashica Half, the Copal Electronic shutter had automatic speeds from $1/500$ to 120 seconds, although the longer speeds were not manually accessible, and indicated only as LT, which meant Long Time.

The aperture priority automatic system controlled the shutter blades with a magnet, which closed the shutter when a capacitor was charged by the exposure. The film speed, aperture value and brightness of the scene, which varied resistance in the CdS cell, all contributed to the charge time of the capacitor. The Yashica Electro Half was introduced in May, 1965, and discontinued six months later.

The Olympus Pen EM, a half-frame camera with a Copal Electronic shutter similar to that of the Yashica Electro Half, was introduced at IPEX in the States in June. It was equipped with an integral electric motor drive which advanced and rewound the film automatically, the first such system fitted to any camera.

In October, Olympus introduced the 35 LE, equipped with a sophisticated, programmed electronic shutter controlling exposure from EV 5.5 (f/1.7, $1/15$) to EV 17 (f/16, $1/500$), and a red lamp in the viewfinder to warn when conditions were outside that range. The camera was also equipped with an electronically-coupled flash which automatically set the correct aperture when guide number and distance had been supplied.

The Single Lens Reflex. 1965.

The Canon Pellix, introduced in March, was the world's first single lens reflex with a fixed mirror. The pellicle mirror was semi-transparent, transmitting through to the film 65 percent of the light striking it, and reflecting 35 percent to the viewfinder, which was somewhat less than the light from conventional mirrors.

Canon Pellix.

The mirror could withstand wide temperature variations and was largely impervious to water. It could be pierced, but the pellicle did not crack, and fingerprints, dust and dirt on the surface could be removed with benzine.

The Canon Pellix was the third Japanese single lens reflex to meter through the lens. The spot meter was operated by the self-timer lever, which, when pushed toward the lens, powered the meter, stopped down the lens and introduced an 8 x 12 mm. CdS cell into the light path just in front of the focal-plane shutter curtain.

The usual match-needle apparatus was visible in the finder. Canon first called it a spot reading meter, later a center area reading meter. The Pellix was soon modified to the Pellix QL with the addition of QL film loading.

In December, Konishiroku introduced the Konica Autorex, the first high quality single lens reflex with a focal plane shutter and automatic exposure control. When a shutter speed was set, the camera selected a correct aperture, which it indicated with a needle on an aperture scale at the right of the viewfinder. The shutter release required substantial pressure, as it also set the aperture in the automatic exposure system.

Konica Autorex.

The dual format Autorex could switch from full to half frame, even with film in the camera. A lever to the right of the pentaprism housing introduced plates at both sides to reduce the film gate to the half-frame format, changed the gear ratio of the film advance and adjusted the frame counter.

The Photographic Industry. 1965.

A number of Japanese cameras were introduced for the Rapid and Instamatic formats in 1965, even as the Rapid system was proving unlikely to succeed, and the Instamatic format was becoming increasingly popular.

The Minolta 24 Rapid, marketed in April, used the Agfa Rapid cassette system and the unusual 24 x 24 cm. German Robot format. The camera had a coupled rangefinder, and the programmed automatic shutter, with a range of EV 8 (f/2.8, 1/30) to EV 17 (f/22, 1/250), was equipped with a manual override not often found on amateur cameras.

Minolta 24 Rapid.

The Yashica Half 17 EE Rapid, introduced in June, had an f/1.7 lens, the fastest available on a half-frame camera at the time. The programmed shutter automatically controlled both aperture and speed, and the camera was virtually identical to the Yashica Half 17i, called the Yashica Half 17 Rapid for export.

Yashica also made the fastest lens available on a 126 Instamatic camera, the f/1.9 on the Yashica EZ-matic 4, introduced in November. The designation 4 referred to the four-shot flashcube socket. It was not until four years later that Kodak AG, the West German subsidiary, developed and introduced a single lens reflex which also had an f/1.9 lens, the Kodak Instamatic Reflex. Until the fast-aperture Japanese cameras made it clear that the frame of the 126 cassette

Yashica Half 17 EE Rapid.

Yashica Lynx 14.

Canon Demi C.

Canonet QL17.

provided sufficient film flatness, Kodak had suggested that cameras for the Instamatic system would be limited to maximum apertures of f/2.8 and smaller.

At the time of its introduction, the full-frame Yashica Lynx had the fastest lens supplied on any fixed-lens camera. The f/1.4 lens was a modified Gauss design, and with an external CdS cell for match-needle exposure control the coupled range was EV 3 to EV 17 at ASA 100. The Yashica Half 14, with an identical lens, had programmed automatic exposure starting at EV 5 (f/1.4, $^1/_{15}$).

The half-frame Canon Demi C, a version of the S, had a shutter behind the lens, permitting the standard 28 mm. f/2.8 to be interchanged with a 50 mm. f/2.8, for which a frame was provided in the finder. On half frame, the 50 mm. lens was equivalent to a 75mm. lens on full 35 mm.

The success of the Kodak Instamatic 126 drop-in cartridge influenced manufacturers to develop easier ways to load 35 mm. film. Canon adopted a what it called a Quick Loading system in the QL 17 Canonet, a medium-priced 35 mm. camera introduced in March. When the film was positioned across the gate and the rear cover closed, the leader was automatically taken up in the spool as the film was advanced. The QL mechanism was eventually incorporated into almost all contemporary Canon 35 mm. cameras.

In November, the Konica EE Matic S was introduced with a takeup spool called the Koni Reel. The leader was inserted into any groove on the spool, and the Reel secured the film on the spool when the film was advanced. Other manufacturers later imitated the design or licensed the patent from Konishiroku, and the system remained in use for decades.

The Koni-Omega Rapid, introduced in February, was manufactured by Konishiroku to specifications from the U. S. distributor, Berkey Photo. Kodak had introduced 220 film in 1964, and the Koni-Omega was the first 6 x 7 Japanese camera able to use both 120 and 220 roll films, which it did with interchangeable backs. A modified Simon-Omega 120 press camera, the Rapid was characterized by the pull/push lever which advanced the film and cocked the shutter. Manufactured at first for export only, it was marketed in Japan in September as the Konica Press.

The medium format, twin lens Minolta Autocord CdS, introduced in March, was the first camera manufactured in Japan to directly accept both 120 and 220 films, which was accomplished by changing the pressure plate for the longer, unbacked 220 roll. Early Autocord CdS cameras which had been marketed for 120 only were retrofitted, without charge, with new counters, winding covers and pressure plates for 220.

Koni-Omega Rapid.

Minolta Autocord CdS.

The Yashica Atoron was introduced in November. A copy of the Minox, it was the first Japanese camera to use the Minox 8 x 11 mm. format cartridge. The Atoron was offered with a number of accessories, but without photofinishing equipment for the tiny format, it sold poorly. Later modified to the Atoron Electro, with an electronic shutter and automatic exposure control, it became the basis of the Atoron Club, an organization of owners, and production continued into the late 1970s.

Yashica Atoron.

The 1965 Petri Fotochrome was designed in the U.S. by Photochrome, Inc., and manufactured under contract by Petri for export only. It was loaded with a roll of reversal color paper on which it made 10 exposures. The process was somewhat cumbersome, the color fidelity was substandard, and the camera looked like a table clock.

Fotochrome.

The Photographic Industry. 1966.

The seventh annual Japan Camera Show, held at the start of the spring photographic season in March, was attended by more than 220,000 visitors. Japanese camera manufacturers had been "forced into a government-approved cartel to cut production and reduce excessive inventory created by the overly rapid expansion," and prices reflected a five percent reduction in the commodity tax, to 15 percent, which had gone into effect April 1.

At the Japan Camera Show, a number of manufacturers showed 35 mm. single-lens reflex cameras which metered through the lens, at full aperture or stopped down, with spot or averaged readings. Current models included the Asahi Pentax SP, Canon Pellix, Topcon RE Super, RE-II, Nikon F Photomic T, Nikkomat FT. Among the introductions were the Canon FT QL, Canon Pellix QL, Petri BTL, Minolta SRT-101 and Yashica TL Super.

The Minolta SRT-101 had two CdS cells on the pentaprism to measure separately the upper and lower halves of the scene. Called by Minolta a Contrast Light Compensator, it was designed to help the averaging system when it encountered bright sky light and small areas of high values.

The Yashica TL Super was the first camera in the world to use a silver oxide battery. Silver oxide batteries were smaller than mercury batteries and had higher output, higher working voltage, and better keeping characteristics.

The Miranda Sensorex, introduced in September, had a CdS cell located behind the center of the reflex mirror, and operated at full aperture with mechanical coupling.

Minolta SR-T101.

Miranda Sensorex.

The Ricoh Super Shot 24 had an unusual system called Dia-Focus. Based on the premise that faces are roughly the same width, rotating the focusing lever matched the width of two Dia-Marks to the face to achieve sharp focus. The system was based on a second, perhaps more elusive premise, that most photographs are portraits; but included zone focus symbols in the finder for other situations.

Ricoh Super Shot 24.

Keystone Reflex K1020.

Marshal Press.

Minolta Autopak 500.

The Marshall Press was a 6 x 8 press camera designed by Seiichi Mamiya, famous designer of the Mamiya Six and the Mamiyaflex. The Marshall had a fixed, triple-convertible Nikkor 105 mm. f/5.6 lens, the only lens of its kind ever made by Nippon Kogaku. Two additional front element groups converted it to 135 mm. and 150 mm., and all three lengths worked with the zoom viewfinder and coupled rangefinder.

For Keystone, U. S., Mamiya made the Keystone Reflex K1020, the first 126 cartridge single lens reflex. The automatic exposure camera used its reflex mirror as a shutter, at $^1/_{125}$ for daylight, $^1/_{50}$ with a flashcube. The Minolta Autopak 500 was a simple 126 cartridge camera with an exposure system capable of determining when light levels required a flash exposure. Owners were encouraged to leave a flashcube in place, assured the camera would use it if necessary. The rather styled plastic Autopak 500 won a design award from the Ministry of International Trade and Industry.

At Photokina in October, 1966, Asahi showed the Metalica, a prototype with a bayonet mount which predicted the K camera, and the Pentax 220, the prototype of the Pentax 6 x 7. Minolta showed the Electro Zoom X, a 16 mm. camera with zoom lens and a built-in motor drive.

In 1966, Polaroid marketed the Swinger in Japan. The all-plastic camera, priced at 8,900 yen, was marketed for novices in an attempt to expand the market for Polaroid instant photography.

The Photographic Industry. 1967.

The eighth annual Japan Camera Show in Tokyo, from February 28 to March 5, was attended by Crown Price Akihito and Crown Princess Michiko. Public attendance was 249,000, the second highest, as 21 manufacturers exhibited 202 items.

Asahi Optical established the Pentax Gallery in December, commemorating the centennial of the Meiji Restoration. Japan's first camera museum, it included permanent and topical exhibitions of antique cameras and related historical materials, and a hall for photographic exhibitions.

In 1967, Japanese cameras for export underwent significantly more intensive testing. Under the new standards, cameras were subjected to intense vibrations at frequencies from 20 to 55 Hz. for an hour, as well as shock tests, on six sides, with peak values of 70g.

The premise of this rigorous testing was to assure that Japanese cameras on world markets would prove to be trouble free, and inspire consumer confidence in Japanese quality. As the number of inexpensive cameras had increased in both domestic and overseas markets, the industry had been troubled by mounting complaints about faulty equipment. Four years earlier, the Japan Camera and Optical Instruments Inspection and Testing Institute had established a committee to deal with this issue. In cooperation with camera manufacturers, JCII developed and instituted the new series of camera function and structural integrity tests which more than assured the capability to perform under normal use.

Mamiya/Sekor 1000DTL.

In 1967, Mamiya redesigned the previous year's 1000 TL into the Mamiya Sekor 1000 DTL, with a dual metering system which offered a choice of average or spot readings. Oddly, this important feature did not become generally available on single lens reflexes until some years after the introduction of this camera.

Yashica EZ-matic Electronic.

Konica EE-Matic Deluxe F.

Two other cameras introduced in 1967 were important for their exposure control mechanisms. In March, Yashica introduced the EZ-matic Electronic, the first 126 camera with an electronic shutter. The EZ-matic Electronic automatically measured reflected brightness during flash exposure, and closed the shutter when a correct value was reached.

The Konica EE-Matic Deluxe F had an eyepoint CdS meter which provided automatic exposures between EV 8 and EV 17. Outside that range, a red flash mark appeared in the finder as a warning, which changed to a white mark when the camera was released from automatic exposure. When a guide number was set on the lens barrel, a flash socket for both flashcubes and AG-1 bulbs popped up. Because of extensive use of ABS plastic, the Konica weighed only 540 grams.

The Koni-Omega Rapid M was a 6 x 7 press camera, a modification of the Koni-Omega Rapid, with the characteristic push/pull lever which wound the film and cocked the shutter.

Koni-Omega Rapid M.

In March, the Olympus Pen FT half frame was introduced with an eight element H-Zuiko Auto-S 42 mm. f/1.2 lens. The latest in the Pen F series of half-frame single lens reflexes, which began in March 1963, had through-the-lens metering and a range of 20 interchangeable lenses, including a zoom. The Pen FT was followed briefly by the Olympus FTL, and the series eventually led to the M-1, later called the OM-1, the extremely popular, compact full-frame single lens reflex Olympus introduced in January, 1973.

The Photographic Industry. 1968.

In 1968, the total production of Japanese cameras increased to 4,063,000 units. The largest number were 35 mm. single lens reflexes, most with some form of through-the-lens exposure measurement. At the annual Japan Camera Show in March, normally indicative of technical trends, there were few of the usual innovative products on display: emphasis was on interchangeable lenses and other components of camera systems.

Since the various cameras had different lens mounts, each with its characteristic flange and diaphragm coupling design, independent lens manufacturers began to introduce lenses designed not to fit cameras, but to fit adapter systems. Mirax Shoji, maker of Soligor lenses, and Sun Optical showed lenses which attached only to their adapters for the popular camera models. The adapter systems were themselves not interchangeable, so the design had obvious advantages and economies for independent lens makers, and soon came into common use.

Japanese camera manufacturers also showed a number of roll film cameras in 1968, partly because color films were becoming more popular, and the larger negative format produced visibly better results with the color films of the time, even at modest enlargements. Japan remained a country where larger format negatives were still championed for their quality, and many of the 120 roll film sizes were historical Japanese formats. These medium format cameras, nominally designated for professional use, were also aimed at the advanced amateur market.

35 mm. viewfinder cameras became more compact as 35 mm. single lens reflexes grew larger, but viewfinder cameras were much less popular than they had been. The industry's efforts continued to guide the public enthusiasms, at the time in the direction of single lens reflexes with substantial complements of accessories, called camera systems, and in the anticipated direction of automatic exposure control. It was the success of the Rollei 35 which began the eventual redesign of the viewfinder camera into what would become the vastly popular point-and-shoot cameras of the 1980s.

Roll Film Cameras. 1968.

The Kowa Six, which became one of the leading Japanese medium format cameras of its time, was introduced at the 1968 Japan Camera Show.

A 6 x 6, 120 and 220 single lens reflex, it was the first leaf shutter camera of its kind in Japan. The Japanese Zenza Bronica, which so resembled the Swedish Hasselblad it had been denounced by the Swedes, was in fact a focal plane shutter design, while most Hasselblads used leaf shutters mounted in the lenses. The leaf-shutter Kowa Six bore a much stronger mechanical resemblance the Hasselblad, but the Kowa body was an upright, vertical design more in the idiom of a twin lens reflex than the admittedly similar shapes of the Bronica and Hasselblad.

The Kowa Six did not have an instant return mirror, but the subsequent Kowa Six MM had mirror lock-up and a multiple exposure system, and the later Kowa Six II had a detachable film back. The camera was simplified and altered into the Kowa Super 66, last listed in the Japan Camera Show catalog of 1978.

Kowa Six.

Fujica G690.

Rittreck Six.

In March, 1968, Musashino Optical introduced the Rittreck Six, a 6 x 6 single lens reflex with a pentaprism finder and an f/2 standard lens. The 120/220 camera also had an instant return mirror, automatic diaphragm control, and operated much as an enlarged 35 mm. design. The Rittreck was distributed as the Graflex in the United States, and later manufactured by Norita Optical as the Norita 66.

In October, Fujica introduced the G690, a 6 x 9 cm. rangefinder camera which resembled two cameras designed by Herbert Nerwin: the circa 1950 KS-6 Graflex 70 mm. combat camera and the Contax II. There were four interchangeable, leaf shutter lenses for the 690: a Fujinon SW 65 mm. f/8.0; the standard Fujinon S 100 mm. f/3.5, and two Fujinon T lenses, a 150 mm. f/5.6 and 180 mm. f/5.6. In the original model, unless a curtain made of shutter cloth was manually closed to protect the film, users could accidentally expose the film while dismounting a lens, and evidently frequently did. The camera was modified into subsequent models G 690 BL, GL 690 and GM 670.

In March, Konishiroku introduced the Koni-Omegaflex M, a studio camera for export only. The 6 x 7 cm. twin lens reflex had interchangeable lenses, and an interchangeable film insert system compatible with the Konica Press, with the characteristic Koni sliding-bar film advance. Curiously, there was a reversed-image focusing screen on the back of the camera. A folding hood could be detached and replaced with a mirror box which corrected the image in the manner of a conventional twin lens reflex. The viewfinder and fresnel lens were coupled to the focusing knob, and moved to correct parallax. Three lenses were available: a 58 mm. f/5.6, a 135 mm. f/3.5, and a 180 mm. f/4.5.

Konishiroku also showed the Konica SF, an innovative prototype 6 x 4.5 cm. pentaprism single lens reflex. The SF incorporated a large Copal square shutter in a shutter-priority automatic exposure system, and the lens mount was compatible with Hasselblad, but the camera was never developed beyond the prototype stage.

Koni-Omegaflex M.

Konica SF.

Chapter Eleven

Electronic Innovation

from an article by Kakugoro Saeki

The Single Lens Reflex. 1968.

Yashica Lynx 5000E.

No aspect of the development of contemporary cameras influenced the industry and its markets as profoundly as the introduction of electronics. The first camera with an electronic shutter was introduced in 1965 by Yashica. In January, 1968, Yashica introduced the Lynx 5000E, a 35 mm. compact with an unusual electronic exposure system. A wheatstone bridge was regulated by an integrated chip, and the aperture ring was turned until a lamp indicated a balanced circuit had been achieved and the correct exposure selected. It was a relatively simple, sturdy system with no moving parts.

The advanced Yashica TL Electro-X was marketed in 1968 for export only, and sold domestically after November, 1969. It was the first camera with an electronically controlled focal plane shutter. The Copal Square SE shutter used a capacitor and transistors as an electronic governor, and a magnet for the curtain release. The shutter, which required a six volt battery, permitted continuously variable, stepless speeds. The camera proved noisy: the shutter, the automatic diaphragm and the reflex mirror were all disturbingly audible.

The Konica FTA, introduced in March, 1968, was a revision of the 1965 Autorex, the first focal-plane single lens reflex with shutter-priority automatic exposure. The FTA had a semi-automatic, match needle exposure system. The metering had been altered and improved to provide a variable reading area,

Yashica TL Electro-X.

Konica FTA.

with a CdS cell on each side of the eyepiece, positioned at a 25 degree angle to the optical axis of the finder. The cells measured the light striking the focusing screen at a slanted angle. With a standard focal length, the meter provided a center-weighted average reading. With a wide angle lens, the meter measured the center, a semi-spot reading. With a long lens, the reading was an overall average. The FTA continued to use the needle trapping mechanism of the Autorex, with the characteristically resistant shutter release. The scale in the finder automatically adjusted for the various maximum apertures of inter-changeable lenses.

The FTA was modified in June, 1970 with a shutter speed indicator in the finder. In April, 1973, an improved version was introduced as the Autoreflex T3. In September, 1974, it was modified with an eyepiece shutter, an electrical accessory shoe and a substantially improved shutter release. The release of the 1965 Konica Autorex travelled 7.5 mm. and required 1000 grams of pressure; by the 1974 T3, the travel had been reduced to 2 mm., the pressure to 300 grams.

Petri Color 35.   *Canon EX EE.*

Compact Cameras. 1968.

The 1968 Petri Color 35 was a compact camera strongly influenced by the original Rollei 35. It had a collapsible lens barrel with indent indication at infinity extension, after which a needle in the finder displayed focus distance. The camera was extremely small, about 100 mm. long by 65 mm. high and 43 mm. deep, and was supplied in three finishes: chrome, all black and two tone. It was the first camera of its type to display all major functions relating to distance and exposure in the viewfinder.

The Canon EX-EE was introduced in August in conjunction with the establishment of a subsidiary, Canon Amsterdam N.V., and marketed in May, 1969. It was sold with a set of interchangeable lenses at a price equivalent to a conventional single lens reflex. The back three elements of the 50 mm. f/1.8 lens were fixed in the camera body, and only the front elements interchanged to produce a 36 mm. f/3.5, a 95 mm. f/3.5, and later, a 125 mm. f/3.5. The shutter-priority automatic exposure camera had the brightest microprism finder of all single lens reflexes, including the Leicaflex SL. It also had an unusually light shutter release and a short film advance stroke.

Kodak Instamatic Reflex, B.R.D.   *Teflex.*

The Photographic Industry. 1968.

More than 400 persons from the Japanese photographic industry attended the 1968 Photokina. Kodak AG, West Germany, introduced the Kodak Instamatic Reflex, a 126 single lens reflex with a Compur electronic shutter and aperture-priority automatic exposure. Rollei introduced a 126 cartridge single lens reflex which metered through the lens. Yashica showed the TL Electro-X, and Asahi introduced the Asahi Pentax 6 x 7, which had been shown as the prototype Pentax 220, with 11 interchangeable lenses, at Photokina in 1966. The Minolta SR-M motor drive camera, the Mamiya-Sekor 2000 DTL and the Convertible Horseman were also shown. Nikon exhibited a Reflex-Nikkor 500 mm. f/8. and a Nikkor 200 mm. f/11, and Minolta showed a Rokkor 16 mm. f/2.8 fisheye.

Nichiryo manufactured several combinations of cameras with prism monoculars or binoculars. The Teflex was a 7 x 50 binocular with a camera based on the mechanism of the Ricoh Auto Half, fitted to the right side. It had three shutter speeds, 1/60, 1/125 and 1/250, and the 165 mm. f/3.5 lens stopped down to f/11. The camera achieved some notariety when it was used as a prop in "The Mechanic", a gangster film starring Charles Bronson. Substantially the same camera, without the left half of the binocular, was introduced for law enforcement applications two years later.

Perma Matic 618.

The 1968 Perma Matic 618, a 126 Instamatic cartridge camera, was the first Japanese camera with a built-in electronic flash. The flash, with an effective range of 5-12 feet, came on in light levels below the range of the selenium exposure meter. The camera sold poorly, partly because it was a bulky design, and was soon discontinued.

The first flashcubes made in Japan were produced in 1968 by Kondo-Sylvania, a joint venture of Kondo Electric and the U. S. firm Sylvania.

The Photographic Industry. 1969.

At the Japan Camera Show in March, most manufacturers showed refined and updated versions of existing models. In New York in June, the National Association of Photographic Manufacturers, in cooperation with the German Photographic Industry Association and the Japan Camera Industry Association, sponsored Photo Expo. Although the displays of new products were not as large as expected, 300 firms exhibited to the 97,000

Kodak Instamatic 44, U.S.   *Asahi Pentax 6 x 7.*

guests. It was the first international exhibition of its kind in the States. Agfa showed the Senso shutter cameras and lenses for macrophotography. The widely publicized Kodak Super 8 cartridge projectors were somewhat disappointing, but the low-priced Kodak Instamatic 44 camera, which sold for less than $10 in supermarkets, was well received.

In July, 1969, Asahi Optical marketed the Asahi Pentax 6 x 7. It was the first camera to combine the design of an eye-level pentaprism single lens reflex with the 6 x 7 cm. format. Similar in appearance and operation to a 35 mm. single lens reflex, it had a bayonet lens mount, the first used by Asahi Optical, an instant return mirror and a single stroke film advance lever. Of the 11 interchangeable lenses announced with the camera, only a 75 mm. f/4.5, 150 mm. f/2.8 and a 200 mm. f/4. were initially available. The Pentax 6 x 7 had an electronic focal plane shutter, with a safety mechanism which locked the mirror when the batteries were low. Despite many years of development, battery life was a critical issue with electronic shutter systems, and a problem in designs as large as the early models of the Pentax 6 x 7.

Olympus 35SP.

35 mm. Cameras. 1969.

In April, Olympus introduced the 35 SP, an automatic exposure compact which offered spot and average metering. Because meter acceptance angles in compact cameras did not correspond to the lens fields, Olympus designed the CdS cell to make an average reading at a 20 degree, and a spot reading at six. The narrow field was engaged with a button on the back of the camera. The 35 SP was somewhat bulky at a time when designs were becoming smaller. It remained in production for two years and was replaced by the more compact Olympus 35 DC.

The Canonet QL 17, also known as the New Canonet, was almost half the size of the popular Canonet. Introduced in July, the compact rangefinder camera could be fitted with an electronic flash that coupled to the automatic exposure system. A detector measured the flash as the shutter was released. If it found the capacitor less than full, the aperture was varied to compensate for the degree of charge. The QL 17 had a quick loading mechanism, and automatically advanced newly-loaded film to the first frame.

New Canonet QL 17.

Minolta Hi-matic 11.

Minolta introduced the Hi-matic 11 in August. A fixed-lens rangefinder compact, it was the first production camera to combine a programmed shutter with automatic exposure control. The camera used what Minolta called a Contrast Light Compensator system, from the SRT-101, and a Seiko ALA leaf shutter in a programmed system which varied the aperture and shutter continuously from EV 6.5, f/1.7 at ¹/₃₀, to EV 17, f/22 at ¹/₂₅₀, at ASA 100. Both aperture and shutter speed were indicated in the finder.

In December, 1969, Konishiroku marketed the Konica Electron, which had been first shown at Photokina in 1968. The fixed-lens, rangefinder compact had aperture-priority automatic exposure. The electronic shutter varied available speed ranges according to the film speed. Flash exposure was controlled by two photocells, one CdS and one selenium. When a flashcube was used, the photocells measured light from the subject and closed the shutter when exposure had been achieved. When the optional Kacomatic-5 electronic flash was fitted into the flashcube socket, the flash duration was too short for shutter control, so the camera quenched the flash when exposure had been achieved. The advanced Konica Electron failed to find a market at a time when cameras were becoming smaller and simpler, and was soon discontinued.

Bell & Howell Autoload 342.

Konica Electron.

Other Formats. 1969.

The Bell & Howell Autoload 342 was a shutter-priority, automatic 126 compact made by Canon exclusively for export. Introduced in April, it had a single-window rangefinder called Focusmatic. The Focusmatic lever to the left of the lens was pressed down and held, the camera was pointed at the base of the object to be photographed, and the lens helecoid was automatically extended when the lever was released. The inexpensive, pendulum-based triangulation focusing system was based on the premise that the height of the photographer was a constant.

The Ricoh 126 C Flex, introduced in July, was the second Japanese 126 single lens reflex. First shown as a prototype at the Tokyo Camera Show in 1968, it had a pentagonal roof mirror formed of plastic elements. Shutter-priority automatic exposure was measured through the lens and controlled by a two-blade Seiko BS-11GA leaf shutter. It was the only Japanese 126 camera with interchangeable lenses. In addition to the standard Rikenon 55 mm. f/2.8., Ricoh offered two thread mount lenses, a 35 mm. f/2.8 and a 100 mm. f/2.8. The 126 C Flex had an electrical accessory shoe, a flashcube socket, and housed a 15-volt battery to power the flash.

The Minolta 16 MG-S was introduced in October, 1969, and marketed domestically in Japan in April, 1970. The 12 x 17 mm. image, larger than other 16 mm. formats, was one fourth the 35 mm. picture area. Kazuo Tashima,

Ricoh 126C Flex.

president of Minolta Camera, said at the introduction, "We were the first manufacturer of 16 mm. cameras and we want to continue the development of the 16 mm. picture format in these times when new mechanisms and innovations are continually producing so much ferment in the Japanese photo industry." Minolta Camera made a variety of accessories for the 16 MG-S, and improved the film quality, but eventually changed to 110 because there was little customer access to photofinishing for the scarce 16 mm. format.

Minolta 16 MG-S.

The Photographic Industry. 1970.

I n 1970, the Japanese photographic industry produced 5,813,236 cameras for both domestic and export markets, with total sales of 97,128,000,000 yen.

The Osaka World Exposition, an important event for the travel and photographic industries, and the Third International Photographic Industry Conference, in Kyoto, were held at the same time in March. The Conference, which included industry representatives from the United States, West Germany and a number of other countries, was opened by Trade Industry Minister Kiichi Miyazawa. Hosting the conference was perceived by the Japanese camera industry as an indication of its importance in world markets.

In 1970, camera manufacturers were marketing interchangeable lenses, prisms and accessories for 35 mm. single lens reflexes as camera systems. Konishiroku introduced a 126 film in the domestic market, and technical advances were beginning to appear in medium format cameras. The annual Japan Camera Show was held at the Takashimaya department store in Tokyo, and the first Photo Accessory Show, sponsored by the Japan Photographic Equipment Industrial Association, was held at the nearby Tokyu Nihombashi department store. It was the first time a complete line of photographic products was shown together to the general public.

In the fall, at Photokina in Cologne, a number of manufacturers showed interchangeable lenses. Nikon introduced a multi-layered, anti-reflection lens coating, the so-called black coating already applied on some of its lenses, and Asahi Optical publicized its Super Multi-layer Coating lenses, which were designated SMC.

A number of cameras were shown with optional black finishes, which were soon regarded as professional versions. Full aperture metering was being recognized as vastly more convenient and no less accurate than stopped-down systems, and automatic exposure systems were being introduced.

The Canon F-1 was marketed in 1970 as a camera system, with a full line of integrated accessories, including interchangeable finders and focusing screens and a motor drive unit. The Servo EE automatic exposure finder was an accessory replacement for the standard prism finder. It coupled to the lens through a slit on the apron of the camera, and used a small motor in the finder to automatically adjust the aperture. Power was supplied by the batteries for the motorized film advance.

Canon was a well-known manufacturer of quality cameras, and Canon rangefinder cameras had been widely regarded in the industry as competitive with Leica. But the company began to experience difficulties trying to mass produce high performance single-lens reflex cameras, and despite repeated efforts, the cameras were not meeting the requirements of professional photographers.

Canon F-1 with Servo EE Finder and Motor Drive.

Fujica ST701.　　　　　*Ricoh TLS 401.*

The 35 mm. Camera. 1970.

The Fujica ST 701 was the first 35 mm. single lens reflex made by Fuji Photo Film. It had a Pentax/Practica-thread lens mount, and stopped-down aperture metering through the lens. The ST 701 was the first Japanese single lens reflex to be fitted with the significantly more sensitive silicon photocell, which provided exposure measurement at much lower light levels. Earlier single lens reflexes used CdS cell metering which, although accurate, tended to retain its previously measured value and responded slowly in low light. Unlike the CdS cell, the silicon element required a transistor or integrated circuit amplifier. In 1974, a silicon cell was fitted in the Canon EF, and it soon became ubiquitous.

The Ricoh TLS 401 had a combination eye-level pentaprism and waist-level reflex finder. A knob on the side of the prism housing caused a small mirror to move up into position, providing waist-level viewing through an eyepiece on the top of the finder cover. The stopped-down metering system had both average and spot measurement. The designation 401 refers to four features combined in one camera, the two finders and the two metering fields.

In September, 1970, Cosina manufactured a single lens reflex designed to use the widely available Exakta lenses. The Exakta Twin TL, made for Ihagee, West Germany, was a somewhat unusual camera with greatly improved versions of many of the original design features of the Exakta. The 46 mm. lensmount, increased from the older 38 mm. bayonet mount to accommodate the larger diameter of faster lenses, fitted older optics with an adapter. In addition to the conventional shutter release, the lens adaptation system included a lever on the left front of the camera which also tripped the shutter.

The Canondate E was an automatic 35 mm. fixed-lens rangefinder camera with an optical system which could imprint day, month and year on the film. Gear wheels on the camera front set the combination of digits which printed in the lower right corner of the frame.

Exakta Twin TL.　　　　　*Canodate E.*

Medium Format. 1970.

The Mamiya RB 67 Professional was introduced in May, 1970. While the Pentax 6 x 7 resembled an enlarged 35 mm. single lens reflex, the Mamiya RB 67 appeared to be an enlarged conventional medium-format single lens reflex. Because the viewing configuration, a successful design for the square format, did not permit the camera to be turned on its side, the RB was fitted with a revolving film back for horizontal or vertical orientation. 6 x 7 cm. was called ideal format because it elongated the square on the length of 120 film until its proportions were those of an 8 x 10 print.

Mamiya RB67 Professional.

The RB 67 had a large shutter cocking lever on the body, but the film was wound with a separate operation of a lever on the revolving film back. Interchangeable lenses were mounted onto the lensboard at the end of a relatively long rack and pinion driven bellows, which permitted significant close focus. The focusing screen displayed a reflex image of the entire 7 x 7 film area, with framing lines for the horizontal and vertical images. The camera was introduced with a 127 mm. f/3.8 standard lens, and three accessory lenses: a 65 mm. f/4.5, a 90 mm. f/3.8 and a 250 mm. f/4.5 telephoto.

The Convertible Horseman, also known as the Horseman CH-842, was a completely modular, lightweight medium format camera. The lensboard assembly, the main body frame and the roll-film backs interchanged to provide a number of configurations in 6 x 7 and 6 x 9 formats. First shown at Photokina in 1968 as the Horseman Reporter, the prototype was announced with additional camera bodies as conversion options. The original frame unit was designed to be replaced with both a view camera and a single lens reflex. The Convertible Horseman was produced for only a short time, and the full line of components was never manufactured.

Convertible Horseman CH-842.

Sakura Pak 100.

Other Formats. 1970.

The Sakura Pak 100 was one of the least expensive cameras produced in modern Japan. It was introduced by Konishiroku at 4,250 yen, without battery, as the manufacturer also began to market 126 cartridge film. The camera body was made of light grey and black plastic, and the Color Hexar 42 mm. single element f/11 was the first plastic lens in a Japanese camera. F/11 was the only aperture, and the shutter had a daylight speed, $^1/_{100}$, and a flash speed, $^1/_{40}$. At f/11, the lens was fixed focus from 8 feet to infinity. The flash range of 3 to 9 feet was made possible by the exposure latitude of the film.

Astral S20.

Yashica Atoron Electro.

Nicnon S.

Eastman Kodak introduced the X series 126 cameras for a new flash cube which fired mechanically. Magicubes did not require an electric contact with the camera: a pin in the flashcube socket triggered a spring in the cube which ignited the flash. Eliminating batteries made possible greatly simplified camera designs, and suggested a more reliable system for the novice.

In December, Seidic introduced the Astral S20 Electric Eye, an export model 126 camera with a 40 mm. f/13 lens and a single shutter speed, $^1/_{60}$. It was the first Japanese camera made for use with the self-igniting Magicube.

The Yashica Atoron Electro, introduced in September, was an electronic shutter version of the 1965 Atoron, a Japanese Minox format subminiature. The fully automatic Atoron Electro was the first electronic subminiature camera. At ASA 100, the programmed automatic exposure range was EV 0, 8 seconds at f/2.8, to EV 16, $^1/_{350}$ at f/13. A yellow warning lamp in the finder indicated slow shutter speeds. The Minox format, developed towards the end of the 1930s in Latvia, required specific processing components, and like Minox, Yashica offered as accessories a developing tank, reels and an enlarging lens. Yashica promoted the incompatible format aggressively, even forming an owners organization called the Atoron Club.

In November, Nichiryo introduced the Nicnon S, an unusual combination of a monocular telescope and an automatic-advance, half-frame 35 mm. camera. A beam splitter diverted a portion of the light from the 165 mm. f/3.5 lens off the monocular path to the film plane. The Nicnon S resembeled a portion of the 1968 Nichiryo Teflex binocular camera, and was popular with law enforcement agencies.

The Photographic Industry. 1971.

In August, 1971, when the United States suspended the gold standard, floating international currency rates had a sudden and significant effect on the Japanese economy and the yen. While the new exchange rates, a de facto devaluation of the dollar, severely effected European photographic manufacturers, the Japanese camera industry was sustained by favorable exports.

In the U.K., Ilford stopped producing color film, and in Germany, Zeiss closed its Braunschweig camera facility. The immediate reason was that German goods were at a competitive disadvantage on world markets because of the continuing strength of the Mark. An underlying factor was the success of Japanese cameras in European markets.

Franke and Heidecke, makers of Rollei cameras, maintained an aggressive competitive position. At a press conference commemorating the company's 50th anniversary, Rollei announced a new plant in Singapore to compete with Japanese cameras.

In 1971, the Japanese Government lifted import controls on color film, and Kodak became a competitor in the domestic market. Fuji and Konishiroku redesigned some Fujicolor and Sakuracolor negative films to develop in Kodak process C-41, in order that the Japanese films might have a broader competitive basis in international markets.

Automatic exposure versions of high quality 35 mm. cameras continued to improve, and a number of models had retail prices above 1,000,000 yen. As price competition eased, Japanese cameras continued to progress on world markets.

The Nikon F, a professional camera virtually unchanged for 12 years, was redesigned as the F2 in 1971. Overseas, the Leica M5 was introduced with exposure metering through the lens, a significant advance in the design of the coupled rangefinder camera.

The Automatic 35 mm. Camera. 1971.

The Olympus 35 EC-2, introduced in October, was an improved version of the 1969 35 EC, also called the Elecon. The Seiko ESF electronic shutter between the lens provided programmed automatic exposure from EV 1, 4 seconds at f/2.8, to EV 17, 1/800 at f/13. The camera automatically engaged programmed flash in low light. An electronic interlock prevented the shutter from operating if the battery was low, and a yellow light in the viewfinder indicated slow shutter speed. Estimated distance was set by zone focusing symbols, although the following year a 21,000 yen rangefinder model was introduced as the ECR. The 42 mm. f/2.8 E-Zuiko lens was quite small, and the 35 EC-2 resembled a half-frame compact.

Asahi Pentax Electro Spotmatic (ES).

Olympus 35 EC-2.

The Asahi Pentax ES was the first single lens reflex with a focal-plane electronic shutter providing aperture-preferred automatic exposure control. The ES had an innovative exposure compensation range of ½X to 4X and an electrical accessory shoe, but the self timer, a standard feature on Pentax cameras since the SV, was omitted to make room for a battery compartment.

With the transition to automatic exposure, a coupling mechanism was added to the thread mount of the Pentax ES for full aperture metering. Although the position of a seated screw-mount interchangeable lens was accurate enough for automatic diaphragm coupling, it was not sufficient to couple full aperture metering. The East German VEB Pentacon addressed the problem with a series of electrical contacts on the Praktica LLC, and the modified Praktica mount had already been used on the Olympus FTL for full aperture metering.

There are traditionally three types of automatic exposure control systems. When shutter speed is manually selected and the camera automatically furnishes an appropriate aperture, the system is called shutter priority. When the aperture is manually selected and the camera determines and furnishes an appropriate shutter speed, the system is called aperture priority. In each case, the photographer is presumed to have determined a priority, over which he has retained control. In the third case, when the camera is permitted to select a combination of both shutter speed and aperture, the system is said to be programmed.

Aperture priority systems became possible with the invention of the electronic shutter. The first was introduced in a production camera in May, 1965, in the Yashica Electro Half. The focal-plane electronic shutter was introduced by Asahi in the Pentax ES. Another nomenclature issue arose when Asahi chose to distinguish ES, electronic shutter, from EE, electronic eye, meaning electronic aperture. Professor M. Tamura of the Chiba University Department of Engineering proposed that all automatic exposure systems be called AE, for automatic exposure. With AE generally accepted by the trade and public, EE, ES, and generic terms like electric eye, as well as trade names using non-standard terminology, were soon dropped by Japanese manufacturers.

The Photographic Industry and the Economy. 1972.

On January 21, 1972, the Fair Trade Commission, which administers the Anti-Monopoly Act, sent investigators to search for and seize documents from four photographic printing paper manufacturers: Fuji Photo Film, Konishiroku, Oriental and Mitsubishi Paper Mills. The raids were conducted on suspicion of price fixing in December, 1971. The Photosensitized Material Manufacturers Association vigorously denied the charges, saying, "Such allegations are inconceivable in the current conditions of bitter competition". But the Commission noted the four companies' new prices were uniform within 10 yen, and asserted that was an unlikely coincidence.

On January 28, the Fair Trade Commission performed 23 more raids, on the main offices of Nippon Kogaku Kogyo and its franchised distributors. The Commission suspected Nippon Kogaku under Article 19 of the Anti-Monopoly Act, which prohibits manufacturers from restricting the business activities of their distributors. Nippon Kogaku was accused of suspending deliveries to retailers who gave discounts of more than five percent, the maximum rate allowed by Nippon Kogaku.

Nagase and Company, the sole Eastman Kodak distributor in Japan, had reduced prices of films and color printing papers by about seven percent in response to the rise of the yen against the dollar. But soon, citing increases in labor and materials costs in the States, Nagase raised them again. The Ministry of International Trade and Industry asked they be rescinded, saying Nagase had profited enough through the exchange rate.

Japanese cameras, transistor radios and electronic calculators were popular in European markets and unpopular in the European press. The influx of Japanese goods was being likened to the invasion of Genghis Khan.

In 1972, more than 60 percent of Japan's camera production was exported. Total sales of 107,976,000,000 yen reflected an expanding market, a general inflationary trend, and a growing consumer preference for more expensive cameras. Through September, still camera production increased 30 percent, and 8 mm. cine equipment increased 64 percent over the first three quarters of the previous year. In October, the government's strict export controls, designed to stabilize the yen and reduce the country's trade surplus, were applied to cameras, lenses and 8 mm. cine equipment. The Japan Camera Industry Association and other, unaffiliated manufacturers organized an export cooperative which set and maintained export levels until August 31, 1973.

Some manufacturers were critical of export controls on cameras, arguing that markets had been well established abroad, the products were in strong demand, and that export sale volumes of cameras were a fraction of steel and electrical products revenues. The argument was not persuasive to the Government as Japan's foreign exchange reserves rose to a record high of $18 billion in December, 1972.

Minolta Autopak 400X.

Chinon M-1.

35 mm. Cameras. 1972.

In January, 1972, Minolta introduced the Autopak 400X, a 126 cartridge camera. To prevent accidental release, the shutter button could be retracted into the camera.

Chinon, a manufacturer of cameras exclusively for export, introduced the Prinzflex M-1 in June. It was a traditional 35 mm. single lens reflex with a small lever mounted next to the shutter release that permitted multiple exposures.

Canon introduced the EX Auto, a modified version of the EX-EE with automatic exposure, automatic flash exposure and automatic maximum aperture indexing. Only the front element of the 50 mm. f/1.8 lens was interchanged to provide a 35 mm. f/3.5, a 95 mm. f/3.5, and a 125 mm. f/3.5.

In July, Olympus introduced the M-1, marketed internationally as the OM-1, which introduced a new class of 35 mm. single lens reflexes. It was more

Canon EX Auto.

Olympus M-1.

Kowa UW 190.

Miranda Sensoret.

Ricoh 35 Electronic.

Mepro Zenit E, U.S.S.R.

compact and lighter than any camera of the type ever made, at 136 mm. wide, 83 mm. high and 86 mm. deep. It had match-needle manual metering, an air-dampened quick return mirror, and was designed so focusing screens were interchangeable through the lens opening. At Photokina, Leitz protested that any other use of M-1 infringed the trademark of the Leica M-1. Olympus renamed the camera OM-1 in January, 1973, and Chinon changed the Chinon M-1 to the Chinon CX.

The Kowa UW 190 was a 35 mm. single lens reflex fitted with a permanently mounted 19 mm. f/4 wide angle lens. In 1964, Kowa had introduced the SW, with a fixed 28 mm. lens. The UW 190, introduced at the Japan Camera Show in Tokyo on February 29, was an adaptation of the Kowa SETR body, which metered through the lens. Although it cost little more than an interchangeable lens, the camera had limited appeal and sold poorly.

Miranda introduced the Sensoret in April. It was a simple 35 mm. compact with a system to display the effective aperture number in the viewfinder when a flash unit was attached. The camera had an electronically controlled, programmed shutter which would not fire the flash above EV 7.5, regardless of the photographer's inclinations.

Ricoh introduced the Ricoh 35 Electronic for export, and later marketed it domestically as the Ricoh Elnica 35. The camera had a mechanical self timer with a light to signal the timing interval. It was the first camera with this feature.

In 1972, Dai'ei, a volume retail chain in Japan, imported the camera body of the Mepro Zenit E, a Russian 35 mm. single lens reflex. With a selenium meter and speeds of $1/30$ to $1/500$, it was marketed at the surprisingly low price of 13,900 yen with a case and a Mepro-Kominar 55 mm. f/2.8 lens made in Japan by Nitto Optical. Although out of date, at a retail price equivalent to the inexpensive compacts it had a substantial impact on the industry. The average domestic retail price of the 25 Japanese 35 mm. single lens reflexes listed in the 1972 Japan Camera Show catalogue was 61,024 yen.

Medium Format. 1972.

Zenza Bronica EC.

In January, Zenza Bronica introduced the EC, the first new Bronica in seven years. It had an electronic focal plane shutter and a two-piece reflex mirror. The top portion, four fifths of the total surface, pulled back and swung up during exposure; the bottom portion swung down. Designed to reduce recoil and use space more efficiently, there was little indication of the join between the mirror sections in the viewfinder. There was historic precedent in Bronica design for unusual solutions to mirror travel vibration: the mirror of the 1959 Bronica was a quick-return element which dropped down flat, rather than the usual practice of swinging up during exposure.

Amateur Photography. 1972.

In 1972, Eastman Kodak introduced Pocket Instamatic 110 format cameras and film, and Polaroid introduced the SX-70 Land camera and film.

Kodak Pocket Instamatic 60, U.S.

More than 60 million cameras had been sold since Kodak introduced the 126 cartridge format in 1963. 110 Pocket Instamatic, Kodak's second cartridge format, was a 13 x 17 mm. image, less than one third the size of 126. Snapshot-size prints from Kodacolor II 110 film were said to be comparable to those from 126 negatives, and 110 negatives were suggested for enlargement up to 5 x 7 inches.

The first Japanese 110 cameras were marketed in September. The Sedic Pocket Carefree 110 cameras closely resembled Kodak cameras, especially the Sedic Model 20, which had a fixed focused lens and a Magicube flash socket.

Sedic Pocket Carefree 110.

Minolta 16 QT.

Minolta had introduced the 16 QT just before the appearance of Kodak's 110 cameras. A subminiature with automatic exposure control and a viewfinder indicator to confirm correct exposure, it used a Minolta 16 mm. cartridge in a 12 x 17 mm. format almost identical to 110. The camera was a less expensive version of the earlier Minolta 16 MG-S, but the film format was not used by any other manufacturers.

In April, Polaroid introduced the SX-70 Land camera, which had been test marketed in Florida since November, 1971, at a retail price of $180. Unlike previous Polaroid Land films, SX-70 integral film emerged from the camera a self-enclosed, self developing print which completed with no attention from the photographer. The picture format was 8 x 8 cm. in a window on a sealed 9 x 11 cm. packet.

In 1972, Meibo Products imported the Snap Shooter, a disposable plastic 126 format camera, from Snap Shooter Corporation of Philadelphia, and sold it for only 600 yen. The camera inspired more competition than sales.

Snap Shooter Simpro-X, U.S.

The Photographic Industry. 1973.

In 1973, Eastman Kodak faced two lawsuits in the United States. Bell and Howell charged that Kodak illegally used its position in the film market to obstruct competition, specifically with the 1972 Kodak Super-8 cine cameras and film. Berkey Photo charged that Kodak had unfairly restrained competition with Kodak Pocket Instamatic cameras and Kodacolor II 110 cartridge film. In both suits, Kodak was being attacked for its marketing practice of coupling new cameras with films specially designed for them.

In late February, Canon opened its long-awaited Canon Salon on the Ginza in Tokyo. Both Nikon and Fuji Photo Film had already opened public salons. In March, Konishiroku celebrated its centennial. Lenses with multi-layer, anti-reflection coating and 35 mm. single lens reflexes which metered through the lens, many shown as prototypes in the previous year, were reaching the domestic market.

At the Japan Camera Show in Tokyo, which opened on February 27, there was a section for manufacturers who were not regular participants. They were given booth space for 40 minutes to distribute catalogues and product literature. However, at the Photo Accessories Show on March 2, the regular distribution of such literature was stopped for the first time, denying the accessories show some of its previous free and easy, bazaar-like atmosphere.

Cosina Hi-Lite EC.   *Fujica ST801.*

35 mm. Cameras. 1973.

In March, Cosina introduced the Hi-Lite EC. A little-known manufacturer of export cameras, Cosina had produced Exakta cameras and possessed significant technology and experience. In March, 1971, Cosina had introduced the Cosina Compact 35, a rangefinder compact. The Hi-Lite EC had aperture-preferred fully automatic exposure in a somewhat simplified system. The reading was made at the moment the lens stopped down, eliminating one of the mechanical interlocks and lowering the cost of the camera. The system used a fast response silicon photocell and an integrated circuit developed by Matsushita Electric.

In April, the Fujica ST801 was introduced. It was an improved ST701 with full aperture metering, and the first camera to display information on LEDs in the viewfinder. The semi-automatic exposure system used seven red LEDs, which were engaged as the shutter button was pressed partway down. Correct exposure was obtained by adjusting the aperture or shutter until the center LED illuminated. Lenses for the ST801 had multi-layer anti-reflection coatings.

Exposure meter of Leica CL.   *Leitz Leica CL*

The Leica CL, jointly developed by Leitz and Minolta, was introduced in world markets in April, and marketed in Japan in November as the Leitz-Minolta CL. It was a compact, lightweight rangefinder camera with a match-needle metering system which had first appeared on the Leica M-5. The M-5 and the CL were the first rangefinder cameras to meter through the lens, with a CDS cell on an arm which was moved in front of the focal plane shutter when the film was wound, and retracted as the shutter was released. The standard lens supplied on the CL was a 40 mm. f/2, designated an M-Rokkor in Japan, a Leitz Summicron overseas. Similarly, the West German Elmar 90 mm. f/4 was designated M-Rokkor in Japan. The CL accepted Leica M series lenses from 35 mm. to 90 mm.

In February, Minolta introduced a camera designed to be the company's best 35 mm. single lens reflex. Known as the XM in Europe, the XK in the States and the X-1 in Japan, it had an electronic focal plane shutter and an automatic-exposure prism which together provided automation from 4 seconds to $^{1}/_{2000}$. The electronic circuitry could be activated by both a fixed-position switch and a quick action switch. Five finder units and nine focusing screens were available.

Minolta X-1, XK in U.S. and XM in Europe.

The Photographic Industry. 1974.

1974 was a difficult year for the Japanese economy, which suffered greatly after the October, 1973 oil crisis. In the inflation that followed, all forms of energy became suddenly expensive, and Japan's strongly Americanized economy, based on consumption, investment and growth, was immediately and severely shaken. New energy conservation policies had less impact on the camera industry than others because cameras were substantially high value products with much larger labor than materials components. At the same time, camera exports, a large portion of the industry, remained stable.

Prices, costs and wages rose dramatically in Japan during the inflation of 1974, and costs rose sharply in the photographic industry. Camera prices had historically reflected overall fluctuations in the costs of general goods and consumer products, and new camera models were traditionally accompanied by modest, incremental price increases. But in a situation reminiscent of the inflation of the early postwar years, the price increases of 1974 were driven by the economy, not the industry, and they were sudden and extreme.

Between December, 1973 and January, 1974, Olympus Optical, Sankyo Seiki, Norita Optical, Miranda and Ricoh raised camera prices about 10 percent. On January 21, Fuji increased color film prices 14 percent. Fourteen other camera and photo product manufacturers announced price increases averaging 16 percent, including Canon, Konishiroku, Slick, Tokina, Zenza Bronica, Tamron, Nippon Kogaku, Hitachi Condenser, Fuji Photo Film, Petri, Matsushita Electric, Mamiya, Yashica and Nippon Polaroid. Asahi Optical, Minolta and Tokyo Kogaku also raised prices, but without formal announcements. The Ministry of International Trade and Industry, alarmed by the sudden inflation, had advised the industry there would be no official objections to manufacturers raising prices if they had valid reasons and if they were careful not to announce the increases.

Prices continued to rise during the summer, and again in September of 1973, and they rose again in 1974. The wholesale price index in January, 1974 was 23 percent higher than the previous year. Manufacturers at the Japan Camera Show in Tokyo, which opened February 28, raised prices as of that day, and again shortly thereafter.

Except for the least expensive models, most cameras introduced in 1974 had electronic shutters, and many had built-in electronic flash units. A number of the new electronic flashes used energy-saving series circuits rather than bypass circuitry for automatic control. Camera manufacturers began to introduce their own electronic flash units to expand their accessory lines, which at the time were called camera systems. By 1974, most interchangeable lenses had multi-layer anti-reflection coating. A number of manufacturers introduced short zoom lenses with focal lengths from wide angle to modestly telephoto, and very wide angle lenses were becoming popular.

Manufacturers introduced few new products during the year, largely because of the economy, but a number of prototypes were shown. Overall sales had slowed because of the price increases, and a new group of inexpensive single lens reflexes began to appear, including the Soligor TM, Mamiya MSX500, Canon TLb, Asahi Pentax SPII and the export Konica Autoreflex A3.

The 13th Photokina, in September in Cologne, was closed to the general public, a policy which continued from that date on. As a result, attendance was just under 100,000, 150,000 less than in 1972; but the trade had complained that the crowds made it difficult to conduct business. The number of participants from abroad remained about 31,000.

Products from countries other than Japan introduced at Photokina that year included the German Minox 110S, a high quality 110 camera with a 25 mm. f/2.8, an electronic shutter with speeds to $1/1000$ and a coupled rangefinder. The Minox 35EL was an extremely compact folding 35 mm. camera with a 35 mm. f/2.8 lens and an electronic shutter. Rollei displayed the SLX, an electronic 6 x 6 single lens reflex, and a 110 camera. The Contax RTS was an electronic 35 mm. single lens reflex jointly designed and produced by Yashica in Japan and Zeiss in Germany.

During 1974, a number of new films appeared. Kodak began marketing 35 mm. Kodacolor II in April, Konishiroku introduced Sakuracolor II in September, and Fuji Photo Film marketed Fujicolor F-II in November.

Kodak introduced two improved transparency films, Kodachrome 25 (KM) and Kodachrome 64 (KR), and two motion picture films. Ektachrome 160 type G, announced in Super-8, could be used in both daylight and artificial light without corrective filtration. Kodachrome 40 was an improved, finer grain version of Kodachrome II Movie Film.

Kodak increased prices of film, printing paper and chemicals from 3 to 28 percent. Fuji Photo Film and Konishiroku also raised prices several times, although in comparatively modest increments.

The Polaroid SX-70 Land camera and film were lavishly introduced in Japan on June 1, but sales were below expectations, in part because of price resistance. The camera sold for 79,800 yen, a 10-exposure pack of film cost 3,300 yen, a flashbar sold for 950 yen.

35 mm. Cameras. 1974.

The Fujica ST901, introduced in February, had been shown as a prototype at Photokina two years earlier. It had aperture-priority automatic exposure control provided by an electronically-controlled focal plane shutter. An LED display in the viewfinder indicated shutter speeds, the first example of this system in a production camera. On automatic exposure control, the camera offered plus or minus 2 EV compensation . Outside the automatic mode, it offered mechanically controlled shutter speeds of B, and 1/60 to 1/1000. A protective baffle was built into the eyepiece, one of a number of features designed to alleviate problems associated with exposure automation using the newly invented electronic shutter. A narrow vertical window over the film chamber revealed a small indicia, containing the film type and number of exposures, printed on Fuji film cassettes.

Fujica ST901.

The Konica C35 EF was fitted with a built-in electronic flash. When a button was pressed on the front of the camera, the flash head snapped up into position and the circuit was turned on. It proved to be a highly influential design in mid-market compact cameras, both for the flash itself and because built-in flash permitted designers to use smaller maximum apertures.

The first 35 mm. camera with built-in electronic flash was the 1964 Voigtlander Vitrona. The first Japanese example was the 1968 Permamatic 618. Both were large, reflecting the size of the components, especially the capacitors, in electronic flash at the time. The Konica C35 EF received a 1975 design award from the Ministry of International Trade and Industry.

Konica C35 EF.

There were a number of new, wider aperture wide angle lenses for 35 mm. single lens reflexes, including the Canon FD 24 mm. f/1.4. At Photokina, Canon showed a prototype FD 85 mm. f/1.2 which reduced flare at maximum aperture by incorporating an aspherical element in the design.

Nikon introduced the Zoom-Nikkor 28-45 mm. f/4.5, one of the first zoom lenses entirely shorter than normal focal length.

110 Cameras. 1974.

Almost 20 firms sold 110 format cameras in 1974, more than 40 models in all, including some exclusively for export. While foreign 110 cameras used flash bulb arrays such as Flip Flash, Magi cube and Flash Cube, a number of Japanese models had built-in electronic flash. The first was the Vivitar 602, made by West Electric of Osaka, a company with many years of experience making flash bulb equipment. Sunpak, Morris Photo Industry and Fuji Koeki, all flash manufacturers, also began to make cameras. Electronic flash was an important factor in the world wide acceptance of Japanese 110 cameras.

A number of new 110 cameras were shown at Photokina, including models from Fuji Photo Film, Yashica and Ricoh. Canon showed a prototype 110ED with a date imprinting device and a 25 mm. f/2. lens, the fastest lens in the format at the time.

Vivitar 602.

Canon 110ED.

Chapter Twelve

The Microprocessor

from an article by Iwao Ogura

The Photographic Industry. 1975.

I n May, 1975, Queen Elizabeth II and Prince Philip made the first royal visit to Japan since the signing of the 1858 Anglo-Japanese Friendship Treaty. Among the industrial facilities they saw was the Canon plant at Shimo-maruko. On September 30th, Their Imperial Majesties Emperor Hirohito and Emperess Nagako made an historic 15-day visit to the United States, the first visit of an Imperial couple to that country.

Even though the Japanese economy was in a mild recession, the average income of a salaried male was 2,290,000 yen and 90% of the nation felt they belonged to the middle class. Japan produced a total of 7,324,000 cameras in 1975; 681,000 more than the previous year, an increase largely in exports.

The annual Japan Camera Show was held February 27th at the Takashimaya department store in Tokyo. The following day, the Photo Accessories Show was held at the Tokyu department store in Nihonbashi, Tokyo. The well-attended expositions gave no indication of a recession, but the catalogues noted that the prices they listed were valid only for the dates of the show. Rapid changes in price, even in a recessive economy, were escalations. Nippon Kogaku announced a 35 mm. enlarger, with lens, at a suggested list price of 160,000 yen, when the average price of domestic Japanese enlargers began at 10,000 yen.

While Japan's gross national product grew not at all in 1974, and actually declined 1% in the first quarter of 1975, in the last three quarters of 1975 it grew by 4.3%, 3.5% and 2.9%, respectively.

According to the Japan Camera Industry Association, production of 35 mm. single lens reflexes in 1975 was down 3% from the previous year, at 2,730,000. Production of 35 mm. compacts was down 14% to 2,360,000 cameras, and production of 110 and 126 format cartridge cameras rose 98% to 1,360,000 in 1975.

35 mm. Cameras. 1975.

Contax RTS.

The Contax RTS was announced at Photokina in 1974 and marketed in November, 1975. The 35 mm. single lens reflex was developed by the Carl Zeiss Foundation and designed by the Porsche Design Group, both in West Germany, and was codesigned and manufactured by Yashica in Japan.

Carl Zeiss began producing microscopes in Jena about 1850. The Carl Zeiss Foundation was formed in 1889 by his partner, Professor Ernst Abbe. Through the 1930s, Zeiss was well known for optical design, engineering and manufacturing, and the Zeiss Ikon subsidiary designed and manufactured Contax and Ikonta cameras. After the war, when Jena was partitioned into communist control, Zeiss moved to Oberkochen. In 1972, with the closing of the Braunschweig plant, Zeiss no longer made, nor had the capacity to make, consumer cameras.

Yashica first made cameras in 1953, and became known for mass-market products. In 1958, Yashica bought Nicca Camera Company and soon introduced the first Yashica single lens reflex, the Pentamatic I. The 1965 Yashica Electro Half was the first camera ever equipped with an electronic shutter, a leaf shutter jointly developed by Copal and Yashica.

The Contax RTS body was produced at the Yashica plant in Okaya City, and the 17 interchangeable lenses were designed and made by Zeiss in Oberkochen. The standard lenses were 50 mm. f/1.4 and f/1.8. Zeiss Planars. There were seven wide angle Distagons, from a 15 mm. f/3.5, and a 16 mm. f/2.8, to a 35 mm. f/1.4; and eight telephoto lenses, from a Planar 85 mm. f/1.4 to a Mirotar 1000 mm. f/5.6. There was a zoom, a Vario Sonnar 40-80 mm. f/3.5, and an S-Planar 60 mm. f/2.8 macro. All the lenses were multi-coated, and designated T*. Eventually, about one third were produced in Japan under license.

RTS, for Real Time System, referred to the electromagnetic shutter release, which was more sensitive than mechanical releases. The electrical switching system simplified remote control and winder actuation, and became a model for electronic shutter cameras.

The 1975 Olympus OM-2 measured light during, rather than before exposure. Electronic sensors were embossed on the curtain of the focal plane shutter in a small black and white lattice pattern. The system coupled to an electronic flash which was also automatically controlled during exposure, an innovation which greatly influenced future designs of single lens reflexes.

The Fujica Date was a viewfinder camera with a date-imprinting system. The information to be printed was displayed in the viewfinder as a reminder the imprinter was turned on.

Olympus OM-2.

Fujica Date.

In 1975, Asahi replaced the Pentax threaded lens mount with a new bayonet design. The K mount was introduced on three single lens reflexes, the Pentax KM, KX and K2, with a series of interchangeable lenses. The cameras were unexceptional, and met with a certain amount of market resistance, particularly from Pentax owners concerned their lenses would become obsolete. But the conversion was significant: Pentax was the major proponent of thread lens mounts. With the new K bayonet, Pentax acknowledged that the more precise alignment of a bayonet design was required to couple electronic cameras and lenses.

Medium Format. 1975.

The Zenza Bronica ECTL was marketed as the world's first automatic exposure, 6 x 6 cm. professional camera. The aperture-priority system included a comprehensive LED display of shutter speeds above the reflex screen, and metering was accomplished by three silicon photo diodes behind the Bronica split mirror. The ECTL was the last Bronica with a focal plane shutter: subsequent models in three 120 film formats, starting with the 6 x 4.5 Bronica ETR, were fitted with Seiko lens-mounted electronic leaf shutters.

The Mamiya M645 was the first of a group of medium-format single lens reflexes to use the revived semi format. The camera made 15 exposures on 120 roll film, and was fitted with a large focal-plane electronic shutter.

Japanese medium format cameras incorporated electronic camera operations and exposure control for some years before the two preeminent roll-film single lens reflexes, the Swedish Hasselblad and German Rolleiflex. Even so, Japanese medium format cameras and lenses remained less expensive than the European models. They became increasingly perceived as competitive, and sales of Japanese products in these quality conscious markets continued to grow.

Zenza Bronica EC-TL.

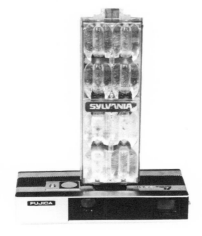

Pocket Fujica 200F.

110 Cameras. 1975.

Kodak announced the 110 system in 1972, and by 1975 there were almost 50 Japanese cameras in the format, and both Konishiroku and Fuji marketed 110 film. The cameras used Magicube flash arrays, which, because they were located so close to the axis of the lens, frequently caused red reflections in the eyes of subjects. Kodak designed an extender to move the flash cube further from the lens. It was supplied free to purchasers of early Kodak 110 cameras, and packaged with later models. Another effort to reduce red eye was the introduction of tall, vertically-stacked flash arrays marketed by General Electric as Flip Flash, and Phillips as Top-Flash.

The Pocket Fujica 200F, a very light 110 camera with a socket for Flip Flash, reached the market almost simultaneously with Kodak cameras designed for the new flash array.

The Photographic Industry. 1976.

I n September 1976, at the 14th Photokina, Pentax announced two new single lens reflexes smaller than the Olympus OM series. Diminuitive size was the only outstanding feature of the Pentax MX, but the Pentax ME incorporated the new Seiko MFC, a vertical-travel metal electronic focal plane shutter. With five sections in the first curtain and six in the second, it was designed so the first blade moved back up after exposure to create a double baffle. Both cameras shared a new quick-loading takeup spool.

The Minolta X-1 Motor was introduced at the spring camera show. With an integral motor drive and a large grip, it was a special-purpose camera for the professional market which developed something of a cult following. With a 50 mm. f/1.4, the X-1 sold for 324,000 yen.

Asahi Pentax ME.   *Flash Fujica Date.*

At Photokina, Fuji announced the world's first high-speed color negative film, Fujicolor FII-400. C-41 compatible and relatively comparable in quality to ISO 100 film, Fuji had substantial expectations for the higher speed film on world markets. The cassette had two uncoated portions on which film speed was encoded. The Flash Fujica Date, announced with the new film, was fitted with an electric contact which could distinguish codes for ISO 100 and 400, and automatically set a speed into the camera.

In 1976, Konishiroku introduced the 24-exposure length of 35 mm. film, which soon generally replaced 20-exposure cassettes as film lengths standardized on multiples of 12 frames.

Rolleiflex showed a prototype automatic exposure 35 mm. camera at Photokina in a configuration reminiscent of a medium-format single lens reflex. The SL-2000 had both shutter and aperture priority, a built-in motor drive and interchangeable film backs. It was not marketed for several years, and other manufacturers had no trouble resisting the configuration for their own 35 mm. cameras.

The Cosina Hi-Lite CSR was an export camera, a fairly standard single lens reflex with aperture priority, semi-automatic exposure control. A separate servo motor, available as an accessory, converted the camera to fully-automatic, aperture priority exposure. The servo mechanism rotated the shutter dial to the correct setting in the context of a preselected aperture.

Cosina Hi-Lite CSR.

Microprocessors. 1976.

As the automation of cameras progressed, various camera functions and controls were designed to be governed electronically rather than mechanically. Electronics became increasingly sophisticated, and the use of digital circuits rapidly increased. Progress in integrated chip technology allowed digital systems to replace the rather simple analog circuits. The Polaroid SX-70 Land camera, made in the States in 1972, was a breakthrough: it performed a series of sequential, data-based control operations with a group of integrated digital circuits.

The 1976 Canon AE-1 was an entirely new, midmarket single lens reflex with a built-in microprocessor. While the exposure operation itself was performed by an analog circuit, the exposure memory, sequential control of various operations, self timer, aperture value control and warning indication were accomplished by digital circuits. Internally, the AE-1 was divided into five modular units, a simplified manufacturing design which permitted the units to be assembled by automation. The cloth focal plane shutter was the first to be modular in construction.

Canon AE-1.

The shutter-priority AE-1, with its built-in microprocessor, incorporated features which soon became standard for single lens reflexes, including a detachable power winder. The dedicted electronic flash coupled directly to the camera's control system, and it was the first camera with an electronic self timer. At 85,000 yen it was something of a bargain, a price Canon was only able to achieve by volume production.

The design and market successes of the microprocessor-controlled Canon AE-1 began a period of competitive product development in the Japanese camera industry. Other major manufacturers soon produced electronic control systems managed by microprocessors, and electronic cameras made possible further manufacturing automation.

In August, a small firm called Yashima Optical introduced the Osanon Digital 750. The continuously variable electronic shutter was set by the automatic exposure system, and speeds were indicated in a digital readout in the viewfinder. But Yashima hadn't the resources to mass produce cameras, and only 2,000 were made before the product was discontinued.

Osanon Digital 750.

110 Cameras. 1976.

By early 1976, monthly production of 110 format cameras had declined 30 to 40 percent. Even as the saturated market shrank, a number of new 110 format cameras were being introduced. In January, Sedic introduced the Tele Focal, an export camera with a built-in long focus lens on a sliding mount. Moving the lens into position, with a small lever on the top of the

Pocket Fujica 350 Zoom.

Minolta 110 Zoom.

Sunpak SP 1000.

camera, also masked the viewfinder. The Pocket Fujica 350 Zoom, introduced in March, was the first 110 format camera with a built-in zoom lens. The 25-42 mm. f/5.6 zoom lens was coupled to a parallax-corrected variable viewfinder.

In May, Minolta introduced the 110 Zoom, the first 110 format single lens reflex with a built-in zoom lens. The 25-50 mm. f/4.5 macro zoom lens was coupled to an aperture priority, automatic electronic shutter with speeds from 10 seconds to $^{1}/_{1000}$, plus bulb and X synchronization. The Hanimex VEF was the least expensive 110 format camera fitted with a built-in close-up lens. Introduced for export in December, the Hanimex also had a parallax correction finder coupled to the close-up lens.

The Sunpack SP 1000 was a 110 format camera with a built-in electronic flash, made by a manufacturer of flash units. The folding viewfinder was also an electronic switch for the flash circuit. The Vivitar 742 XL was a 110 camera fitted with a programmed electronic shutter and a coupled rangefinder. The distance and flash scales were illuminated. The Sedic School 110 was a simple camera in kit form designed to be assembled by school children.

Vivitar 742 XL.

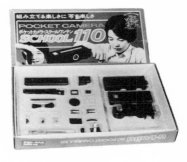

School 110.

Medium Format. 1976.

The Zenza Bronica ETR, marketed in April, was an advanced 6 x 4.5 cm. single lens reflex in the idiom of the Mamiya M645. Both backs and lenses were fully interchangeable, and the lenses mounted electronic leaf shutters. The control circuit and the power source for the electronic shutters were housed in the camera body and coupled to the lenses by a series of contacts. Early models were not equipped with quick return mirrors.

35 mm. Cameras. 1977.

As electronic automation in 35 mm. cameras became more sophisticated, the increasingly complex information exchanges between camera body and lens became impossible with thread mounted lenses. Most major camera manufactures developed their own bayonet mount systems, but Ricoh introduced the XR-1 in June with the Asahi K mount. Saburo Matsumoto, president of Asahi Optical, said "I agree to Ricoh's request of their using our K mount on their new SLR camera because I personally prefer not to be narrow minded and exclusive about this. I would rather have this mount become an international standard." Although the Ricoh XR-1 was not particularly innovative, it received a design award and a special prize for the 20th anniversary of the G-mark product award because it was designed with a compatible lens mount, making available a wide choice of optics.

Minolta XG-E,

The Minolta XD, for Dual priority, was introduced in August. It was the first 35 mm. single lens reflex with both aperture and shutter priority automatic exposure. Minolta also introduced a new lens group, MD Rokkor, with this camera. The Minolta XG-E, also marketed as the XG-2, was an aperture priority and a manual camera.

Automatic Focus. 1977.

In November, Konishiroku introduced the Konica C35 AF, the first production camera in the world with a built-in autofocus system. The compact, accurate autofocus Konica was based on a microchip designed and manufactured in the States by Honeywell. The C35 AF also had programmed automatic exposure and a built-in electronic flash.

At Photokina in 1963, Canon had shown a prototype autofocus 35 mm. camera, and at PMA in Chicago in 1971, Nikon displayed a lens containing an autofocus mechanism. Neither reached production. At Photokina in 1976, Leitz showed a focus aid called Correfot, and Asahi Optical displayed an autofocus zoom lens using the Honeywell Visitronic module.

Manual optical rangefinders measure distance by triangulation as the operator matches double images. The Honeywell Visitronic module electronically compared images on photocells in the context of their relative positions. When the shutter was released, the lens was pulled back toward the infinity position. A coupled mirror moved and scanned, and when the image on a group of scanned cells correlated with the image on a fixed photocell, the lens was mechanically stopped and the shutter released.

The Photographic Industry. 1978.

Twenty-nine firms, including Polaroid and Rollei, participated in the annual Japan Camera Show from March 2 to March 7, and four other exhibitions were held at the same time. The Camera Accessory Show was at the Tokyu department store in Nihonbashi from March 3 through March 8, and on the same dates the Matsuya department store hosted the World Second-hand Camera Fair. The Leica Fair was held at the Matsuzakaya department store March 2 through March 7, and the Enjoyable Photo Group exhibited on March 5 at the Kitanomaru Scientific and Technical Museum.

At the 15th Photokina, there were a number of autofocus 35 mm. compacts and autofocus amateur movie cameras, including the Sankyo Sound XL 320, Supertronic VAF, Chinon AFXL and Bell and Howell 1225 AF. There were 16 still and cine autofocus cameras fitted with the Honeywell Visitronic module. Leitz sued Honeywell for infringing two German patents relating to autofocus systems, and on the same day Honeywell denied infringement, asserted Leitz' patents were effective only within West Germany, and countersued.

An increasing number of manufacturers adopted the Asahi Pentax K mount for interchangeable lenses. First produced in 1975, it was used by Ricoh on the XR cameras in 1977. Topcon, Cosina and two European cameras made in Japan, the Swiss Carena and German Bauer, were introduced at Photokina with the K lens mount.

When Pentagon in East Germany introduced a Praktica with a bayonet mount resembling the K design, the forty year old thread lens mount was effectively discontinued.

35 mm. Cameras. 1978.

As the Japanese trade shows opened in 1978, Minolta was introducing the XD, and Canon, the A-1. Both firms advertised heavily, stressing the number of automatic modes each camera offered.

It had been relatively simple to design an electronic combination of aperture priority and shutter priority automatic exposure, and by 1978 programmed exposure systems were in general use in mid-market 35 mm. compacts. The Canon A-1 was the first single lens reflex in the world with a built-in computer that programmed all exposure functions. Programmed exposure in the A-1 had been developed out of earlier Canon shutter priority systems. In addition to aperture priority and program modes, Canon added automatic flash exposure and a semi-automatic control mode in the A-1.

Canon A-1.

Konica FS-1.

While both the Contax 137 and Konica FS-1 were announced at Photokina in 1978, the Konica passed JCII export inspection on December 13 of that year and the Contax did not until March 13, 1980. The Konica thus became the first 35 mm. single lens reflex marketed with an integral motor drive. It also had a semi-automatic loading device which advanced film to the first frame.

Ricoh FF-1.

Date imprinting module, Konica C35 EFD.

The Ricoh XR-500, the Canon A-1 and the Minolta XD received the G-mark product award in Japan in 1978. The Ricoh won because of the aesthetics of the compact, black-finished body, and because it was surprisingly inexpensive. With a 50 mm. f/2 lens, the Ricoh single lens reflex sold for only 39,800 yen, less than many compacts. It was advertised on price as the San-Kyu-Pa, the Three Nine Eight. Fitted with a vertical travel, metal Copal focal plane shutter, it had speeds from ⅛ to ¹/₅₀₀ and match needle, full-aperture metering.

The Vivitar 35EM was a 35 mm. compact with a single lever on the front which opened the lens cover, moved the lens into position and prepared the shutter release. The Ricoh FF-1 was an ultra compact full-frame 35 mm. strongly reminiscent of the Minox 35 introduced several years earlier. It had estimated scale focusing and the lens extended when a folding door was opened.

The Konica C35 EFD was a C35 EF with a built-in calendar and clock mechanism that automatically recorded on the corner of each frame. The Yashica Auto Focus was the first 35 mm. compact equipped with a focus lock.

Yashica Auto Focus.

Asahi Pentax Auto 110.

110 Format. 1978.

The Asahi Pentax Auto 110, marketed in July, was the only single lens reflex ever made in 110 format with a full line of accessory interchangeable lenses. Exposure control was fully automatic, and an optional motor drive was available. The camera was announced with three interchangeable lenses, the 24 mm. f/2.8 standard lens, an 18 mm. f/2.8 wide angle and a 50 mm. f/2.8 telephoto. A 70 mm. f/2.8 telephoto, a 20-40 mm. f/2.8 zoom and a fixed-focus 18 mm. f/2.8 were introduced later. All the Pentax-110 lenses were bayonet mount, and had no aperture: two metal shutter blades in the camera served both functions.

The programmed automatic exposure system kept the aperture at f/2.8 until EV 9, where it began at ¹/₃₀ and stopped down the aperture and increased speeds until ¹/₇₅₀ at f/13.5. The camera had transistorized, rather than mechanical, X synchronization for the optional dedicated automatic electronic flash.

The Minimax 110EE, made by Sugaya Optical, resembled a scaled-down 35 mm. rangefinder camera. It was supplied with a 32 mm. f/2 lens and a programmed automatic electronic shutter.

Minimax 110EE.

Zenix Zoom TS.

The Zenix Zoom TS was a 110 format camera fitted with a fixed-focus zoom from standard to medium telephoto focal lengths. It was the least expensive camera of this type with a zoom lens. The Zenix TL-5 was a 110 format camera with a sliding lever with which the user could choose a wide angle, standard or telephoto lens. It was the least expensive multiple focal length camera in this format.

The Pocket Fujica 550 Auto had a thyristor quench circuit in the built-in electronic flash which adjusted the light output according to the distance at which the camera was focused. It was the only 110 format camera equipped with this feature.

The Coca Cola camera was a simple 110 format camera housed in a facsimile of a Coca Cola can. It was manufactured by Sedic, Limited, for the Coca Cola Company and was used for promotional purposes. There were a number of other promotional cameras in configurations of products, including the famous Bridgestone Tire camera and the Turtle camera.

Coca Cola Camera.

Plaubel Makina 67.

Medium Format Cameras. 1978.

The Plaubel Makina 67 was a modern, 120 roll film version of an historic design. Its structural resemblance to the 1932 German Plaubel Makina was belied by the contemporary supergraphics on the housing and the rather large identification of the 80 mm. f/2.8 Nikkor lens around its rim. The Makina 67 had an exposure meter enclosed in the optical system of its coupled rangefinder.

The Fujica GW 690 Professional was a 6 x 9 cm. format, 120 roll film rangefinder camera. Fuji produced a succession of professional roll film cameras, most with rangefinders and built-in exposure meters, some in folding designs and some reminiscent of large Leicas. They were extremely well regarded in their rather specialized markets. The GW 690 was fitted with an unusual counter capable of recording the camera's total exposures to 999.

The Art Panorama 240 made three exposures on 120 roll film in 60 x 240 mm. format, four exposures when the frame was 170 mm. long. With aspect ratios up to 4:1, it was the widest angle camera of this type produced by any manufacturer.

Fujica GW 690 Professional.

Art Panorama 240.

35 mm. Cameras. 1979.

Among the exports on which Japan relied to maintain foreign currency income in 1979 were 35 mm. single lens reflexes and compact autofocus cameras. Price increases in OPEC crude oil, and fluctuating foreign exchange rates, made the United States and European markets increasingly important to Japan's fiscal planning.

With a new series of 35 mm. single lens reflexes, Fuji discontinued the threaded lens mount and introduced a new bayonet design. The AX-1, AX-3 and AX-5 cameras were sold initially on the export markets, and introduced domestically in Japan in March, 1979. Fuji, learning from Asahi's experience, enlarged the inside diameter of the bayonet lenses to 49 mm., permitting the AX-5 to use threaded lenses with an adapter. The AX-5 was a multi-mode, programmed single lens reflex which incorporated most of the electronics available in cameras at the time. It was able to shift the program when lighting conditions made it impossible to accommodate a manually entered value. It had an automatic exposure lock, and an electromagnetic self timer which made a series of audible signals during the countdown. An accessory back used a "memory pen" to enter up to 30 characters in an 8 x 28 mm. space at the lower left of the frame.

The Nikon F-2 H-MD was a limited production camera designed primarily for use with a high speed motor drive. It was capable of operating at up to 10 frames per second. Because traditional, moving reflex mirrors could not operate at such speeds, the H-MD was fitted with a fixed, semi-transparent mirror. While 35% of the light reaching the mirror was reflected into the viewing system, the remaining 65% passed through to the film plane. The design made significant use of titanium around the outside of the body on the finder cover, the bottom plate and front apron. The Nikon competed directly with a Canon introduced two years earlier, a pellicle mirror reflex capable of 9 frames per second.

Fujica AX-5.

Nikon F-2 H-MD.

Pentax ME Super.

The Pentax ME Super was equipped with both fully automatic and metered manual exposure systems. In the manual mode, the shutter speed was changed by pushing either an up or down button on the top of the camera, and the value was indicated by an LED in the viewfinder. The data display in the viewfinder also indicated aperture and operating mode. The Pentax ME Super had a maximum shutter speed of $^1/_{2000}$.

The Mamiya ZE was the first Japanese single lens reflex to use an electronic coupling system to transmit information between the camera body and interchangeable lenses. Previous interactions between lenses and camera bodies had been by mechanical pins, cams or levers which frequently initiated electrical signals used for operations circuits. While many manufacturers were reluctant to make changes which would render their lenses obsolete, Mamiya, with few previous 35 mm. single-lens reflex models, was able to aggressively pursue the new mount configuration.

The body of the Mamiya ZE had only three electrical contacts, but the interchangeable lenses introduced with the camera had ten. They were potentially capable of transmitting information about maximum and minimum aperture value, and correction values for effective apertures and focal lengths, to subsequent generations of cameras beyond the ZE, which used focal length data to program shutter speeds for hand holding.

The Contax 139 Quartz, introduced in April, was a lighter, more compact version of the Contax RTS. It was the first camera fitted with a quartz oscillator, which provided extremely accurate shutter speeds. The aperture-priority automatic system calculated exposure time by analog means, then passed the signal through an analog/digital converter. The system then digitally controlled shutter speed, data indications, self timer, electronic flash quench, a number of check functions and the operating sequence.

Contax 139 Quartz.

Compact Cameras. 1979.

The Hanimex 35 Reflex Flash, made by Sedic Company, Limited, was a very inexpensive 35 mm. single lens reflex fitted with a built-in electronic flash. In finish and design, it resembled a 35 mm. compact converted to reflex viewing. The Fujica ST-F was a similar camera.

The Cosina VAF Auto Focus was an autofocus camera fitted with the Honeywell module. Autofocus cameras incorporating on Honeywell units experienced difficulty focusing in low light, and making certain kinds of subject distinctions. The Cosina was designed so the autofocus system could be disengaged when necessary, and distance could be entered manually.

Hanimex 35 Reflex Flash.

Cosina VAF Auto Focus.

Flash Fujica Auto Focus.

The Flash Fujica Auto Focus also used the Honeywell module. To address the same problem as the manual option on the Cosina, the Fujica had a small, powerful light source, called a Beam Sensor, fitted to the camera as a focusing aid.

Low light failure was a generic weakness of the passive autofocus systems. The next generation of 35 mm. compacts was equipped with active infrared autofocus, sending an infrared signal and receiving the reflected light to measure distance. The Canon AF 35 M, known in the States as the Sure Shot, and in Japan as the Auto Boy, was the first automatic focusing camera to employ an infrared sensing system designed by Canon. The camera focused automatically within 27 feet, beyond which the limitations of the infrared system required it to elect infinity focus. In addition to automatic exposure control, a built-in motor drive advanced and rewound the film. It was one of the most popular cameras ever made.

Canon AF 35 M.

Ricoh AD-1.

The Ricoh AD-1 was fitted with an integral spring-wound automatic film advance. It was a larger version of the 15-year-old spring wound Ricoh Auto Half, capable of advancing more than 10 frames on a single winding. Unlike most spring systems, it was also able to operate at up to two frames per second. It was a simple and inexpensive camera designed to provide automatic film advance at a modest price.

When it was introduced in 1979, the Olympus XA was the most compact 35 mm. camera ever made. The innovative 35 mm. f/2.8 F-Zuiko lens was designed with a particularly short back focus, and only an internal element moved during focusing, the front and rear surfaces remained stationary. The design made the six element lens compact, but the optical quality was only satisfactory. Designed with a sliding cover over the lens and viewfinder, the XA offered aperture-priority automatic exposure with a coupled rangefinder and a detachable electronic flash.

Olympus XA.

The Carena EF-250, made by Zenix Industries, was a 35 mm. compact with a built-in electronic flash which swung out into position. The lens emerged when a pair of small doors was opened.

The HD-1 Fujica was an all-weather camera. The lens was sealed with a glass protective cover, and twenty points on the camera were weatherproofed with O-rings and silicone rubber packing. Fuji Photo Film marketed the camera as a "daily waterproof", a term used generally in wristwatches at the time. The dedicated electronic flash unit was also water resistant, and contact was accomplished with an infrared LED on the camera and a detector in the flash unit.

Carena EF-250.   *HD-1 Fujica.*

110 Cameras. 1979.

Minolta introduced two new 110 cameras at the end of that format's development. The Minolta Weathermatic A was an all-weather design in a distinctive bright yellow body. The only underwater camera made for the 110 format, it floated on water and could be used to depths of 15 feet.

The Minolta 110 Zoom SLR-Mark II was a premium camera for the 110 format fitted with a Zoom Rokkor Macro 25 mm. to 67 mm. f/3.5 lens. The normal-to-telephoto zoom at macro position focused to three inches. The Minolta had aperture priority automatic exposure, a variable diopter eye piece with a shutter and a dedicated flash with a detachable filter panel for macrophotography. The camera sold for 65,000 yen with case.

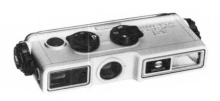 

Minolta Weathermatic A.   *Minolta 110 Zoom SLR Mark II.*

Chapter Thirteen

The Single Lens Reflex

from an article by Iwao Ogura

The Photographic Industry. 1980.

There were three international exhibitions of new photographic products in 1980, Photokina in Germany, the Japan Camera Show in Tokyo, and PMA in the United States. Japanese manufacturers had decided they had become similarly important, and began to announce new products at whichever was convenient. The Japan Camera Show was held, as usual, in late February at Takashimaya department store in Tokyo. PMA, also annual, was in Las Vegas, Nevada, at the end of March. Photokina, the oldest international trade show and the traditional venue to display prototypes and announce new products, continued to be held biannually in the fall in Cologne, Germany.

Two important 35 mm. single lens reflexes were introduced for the professional market in 1980. In late February, the Nikon F3 replaced the 1971 F2. Designed by George Allo, the body appeared somewhat more styled than the F2, although when the camera was fitted to its motor drive the proportions appeared completed. The F3 was fitted with Nikon's horizontal-travel, single-axis focal plane shutter, the same shutter as the F2, but the metering, microprocessor and control mechanisms of the automatic exposure module were fitted inside the camera body, not in the interchangeable prism.

Nikon F3.

The center of the quick-return mirror was a beam splitter. Behind it, a small secondary mirror directed light to a receiving element at the bottom of the camera body. The beam splitter was provided on a coated surface to avoid polarization error.

The liquid crystal display at the upper left of the viewfinder consumed substantially less power than an LED display but required a small lamp to illuminate it in low ambient light.

The Pentax LX, introduced in June, was named in recognition of the 60th anniversary of the company. It was the first Asahi 35 mm. single lens reflex designed and sold for the professional photographer. It was especially well sealed against dust and humidity. Black filler was injected between the outer cover and the body, a sealed bearing was used on the winding lever shaft, and a rubber sponge replaced the usual polyurethane foam where the back cover fit into the body. The LX had direct through-the-lens flash metering, and eight interchangeable finders, but the interchangeable lenses were not similarly weatherproofed.

Pentax LX.

Zenza Bronica SQ.

Contax 137 MD Quartz

The Contax 137 MD Quartz, introduced at the Japan Camera Show in February, was one of the most fully automated, high quality cameras available at the time. It was a sophisticated single lens reflex in a compact black body which continued the Porsche Design idiom begun with the Contax RTS. A small circular window on the back cover displayed a rotating, magnetically driven indicator that revealed the film was advancing properly.

The Zenza Bronica SQ was introduced in August. A sophisticated, electronic 6 x 6 single lens reflex, it was offered with an optional aperture priority, automatic-exposure pentaprism. When film speed was set on an interchangeable film magazine, the information was electronically transmitted to the metering system as the magazine was attached to the camera.

Compact 35 mm. Cameras. 1980.

Mamiya ZE 2 Quartz.

Olympus XA2.

The Mamiya ZE-2 Quartz, introduced a year after the ZE, issued warning signals of potential camera movement. An electronic sensor coupled each lens to the camera through six gold contact points. The sensor automatically selected the slowest hand-held shutter speed possible for that focal length.

In April, Olympus announced the XA-2, a simplified, less expensive version of the XA compact. It was fitted with a slightly slower, four-element f/3.5 lens with three-position zone focusing. The lens returned to the its hyperfocal setting each time the sliding front cover was closed. In Japan, the XA-2 was awarded the 1981 Good Design Grand Prix.

In July, Chinon introduced the Bellami compact, which was designed to fit in a shirt pocket. When the film advance lever was pulled away from the body, it activated a mechanism which opened two doors on the front and moved the lens assembly into position. When the lever was fully closed against the body, the lens retracted and the doors shut.

In November, the Hanimex 35 Micro Flash was made for export by Fuji Koeki. It was a particularly small compact with an electronic flash unit built into the front protective cover.

Chinon Bellami.

Hanimex 35 Micro Flash.

The Photographic Industry. 1981.

In 1981, trade conflicts continued as Japan negotiated with the United States and Europe over tariff barriers and foreign access to Japan's domestic market. The Japanese balance of trade turned positive, and that year showed a surplus of more than 10 billion dollars. As the value of the yen fell against the dollar, Japanese products became more attractive on world markets. The 199.63 yen value of the dollar on January 6, 1981, strengthened to 221.80 yen by May 14.

Stronger export markets, a firm domestic market and advances in electronics all contributed to the development of new, more sophisticated 35 mm. single lens reflexes.

In March, 1981, Mamiya marketed the ZE-X, which had a particularly sophisticated automatic exposure control system. The camera could be used in either aperture or shutter preferred automatic modes. If the system determined the photographer's selection of shutter speed or aperture value was incorrect, a crossover network would automatically override. The microprocessor could shift the entire exposure diagram, and change the preset value until it reached the appropriate automatic range.

Mamiya ZE-X.

Canon New F-1.

In September, Canon introduced an electronic version of its professional single lens reflex. The New F-1, successor to the mechanical 1971 F-1, was marketed as a system with a wide range of interchangeable parts and accessories. There were 17 components relating to power winders, motor drives and remote control; 11 viewfinder components, in addition to focusing screens; 32 components for macro and micro photography; 51 interchangeable lenses or optical attachments; and 10 flash related accessories, all available at the time of the introduction.

The electronic F-1 offered four accessory-based means of exposure control. An eye level finder provided manual match-needle metering similar to the earlier F-1. The addition of an AE motor drive or an AE power winder, in combination with the finder, added shutter priority automatic exposure. When an AE finder was mounted without the motor drive or power winder, the camera provided manual and aperture-priority automatic exposure. When an AE motor or winder was combined with the AE prism, both shutter and aperture-priority automatic were available.

Interchangeable focusing screens offered three options: center-weighted average metering, selective area metering and spot metering. The screen configurations, micro beam splitters with differing areas of reflectance located between the focusing plate and the condenser lens, had taken Canon seven years to develop. A total of 32 combinations were available, as screen patterns were offered in each of the three types of metering.

Minolta X-700.

Pentax ME-F.

In October, 1981, Minolta introduced the X-700, which was designed to operate simply while offering multiple functions. It had programmed automatic exposure, a programmed multiple function back and programmed motor drive. When the accessory Minolta Autoflash 360PX or 280PX was fitted, the camera engaged a programmed autoflash mode in which aperture was automatically selected and flash was measured through the lens. A multiple function data back was available. The X-700 was the first winner of the European award for Camera of the Year.

In November, 1981, Asahi introduced the Pentax ME-F, the world's first 35 mm. single lens reflex equipped with an automatic focusing system. The system Asahi called Through The Lens Electronic Focus Control consisted of two rows of linear MOS image sensors behind a micro beam splitter. When contrast in the two rows was equal, the plane of maximum contrast -the best focus- lay in the middle between the rows, on the film surface.

Signals generated by the system drove a servo mechanism in Asahi autofocus lenses, and an LED indicator confirmed correct focus. When a switch on the lens mount was used to turn off the servo mechanism for manual focusing, or a conventional lens was fitted, the LED indicator in the finder continued to confirm focus.

In July, Ricoh introduced the XR-S, a single lens reflex with solar cells on both sides of the prism to recharge a silver cell battery. While solar cells alone could not produce the current required to operate the camera, Ricoh asserted the partial charging they provided would extend the life of the battery from two to at least five years. The camera's case was fitted with a transparent section to expose the cells to daylight while the case was closed.

In June, Makina, primarily a manufacturer of interchangeable lenses, marketed an export camera called the Makinon MK. At the time, it was the only 35 mm. single lens reflex with interchangeable lenses and a built-in electronic flash. The flash was coupled to the automatic exposure control system, and the camera used the Pentax K lens mount.

Ricoh XR-S.

Minolta CLE.

Compact Cameras. 1981.

By 1981, Japanese designers were trying to simplify camera operation and build smaller, more compact products. Minolta introduced a successor to the compact camera it built for Leitz, the Leica CL, which had been sold in Japan as the Leitz Minolta CL. The original model had a mechanical shutter and measured through the lens for a match-needle metering system. The Minolta CLE had an electronic shutter, with aperture-priority automatic exposure with speeds from 1/2 second to 1/1000. The CLE measured light reflected from the film, or from a pattern of scattered white surfaces on the shutter curtain designed to simulate the reflectance of the film surface. Proper exposure for the dedicated flash was also metered through the camera. The coupled rangefinder had parallax-corrected frames for 28 mm., 40 mm. and 90 mm. lenses.

Two compact cameras were introduced in March. The Minolta Hi-Matic AF-D had an active infrared autofocus system. A flashing LED and a warning tone indicated when the camera was too close for the autofocus system, or too far from the subject for proper flash exposure.

Minolta Hi-matic AF-D.

The Konica C35-EF3 was made smaller by setting the film rewind crank into the top. It popped out when the back was opened to remove the film.

In April, Hosoi Seisaku-sho introduced the Raynox FC-35 Auto Flash, manufactured for export only. It was a low priced, compact 35 with built-in electronic flash. The flash operated automatically when there was insufficient light for an exposure, and the circuit shut itself off automatically until the meter indicated it was required.

In June, 1981, Canon introduced the AF 35 ML, an autofocus compact sold in the U.S. as the Super Sure Shot. Fitted with the fastest lens available on a camera of this type at the time, a 40 mm. f/1.9, and an autofocus system using 240 CCD line sensors, it was the first camera to combine automatic focusing with automatic film advance. In daylight, it was capable of making one exposure per second.

Canon 35 AF ML.

The Fujica Auto 7 Date, marketed in September, was one of the most completely automated cameras of its time. It was named for its seven built-in automatic systems, including an electro-optical date imprinter. It was the first camera in which the rewind mechanism was tripped by the tension of the film at the end of the roll, and also offered programmed automatic exposure, automatic focusing, automatic film advance, automatic flash and automatic film loading.

The Chinon Infrafocus AF, announced in October, was a compact 35 with an infrared autofocusing system significantly more sophisticated than most. The autofocus operated continuously from three feet to infinity.

Fujica Auto-7.

Electronic Still Cameras. 1981.

A number of technological and market forces were converging in 1981, leading towards a blend of video and traditional optical/chemical photography. For some years, electronics had been incorporated in cameras, first to measure light then to control it. By 1981, electronic systems based on microprocessor chips were measuring and automatically controlling both light and focus, systems which would have been impossible mechanically. CCD sensors, a video technology, were becoming the predicate mechanisms for sophisticated autofocus cameras, which would be ubiquitous within a decade. It was only a matter of time until electronics expanded from the role of controlling still photography to recording it.

At the time, the general consensus was that video recording produced a printed image inferior to the silver or dye image of chemical photography because it looked like a television picture. The still electronic image contained the video equivalent of grain. The black lines, like the black dots called grain in photographs, were actually the spaces between the image- forming components, in this case raster scan lines. While photography was a means of making a print, and video, still or continuous, was a means of making a displayed image, the notion of electronic still-video photography still implied that a print from a video system had to rival a photographic print, as it would be put to the same uses.

In 1981, VCR sales of 850 billion yen exceeded sales of color televisions, and video discs were being promoted as picture-producing records. Within a decade, major Japanese camera manufacturers would be marketing their own brands of video cameras, many supplied by other manufacturers, many in the then-new 8 mm. format. Following Canon, Pentax, Nikon, Olympus and Konica sought joint ventures with electrical manufacturers such as Hitachi, Victor and Matsushita.

In August, 1981, Sony announced an electronic still video system called Mavica, an acronym for magnetic recording still video camera. The original system included a single-lens reflex camera which recorded onto a small floppy disc, a disc player, a transfer printer, and a telephone image transmission device.

Sony Magnetic Video Camera, Mavica.

Sony electronic still video disc.

The disc format had been subject to negotiation and agreement by a wide range of world manufacturers. A small plastic housing 60 x 54 x 3 mm. contained a floppy disc 47 mm. in diameter. At the moment of exposure, the floppy disc turned at 60 revolutions per second.

The camera recorded still images through a three-color separation filter forward of the CCD MOS image sensor. The image signal was recorded on the floppy disc by becoming a luminance signal, which was FM modulated, and two color differential signals, B-Y and R-T, which were also FM modulated with a low frequency subcarrier. With a line sequential scanning system for the color difference signal, the method resembled the European SECAM system. The initial unit's 200,000 pixel resolution was similar to that of broadcast television.

Because of the field refresh frequency, the shutter had a minimum speed of 1/60. The maximum speed with the mechanical shutter was 1/1000, with the electronic shutter, 1/2000. The high shutter speeds were made possible by the persistence of the image sensor, which also allowed the use of electronic flash.

By 1984, both Sony and Canon were demonstrating still photographic systems at the Summer Olympics in Los Angeles, and image signals transmitted to Japan by telephone were printed in monochrome in the Asahi Newspaper and in color in the Yomiuri Newspaper.

Fuji Instant Camera Model F50-S.   Fuji Instant Camera Model F10.

Japanese Instant Cameras. 1981.

I n April, 1976, in the States, Eastman Kodak announced an instant photography system. It went on sale in Canada in May, in the States in July, and in Japan the following year. In October, 1981, Fuji Photo Film announced two instant cameras, Fuji Instant Camera Model F-50-S and Fuji Instant Camera Model F-10. The Fuji cameras used the film system developed by Eastman Kodak, and Fuji and Kodak cameras accepted each other's film packs. They were not interchangeable with Polaroid SX-70 Land film.

The Fuji F-50-S had folding bellows, a built-in electronic flash and programmed automatic exposure. There was a manual override for density which was maintained with flash. The exposed print was ejected upward out of the top of the camera by a motor. The Fuji Instant Color Film FI-10 pack contained 10 exposures, each with an image area about 91 x 68 mm. The prints had a finely textured matte finish.

The Model F-10 was a rigid camera with a detachable electronic flash attachment called Fuji Instant Strobo S. Although this was a simple box type camera, it included AE and density control features similar to the F-50.

In 1982, Polaroid and Konica reached a marketing agreement, while Polaroid continued an eventually successful litigation against Eastman Kodak for patent infringement. Under injunction, Kodak eventually removed all of its instant cameras and film from the market.

ISO Film Speed Indication. 1981.

I n May, 1982, Kodacolor HR Disc film was marketed with ISO film speed designation, the first Kodak film rated by that method. By 1983, Japanese films were being marketed only with ISO speeds designations.

Historically, there had been a number of attempts to quantify and standardize film sensitivity, starting with Hurter and Driffield in 1890, and Scheiner in 1894. In 1931, when Germany was the world's leading camera and film manufacturing country, the Deutscher Normenausschuss, the country's standards organization, developed the Deutsche Industrie Norm which became the recognized system of grading film sensitivity. The DIN scale is logarithmic: every three numbers represent a doubling or halving of the value.

After World War II, Eastman Kodak became the preeminent film manufacturer, and in 1947, based on research done at Kodak, the American Standards Association established ASA film speed ratings. In 1954 the ASA was revised, and in 1957 the DIN standard was revised, but the definitions and methods of measurement were so different it was impossible to make a direct correlation between the two.

In the early 1960s, the ASA standard was revised and it became similar to DIN. In response, DIN was revised to conform to ASA in October, 1961. Although the two leading methods of measuring film speed had been unified, it was more than ten years until ISO replaced ASA/DIN ratings. At the ninth meeting of the International Standards Organization ISO/TC 42 (Photography), held in Tokyo in the fall of 1979, Japanese film manufacturers agreed to convert from ASA/DIN.

Nikon FM-2.   *Chinon CE-5 AF.*

The Single Lens Reflex. 1982.

The Nikon FM 2, introduced in December, 1982, was a manual metering camera with shutter speeds to 1/4000, and X flash synchronization to 1/200. To achieve the high shutter speed, Nikon increased the curtain speed with a new, lightweight focal plane shutter blade made of a honeycomb structure of titanium.

The Nikon F3AF, a prototype autofocus version of the F3, and two autofocus lenses, 80 mm. and 200 mm., were shown at the Japan Camera Show at the Takashimaya department store in Nihonbashi, Tokyo, on February 25. The lenses focused quickly, using a built-in motor and split-image range detection focusing, the electronic equivalent of the optical rangefinder.

In March, Canon introduced the AL-1, an advanced AV-1 with an added manual exposure control and a focusing aid similar to the image contrast detector of the previous year's Pentax ME-F.

The Chinon CE-5 AF, marketed in August, was the first 35 mm. single lens reflex with active infrared autofocusing coupled to a zoom lens. The electronics of the system are coupled to the camera body and activated by the exposure release. A 50 mm. AF Chinon f/1.7, and an AF Zoom Chinon 35-70 mm. f/2.8 were designed with the camera, which had a vertical focal plane shutter with speeds to 1/2000. In the illustration, the infrared emitting diode is seen on the left, the receiver is in the larger housing on the right of the lens.

The Olympus OM-30, called the OM-F in the States, was introduced in November. It incorporated the Honeywell TCL module in a passive focus aid.

At the time, automatic focusing systems for single-lens reflex cameras were broadly classified as active, in which an ultrasonic wave or an infrared light is sent out from the camera and then measured; and passive, in which measurement is made of the brightness distribution of the object. Passive systems were roughly divided into contrast detection and split image detection. The first production contrast detection system was the Asahi Pentax ME-F, and the first production split-image detection system was the OM-30. In the Olympus, the focusing sensor was a linear MOS image sensor which scanned in the horizontal direction. A green LED and a tone indicated accurate focus; a red LED to one side or the other indicated the direction in which the lens should be turned to correct focus.

Olympus OM-30.

The OM-30 was supplied with an unusual accessory: a trigger cord which connected the focusing aid mechanism to the power winder. An object could then be automatically photographed when it came into a prefocused position in front of the camera.

At Photokina, Ricoh introduced the XR-F, an export single lens reflex with aperture-priority automatic exposure. It was equipped with an electronic focusing aid using the Honeywell module.

The Compact Camera. 1982.

The Minolta AF-C, announced in October, was an extremely small automatic exposure, automatic focusing compact of simplified design. The active infrared system moved only the rear elements of the taking lens, the front of the lens remained stationary. A sliding front cover served as a lens cap, and the camera was fitted with a focus lock.

The Fujica DL-20 was an inexpensive, automatic compact with semi-automatic film loading. DL refers to drop-in loading, a system in which the film cartridge was placed into the camera, the back was closed, and the camera engaged the film and automatically advanced it to the first frame. An automatic rewind mechanism sensed the end of the roll and rewound the film. The lens was opened and the viewfinder exposed by rotating a ring on the front of the camera. Closing the camera returned the lens to the hyperfocal position.

The DL-100, with the same film loading mechanism, was an automatic focus, automatic exposure compact with a built-in flash. Introduced with the DL-20 in September, the DL-100 was designed by Mario Bellini, an Italian industrial designer.

Minolta AF-C.

Fujica DL-100.

Telepac TS-35.   *Contax Preview.*

The Photographic Industry. 1982.

A number of unusual new cameras were introduced in 1982. The Telepac TS-35 was announced in March by Yashio and Company, Ltd. It was an interesting combination of a pair of prism binoculars with an automatic-exposure 35 mm. camera with a 300 mm. telephoto lens. The 9 x 30 binoculars covered a field approximately equivalent to that of the telephoto lens, and although they functioned independently, the focusing mechanisms were coupled.

The Contax Preview was specialty camera designed to accept Contax and Yashica lenses on a housing fitted with a Polaroid Land pack film back. The camera made standard 24 x 36 mm. images on 3 1/4 x 4 1/4 inch format Polaroid Land pack films. Introduced in August, 1982, the Preview had a right-angle reflex finder.

The Nimslo-3D camera was designed by an American firm and originally manufactured in the United Kingdom. Early in 1982, Sunpak, the Japanese manufacturer of the electronic flash for the Nimslo, contracted to re-engineer the camera to reduce costs and improve quality.

Rather than two lenses placed at an interocular distance, the traditional configuration of stereo cameras, the Nimslo had four 30 mm. f/5.6 lenses arranged horizontally, about 20 mm. apart at the optical centers. The lenses simultaneously made four 17.5 x 22 mm. negatives, which were printed together in register on lenticular paper to create a sense of apparent depth.

The Fuji Instant Camera F-55 V was introduced in December, 1982. Substantially a modified F-50S, the V model, for Voice, was the first camera ever manufactured with a voice command system. A synthesizer produced a woman's voice, speaking in Japanese, which instructed users to eject the darkslide, adjust focus, use flash and change film. The camera also played two melodies. The voice could be turned off.

Nimslo-3D.   *Fuji Instant Camera Model F-55 V.*

Medium Format Cameras. 1982.

The 1970 Mamiya RB 67 became the RB 67 Pro S in 1975, and in May, 1982, it was revised as the RZ 67 Professional. On RB models, the shutter was cocked with a large lever on the side of the camera, the film wound separately with a lever on the revolving film back. The RZ 67, with an electronically controlled shutter, advanced the film with a single stroke of the body- mounted lever. The camera was coupled to the interchangeable lenses by a series of electrical contacts, and an optional prism finder provided semi-automatic exposure control.

The Zenza Bronica SQ-AM, marketed in August, was the first medium format 120 camera of Japanese manufacture with an integral motor drive. A continuation of the SQ and SQ-A, the automatic exposure SQ-AM could operate at slightly more than one frame per second.

Mamiya RZ67 Professional.

Zenza Bronica SQ-AM.

Kodak Disc Format. 1982.

On February 3, Eastman Kodak Company announced the Disc system, which included three cameras which used a new film format, Kodacolor HR Disc Film, and a comprehensive line of photofinishing equipment. It was made available for sale in Japan and the United States in May. The 8.2 x 10.6 mm. negative was less than half of the size of the 110 format negative. The f/2.8, 12.5 mm. lens gave disc cameras a fixed focus range from 4 feet to infinity.

The Kodacolor HR Disc was an ISO 200 color negative emulsion coated on an .18 mm. thick polyester base, to provide the necessary flatness for the unusual film configuration. Sales began well, but the negative required a 13x enlargement to make a standard print, while the increasingly popular 35 mm. compact cameras required less than 4x enlargement to make a standard print. The grain appeared coarse when compared to prints made from 35 mm. negatives, and in Japan, prints from Disc negatives were twice the cost of prints from 35 mm. In its second year, sales dropped drastically.

Fuji Koeki manufactured a disc camera for Osram, and Minolta, Konishiroku and Fuji Photo Film began to produce disc cameras, but most had stopped within a year.

At Photokina, Fuji Photo Film introduced Fujicolor HR Disc film. Eastman Kodak announced Kodacolor VR-1000, a high resolution 35 mm. color negative film which showed only slightly more grain than 400 speed film at modest enlargements. Polaroid announced a 35 mm. instant slide system, consisting of black and white and color self-processing 35 mm. transparency films, a processor and a slide mounter.

Disc cameras were shown by a number of manufacturers, although most were OEM products of W. Haking Industries Ltd., of Hong Kong. The sole Japanese product was the Osram Flash Disc Autowinder, made for the German electrical conglomerate Osram by Fuji Koeki, an entirely different company than Fuji Photo Film. Osram electronic flash units had been produced in Japan for some time.

Also at Photokina were two further indications of the merging of photography and video. Kodak showed a video image reproducing device to display Disc negatives as positives on a television, and all the major Japanese video manufacturers displayed products at the German photographic trade show.

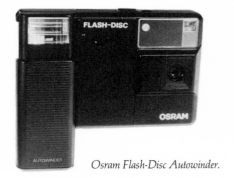

Osram Flash-Disc Autowinder.

Chapter Fourteen

The Automatic Camera

from an article by Kakugoro Saeki

35 mm. Cameras. 1983.

The Canon T50, introduced in January and sold domestically in March as the Automan, was a completely automated single lens reflex made on a highly automated assembly line. A remarkable number of parts were made of specialized plastics, including the lightweight, polycarbonate body and the shutter. The camera had a single programmed-automatic exposure mode, an integral automatic winder, and a new, compact FD 35-70 mm. f/3.5-4.5 zoom lens. The Canon T50, perceived as an intermediary between a compact and a fully equipped single lens reflex, won the 1983 Design Grand Prix for all categories.

A compact, dedicated electronic flash for the Canon T50, the 244T, could be set for ISO 100 and ISO 400 only. When attached to the camera, the shutter speed was automatically set to $^1/_{60}$. When the shutter button was partially engaged, the electronic flash discharged a near infrared beam for distance measurement, and the results were used to automatically set an aperture between f/2.8 and f/5.6.

Canon T-50.

Each of the two five-blade curtains on the vertical focal plane shutter was formed of metal-plated 0.12 mm. plastic sheets; all ten blades weighed only 1.4 grams. With speeds from 2 seconds to $^1/_{1000}$, the program varied shutter values from 2 seconds to $^1/_{60}$ at full aperture, and thereafter both shutter and aperture were diminished along a slope of 1:2.

Two other plastic-bodied single lens reflexes were soon introduced, the Asahi Pentax A3 and Minolta Alpha 7000.

The Nikon FA was announced in August and offered for domestic sale in September. It was the first multiple mode, automatic exposure single lens reflex made by Nikon. A lever on the shutter speed dial was used to select program, shutter priority, aperture priority and manual modes. There were two program modes: standard, and one which provided higher shutter speeds for longer focal length lenses. The standard program began at full aperture, at f/1.4, and shifted up to f/16, $^1/_{1000}$ on a 1:1 slope, where it stayed at f/16 as it continued to $^1/_{4000}$. With Nikkor AI S lenses 135 mm. or longer, or with Nikon teleconverters, the second program shifted by 1.5 EV towards higher shutter speeds.

Nikon FA.

While aperture priority and manual modes operated in the usual manner, the shutter priority mode was capable of aperture control in extreme lighting conditions. When an aperture value beyond those of the lens was required, the camera varied the shutter speed to achieve correct exposure.

The multiple-pattern metering system used compound silicon photodiodes at both sides of the eyepiece. It measured five sectors, a central area and the four corners, and was programmed with 20 patterns of brightness differentials between the central and peripheral areas. It eliminated portions brighter than EV 16 and darker than EV 1 under ISO 100, and selected optimum exposure from the average, center weighted, highlight or shadow readings. In the automatic mode, a switch could override the matrix pattern and engage center-weighted metering.

Shutter speeds were indicated in the viewfinder by a liquid crystal display, and a tiny optical window made an aperture indication on the lens barrel visible in the viewfinder. The FA won the first "Camera Grand Prix" of the Camera Industry Press Club.

The Olympus OM-4 was announced in September and marketed in October. It was an aperture priority, automatic exposure single lens reflex with an additional spot metering program. Approximately 20% of the light was diverted by a beam splitter to a silicon photodiode which was changed from full to spot metering by switching the circuit. A liquid crystal display panel at the bottom of the viewfinder indicated information in white. Spot metering measured about 2%, an area equivalent to the center of the microprism. With a normal lens, the spot metering angle was about 3 degrees. Each time the spot button was pressed, the camera emitted an electronic sound. When more than eight spot metering selections were made, the earlier selections were sequentially canceled. The outer ring of the shutter release button was a memory switch: turned anticlockwise, it retained a spot reading for one hour after an exposure was made. When the ring was turned clockwise, all data was cancelled, so it could also be used for clearing the memory as needed. There was also a "clear" button on the lens mount.

Olympus OM-4.

Chinon CP-5 Twin Program.

Two logical evolutionary steps in data-based exposure management were programs which varied according to the lens in use, and multiple specific programs which could be selected according to circumstance. The Chinon CP-5, introduced in August and sold domestically in March, 1984, was designed with two program modes, one called Creative, one called Sports. There were two other operational modes, aperture priority automatic and manual. In program one, Sports, exposure varied up to 1/60 at full aperture, then varied up to f/16 and 1/1000 on a slope of 4:6.5. Program two, Creative, varied both values to f/16 and 1/1000, after which the aperture stopped to f/22. The CP-5 was otherwise substantially the same as the Chinon CE-5 and CG-5.

Medium Format Cameras. 1983.

M any of the advanced functions introduced in 35 mm. cameras, including more precise light metering systems, were soon added to professional roll film cameras in the various medium formats.

The Fujica GS 645 Professional was introduced in April, 1983. A folding, bellows camera with a coupled rangefinder, it made 15 exposures 6 x 4.5 cm. on 120 roll film. Because the film ran from left to right, the less-than square frame was vertically oriented and the camera made a vertical photograph in its normal position, and was turned sideways for horizontal exposures. When the front was closed over the retracting lens and bellows, the plastic body became relatively flat and quite compact. The built-in metering system provided over, under and correct exposure indication, and the bright frame rangefinder offered parallax compensation. The 75 mm. f/3.4 EBC Fujinon S was mounted in a Copal #00 shutter with speeds to ¹/₅₀₀, and a self timer.

The Fujica GS 645 W Professional, marketed in October, had no rangefinder, was manually focused by estimation, had no bellows and did not fold. It was fitted with a 45 mm. f/5.6 EBC Fujinon W, which offered an angle of view on 6 x 4.5 equivalent to a 27 mm. lens on a 35 mm. camera. The 645 W had the same exposure system as the GS 645, and had a characteristic protective bar surrounding the lens.

Fujica GS645W Professional.

Minolta AF-SV.

Vivitar TEC 35 Autofocus.

Compact 35 mm. Cameras. 1983.

T he Vivitar TEC 35 Autofocus, introduced in February, was made for Vivitar by the West Electric subsidiary of Matsushita Electric Company. It was sold in Japan as the National Chance C-700 AFS. It was the first camera to be fitted with a liquid crystal display on the top to indicate the film speed setting and the frame number. In low light, a sensor circuit automatically positioned the electronic flash unit and began to charge the capacitor. If the light level increased, or if an exposure was not made within 60 seconds, the flash unit retracted into the camera. The active infrared autofocus system operated by discharging a tiny electronic flash covered with an infrared filter, then measured the intensity of the reflected light.

The Minolta AF-SV, also known as the Talkman, was introduced in June. The camera was equipped with a female voice which, in Japanese or English depending on the market, said "Load film", "Too dark, use flash" and "Check distance"

Olympus Quick Flash AFL.   *Goko UF.*

as required. A transparent cover was fitted over the film takeup spool. During loading, the leading edge of the film was placed under it, and the film partially advanced to confirm proper placement. Film advance and rewind were motorized.

The Olympus Quick Flash AFL was marketed in October. Fitted with two lithium cells, the brief recycle time permitted the camera to make flash exposures at 1.5 second intervals. The lithium cells also powered the automatic exposure and focusing systems, and the film advance and rewind. Because of its self-contained design, the camera was advertised as caseless, and it was featured on Japanese television commercials under the nickname Picasso. The batteries were advertised as lasting up to five years, based on the use of one 24-exposure cassette per month, half of all exposures taken with flash. The active infrared autofocus operated to .85 meter, and was equipped with a focus lock. An additional model was available with time and date imprinting in the Japanese, U.S. and U.K. notational conventions.

The Goko UF was a very simple 35 mm. camera with a built-in flash. It was a fixed-focus camera with an unusual optical design. When the electronic flash was activated, one of the lens elements was moved out of position, refocusing the camera to ten feet, the distance covered by the flash.

Disc and Miniature Cameras. 1983.

Minolta Disc-7.

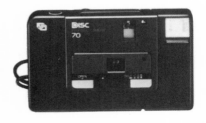

Fuji Disc Camera 70.

In April, Minolta introduced the Disc 7. The camera had a square convex mirror on the front, and was fitted with a telescoping arm which somewhat resembled an automobile radio aerial. When the camera was held at the extended length of the arm, the mirror provided a quite accurate visual field for self portraits. An accessory 50 cm. collapsible extender had a built-in shutter release. In addition to the Disc 7 and the Disc 5, which did not have the mirror, Minolta marketed two cameras in department stores: pastel pink and blue disc models with the name of French fashion designer Courreges emblazoned on the front. In the States, Consumers Reports gave the Minolta Disc cameras high ratings.

The Konica Disc 15 Auto-Focus was introduced in May as an export camera. Although it had only two focus positions, infinity to 1.2 meters, and 1.2 meters to .35, it was the only disc camera produced with an active infrared autofocus system. A conversion lens was coupled to the autofocus system and was shifted into place automatically.

In June, the Fuji Disc Camera 70 was introduced. A lever on the front offered continuous, single exposure, three exposure and self timer operation. At the continuous position, all 15 frames could be exposed successively when the shutter release was held open.

The Enica SX was a subminiature in Minox 8 x 11 mm. format, which used standard Minox film. Made by Niko Kogyo, it was the first camera in Minox format equipped with a built-in electronic flash. It was fitted with a fixed focus 14.3 mm. f/3.8 with a single shutter speed of $^1/_{120}$. The camera was distinguished by an attractive, high quality finish of a patterned, anodized aluminum.

Although the market for 110 format had largely been replaced by the disc, an unusual camera in the cartridge format was marketed in January by West Electric Co. The National Macro Camera C-M30 was designed so that a standard E-size print from a negative made at the macro position provided a total, combined magnification of 30X. The camera otherwise resembled an ordinary 110, and could be used conventionally with a fixed-focus range from 1.5 meters to infinity. Among the optional accessories was a macro hood designed for relatively large subjects. It attached to the front of the camera, and the lens was focused to the front edge of the hood. An adjustable macro stage could be fitted to the hood to hold objects to be photographed. A macro stand was available, on which focusing was accomplished with a ring attached to the stand. A diopter adjustment was fitted to the finder eyepiece.

Enica SX.

National Macro Camera C-M30.

The Photographic Industry. 1983.

In the recession of 1982, Japanese 35 mm. single lens reflex production dropped to 80% of the previous year, at 5,390,000 cameras. Similarly, the 690,000 unit domestic market was 81% of the previous year.

Two new standards were set in 1983. One was the DX encoding system for 35 mm. cassettes announced by Eastman Kodak Company at the Photo Marketing Association trade show in the States. It was not unlike an earlier Fuji system which permitted Fujica cameras to distinguish between Fuji 100 and 400 speed films on specially encoded cassettes, and to set the speed into the camera.

The DX encoded 35 mm. cassette had a series of insulating or conducting blocks which contained film information recognizable by sensors in the camera. The code described film speed in one of 24 steps from ISO 25 to 5000, length of the roll and film latitude control. A bar code adjacent to the DX code was for photofinishers, and a bar code preprinted on the film was used in specific photofinishing operations. All Japanese films were converted to the DX system, and new cameras at all market levels were designed to recognize and incorporate DX code information.

The other standard was the magnetic disc for electronic still photography. Most of the parameters were announced in 1983, including the 47 mm. diameter of the disc and its housing configuration, and the two image-writing densities, 25 frames and 50 frames. In June, 1984, the Electronic Still Camera Standards Committee, comprised of 32 manufacturers worldwide of electronic equipment, cameras and magnetic media, published the final comprehensive standards.

35 mm. Cameras. 1984.

The Ricoh XR-P Multi-Program was introduced in February, 1984. It was the most expensive Ricoh, with a wide range of operating modes, including three programmed automatic options, aperture priority automatic and manual. In addition to the basic program, there was a high speed program mode called Program Action, and a depth of field program, Program Depth. The three, notated as P, PD and PA, were selected on the left side of the shutter release. On the shutter dial, in addition to B and speeds of 4 seconds to $^1/_{2000}$, there was a setting marked TV, which engaged shutter speeds for the writing rates of various screens. With the shutter set at TV and the program selector at P, the speed was $^1/_{30}$, for Japanese and U.S. systems. PD was $^1/_{25}$, for European television systems, and PA was $^1/_4$, for computer and word processor screens.

The electronic self timer was controlled by a dial which also operated an interval timer. Combined with the winder, the camera could be set to produce exposures at 2, 15, and 60 second intervals. The same control, set at null, operated as a second shutter release.

Ricoh XR-P Multi Program.   *Pentax 645.*

Medium Format. 1984.

In June, Asahi introduced the Pentax 645, a medium format, eye-level single lens reflex with a number of exposure modes and a built-in motor drive.

Although in the traditional configuration of a 120 single lens reflex with a prism and a handgrip, with film holders fitted to the back, the Pentax 645 was operationally more like a contemporary 35 mm. camera. It offered multiple mode automatic exposure, it was an eye level camera in a rectangular format, and it had an integral power winder. While the 645 looked like a traditional roll film reflex, and the larger 1970 Pentax 6 X 7 looked like an enlarged 35 mm. single lens reflex, the two Pentax cameras shared the the same design premise: they were medium format cameras with handling and operational features contemporary to the development of 35 mm. cameras at the time of their introduction.

The Pentax 645 accepted 120 or 220 film in frames which were not interchangeable, lightproof backs. The frames, which were supplied in fitted plastic cases, permitted rapid reloading but not mid-roll exchange of films. Like all contemporary 645 cameras, the Pentax made 15 and 30 exposures on the two lengths of roll film.

A liquid crystal display on top of the camera displayed aperture and shutter speed, operational mode, film speed and an exposure counter. The camera could be operated in programmed automatic, aperture and shutter priority automatic and full manual. Modes, exposure compensation and film speed were controlled by engaging each category with its own button, then changing the engaged category with a pair of up and down buttons. The same pair of up/down controls were used to electronically select aperture and shutter speed values.

The camera body was made of glass-filled polycarbonate, in a substantially greater density than used for 35 mm. cameras. The grip contained six AA batteries, and the camera body housed a lithium battery for exposure data memory circuits.

Yashica T AF-D.

Pentax PC35 AF-M.

Compact 35 mm. Cameras. 1984.

The Yashica T AF-D was marketed by Kyocera in June. It was fitted with a Zeiss Tessar TP 35 mm. f/3.5, and was heavily advertised on television as offering a premium lens on a compact camera. The camera was caseless: a sliding cover closed over the shutter release, and the lens was enclosed by a black plastic cover which opened as the shutter was released and closed again after the exposure. Programmed automatic exposure control was managed with an electronic shutter with speeds from $1/30$ to $1/700$, a relatively high maximum speed for a compact.

The Asahi Pentax Autoron II, sold overseas as the Pentax PC 35AF-M, was announced in June and marketed domestically in July. It was Asahi's second 35 mm. compact camera; for the company's first 30 years, from 1952 to 1982, Asahi made only single-lens reflexes. The PC 35AF-M had a built-in motor to advance and rewind the film, and was the first camera equipped to read DX encoded film cassettes. Film speed could also be set manually, and a small rectangular window on the back of the camera displayed a portion of the cassette on which film type, speed and length were printed.

In October, Fuji introduced the DL-200, which was called the Cardia in Japan, and the DL-200D. Fuji had changed the name of its cameras from Fujica to Fuji, and had called a series of cameras FACE, for Fuji Automatic Camera Evolution. Fuji had also introduced a system called CQC, for Camera Quality Control, which implied an ability of the camera to control the quality of the photographs.

The DL-200 was the first camera in that series. It was equipped with the Fuji drop-in film loading system: when the back cover was closed a motor wound the entire roll of film out of the cassette onto the spool. As each frame was exposed, the film was wound back into the cartridge frame by frame. The

Fuji DL-200.

system, which soon became popular in compact 35 mm. cameras, protected exposed frames from accidental ruin if the camera back was opened in mid-roll.

The DL-200 also metered through the lens, with two receiving cells placed near the film gate controlling the shutter speed. The electronic flash circuit was switched on by opening the lens cover. With a guide number of 10, the lithium batteries could recycle the unit in 3 seconds. In low brightness or backlighting, daylight-synchronized flash or full flash could be controlled manually. The camera was equipped with DX sensors; if film was not DX encoded, the system defaulted to ISO 100.

In May, Fuji introduced the model 800X instant camera, the first of three related models designed to accept film rated up to ISO 800. The 800X was fitted with a glass lens, the 800S had a plastic optic. The third model was the autofocus 800AF. With an accessory closeup unit which included a finder, an electronic flash, a measuring tape and polarizing filters for both lens and flash head, the 800X focused at 50 cm. at the infinity position, 18.3 cm. at the close focus position.

Fuji Instant Camera 800X.

Minolta 7000AF, 7000 MAXXUM in U.S.

35 mm. Cameras. 1985.

The Minolta Alpha 7000 was called the Maxxum in the U.S. and the 7000 AF in Europe. It was introduced in all three markets simultaneously in February, 1985. The twelve new lenses announced with this multi-mode camera had integral read-only memory and five electrical contacts to identify themselves to the camera. The contacts also could provide data on focal length, maximum and minimum lens aperture, variances in maximum aperture in certain zooms, and coefficients of lens extensions. The lenses had no aperture controls, and were driven during autofocus by a motor in the camera. The fixed focal length lenses included an AF 50 mm. f/1.4; an AF 50 mm. f/1.7; a macro AF 50 mm. f/2.8; an AF 24 mm. f/2.8; an AF 28 mm. f/2.8; an AF 135 mm. f/2.8 and an AF 300 mm. f/2.8. There were more zoom lenses, including an AF 28-85 mm. f/3.5-4.5; AF 28-135 mm. f/4.0-4.5; AF 35-70 mm. f/4.0; AF 35-105 mm. f/3.5-4.5; and an AF 70-210 mm. f/4.0.

Two 8-bit chips controlled camera functions and the phase differential-detection autofocus, a system similar to the Minolta X-600 and the Nikon F3AF. The 7000 was capable of focusing the 50 mm. f/1.7 from one meter to the infinity stop in 0.3 seconds.

A dedicated electronic flash unit provided autofocus up to 5 meters by projecting near-infrared vertical stripes, which were read just prior to the flash exposure.

Canon T80.

LCD Pictograph panel. Canon T80.

The 7000 had automatic exposure programs for wide angle, normal and telephoto lenses, and for the changing focal lengths of zoom lenses. It also offered aperture priority and shutter priority modes, and manual. The camera operated on four AA batteries, and was fitted with a lithium cell for memory backup. An accessory data-imprinting camera back could record time, date and other data on the film between frames and also function as an intervalometer. An advanced back allowed a choice of program curves, indicated program diagrams on a liquid crystal display, and could automatically and continuously change the exposure value of up to nine frames in minimum steps of .25 EV.

The 7000 enjoyed substantial sales, and won two industry awards in 1985, the second annual "Camera Grand Prix" of the Japanese Camera Industry Press Club and the fourth annual "European Camera of the Year" award.

The Canon T80 was announced in January, 1985, and marketed in April. It was an autofocus single lens reflex with a large liquid crystal display with an array of pictographs displaying 17 different types of information. There were liquid crystal displays on the T50 and T70 Canons, but the T80 was the first camera to show the data in pictorial form, an idiom that would be extended in the subsequent EOS series cameras. There were seven program modes, including standard, depth of field program, stop action, a floating program for panning, and electronic flash and stop-down aperture automatic. Three autofocus lenses were announced for the T80: a 50 mm. f/1.8, a 35 to 70 mm. f/3.5 and a 75 to 200 mm. f/4.5.

Compact Cameras. 1985.

The Kodak VR-35 K-10, and the subsequent K-12 and K-14, were 35 mm. compacts manufactured in Japan by Chinon Industries for Eastman Kodak. Eastman Kodak had produced 35 mm. cameras in the past, but for some years Kodak had marketed only consumer cameras in the 126 and 110 cartridge formats, and the disc format. With the K series, Kodak began to address the amateur market defined by Japanese 35 mm. compact cameras.

When a colored acrylic lens cover was raised, a small electronic flash built into the upper end of the cover was positioned above the camera. The power source for the camera and the flash could be either a dedicated 9V lithium battery or a standard 9V alkaline battery, for which there were different contacts inside the battery chamber.

Although the K-10 had a 3-element f/3.5 35 mm. Ektanar lens, the K-12 and K-14 were equipped with an f/2.8 35 mm. Ektar, the first mass produced, precision-molded glass, aspheric 4-element lens. The aspheric element was fabricated in Rochester, N.Y., and shipped to Japan for assembly.

Kodak VR-35 K10.

Ricoh FF 70D.

The Ricoh FF-70D was introduced in March. It was the first camera which could read and display both film speed and exposure length from a DX-encoded cassette. A large liquid crystal display on the top of the camera showed exposure count, film speed and type, confirmed film advance and displayed battery check.

In March, Fuji announced the Auto 8QD and the TW-3. The Fuji Auto 8QD had a date imprinting device which changed the imprint to conform to vertical and horizontal camera positions. When the camera was turned for a vertical photograph, a pendulum-like action caused the date mechanism to rotate 90 degrees, and the information was imprinted along the short edge of the film. In Japanese, the camera was called Tateyoko, which means vertical and horizontal.

The Fuji TW-3 was a half frame camera with automatic motor wind, drop-in film loading, DX film speed setting and a built-in electronic flash. It had two lenses, which were selected by a turning a ring on the front of the camera. The wide angle lens was an f/8 23 mm. fixed-focus, with nominal sharpness from one meter to infinity. The longer lens was an f/8 69 mm. with 4 focus zones: 4 to 6 meters, 6 to 12 meters, 12 meters to infinity and a lever-actuated, half meter close focus position. A Z-shaped optical axis reduced the dimensions of the 69 mm. lens.

Fuji Auto-8 QD.

Fuji TW-3.

Chapter Fifteen

The Japanese Photographic Industry

from an article by Takashi Hibi
and William S. Fujimura

Japanese Photographic Optics.

Cameras were made in Japan as early as 1868, but photographic lenses were not commercially produced until well into the twentieth century. The Japanese optical industry began by making ophthalmic lenses with imported optical glass, progressed to making photographic optics, and developed optical glass melting capabilities and began producing lenses independently shortly after the outbreak of the first World War.

In 1873, the government of Japan sent Matsugoro Asakura to Austria to learn optical fabrication. He returned in 1875 and began to build the country's first optical facility. Although he died before it was completed, by the fall of 1867 his students had produced ophthalmic lenses from imported glass.

By 1883, his son, Kametaro Asakura, had begun work on a photographic lens at his Yotsuya Denmacho ophthalmic manufacturing plant in Tokyo. He made what is generally considered Japan's first photographic lens, which won first prize at the Third National Industrial Exhibition in 1890.

Ryuzo Fuji graduated in mechanical engineering from Tokyo Institute of Technology and became a naval engineer. Assigned to study science in Europe, he spent three years in Germany studying optical design and lens fabrication. His younger brother Kohzo graduated from Tokyo Imperial University in applied chemistry, and became director and manager of the Aichi Cement Company. In 1908, the two brothers started their own company, which they called Fuji Lens Factory.

They rented the dirt-floor foyer of a residence in which they began to produce prisms and lenses. In March, 1909, they created Japan's first modern optical plant in the Shiba district of Tokyo, which they equipped with German optical fabrication equipment and Zeiss measuring instruments.

All nineteenth century Japanese efforts to design and fabricate lenses used imported glass. While commercial glass melting techniques were brought to Japan in 1887, and the country produced glass for windows and bottles, optical glass was imported from Germany, France and England. German supplies stopped immediately when World War I began, and blockades interfered with shipments from other countries. In 1915, the Department of the Navy began a program to manufacture optical glass, and the Department of Agriculture and Commerce's Osaka Industrial Materials Testing Laboratory began in research optical glass melting in 1921.

Camera and Lens Manufacturers.

Asahi Optical Company, Limited.
(Asahi Kogaku Kogyo Kabushiki Kaisha).

Asahi began in 1919 as Asahi Kogaku Goshi Kaisha, in the Tosima district in Tokyo, manufacturing ophthalmic lenses designed by Kumao Kajiwara. In 1923, Asahi marketed its first photographic optic, the AOCO motion picture projection lens. In 1929, Asahi began to design and manufacture lenses for still photography, and by 1943 the company was a major supplier of lenses for other camera manufacturers.

Asahi made a number of lenses for Minolta between 1931 and 1937. In 1931, the 105 mm. f/4.5 triplet Corona Anastigmat was supplied for the Eaton and Happy cameras. In 1933, Asahi made the 105 mm. f/4.5 triplet Actiplan Anastigmat for the Minolta. In 1935, the Semi Minolta was fitted with a 75 mm. Corona Anastigmat. In 1937, the Auto Semi Minolta was supplied with a 75 mm. f/3.5 Promar Anastigmat, a 4-element Tessar design, and the Auto Press Minolta was fitted with a 105 mm. version of the same lens.

For Konishiroku, Asahi made two lenses for the Pearlette in 1932, an f/8 Achromatic Doublet and an f/6.3 75 mm. Optor Anastigmat. In 1933, Asahi made an f/4.5 105 mm. Optor for both the Idea and the Pearl Eighth Year Models.

Most of Asahi's facilities were destroyed during the war, and the company was closed until 1948, when it reopened as Asahi Optical, manufacturing binoculars for export. In May, 1952, Asahi introduced a camera for use with a telescope it marketed: the 35 mm. single lens reflex had a waist level focusing finder and the first Asahi Takumar lens, an f/3.5 50 mm. All Asahi lenses between 1952 and 1976 were called Takumar, Super Takumar, Auto Takumar, or SMC Takumar. SMC, Asahi's seven layer anti-reflection coating designed by OCLI in California and developed for production by Asahi, was introduced in 1970 on lenses for the 6 x 7 Pentax. In 1976, for the new K and M cameras, Asahi made a series of bayonet-mount lenses designated SMC Pentax, to distinguish them from thread-mount Takumars.

Canon, Incorporated.
(Canon Kabushiki Kaisha).

Canon was founded by an obstetrician and amateur photographer named Mitarai in November, 1933, as Seiki Kogaku Kenku Sho. In 1935, the company showed a prototype 35 mm. rangefinder camera called the Kwanon, and introduced a production model called the Hansa Canon. The lens was a Nikkor; the company, called Seiki Kogaku Kogyo after August, 1937, made its first lens in 1939, a 50 mm. f/1.5 Seiki Serenar for an X-ray camera. After the company was named Canon in September, 1947, lenses were also called Canon.

Chinon Industries, Incorporated.

Sanshin Seisakusho was founded in Chino City in the summer of 1948 by Hiroshi Chino, to manufacture lens barrels and mounts for Olympus, Ricoh and Yashica. In 1959, the company marketed its first 8 mm. cine zoom lenses; in January, 1973, the name was changed to Chinon Industries. The optical division continues to make lenses for Chinon cameras, as well as a variety of zoom lenses for video cameras.

Fuji Photo Film Company, Limited.
(Fuji Shashin Film Kabushiki Kaisha).

Fuji Photo Film was founded in January, 1934, to produce sensitized materials. By 1938, it announced it would make a complete range of photographic goods, and would make optical glass for photographic lenses. During the war, Fuji made aerial cameras and lenses, and later made high grade optical glass and Rectar studio camera lenses. After 1954, all Fuji lenses were renamed Fujinar or Fujinon.

Konishiroku.
(Konishiroku Shashin Kogyo Kabushiki Kaisha).

Konishiroku was founded, as Konishi Honten, in 1873. It was also known as Rokuohsha, which was a division established in 1902 to make sensitized materials, which later produced cameras, lenses and other photographic apparatus. In the States, the company is known as Konica.

In 1928, Hirowo Mohri began designing a four-element lens in the Tessar style, and by the spring of 1931 produced, with Jena glass, a 135 mm. f/4.5 lens called Hexar. *Roku* means six in Japanese, and the *hex* of Hexar refers to the name of the founder, Rokuemon Sugiura. The design was a success, some said the equal of the Zeiss Tessar. The first Hexar was supplied on the Tropical Lily camera, announced by Konishiroku in June, 1931. The Hexar name was used for many different lenses until 1959, when the name was changed to Hexanon.

Minolta Camera Company, Limited.
(Minolta Camera Kabushiki Kaisha).

Minolta was founded by Kazuo Tashima in 1928 as Nichi-Doku Shashinki Shokai. In 1931, the name was changed to Molta Goshi Kaisha, and in 1937, when the company began to manufacture lenses, the name was changed to Chiyoda Kogaku Seiko Kabushiki Kaisha. The first Minolta Rokkor lens was an f/4.5 200 mm. for a 1940 portable aerial camera. By order of the Imperial Japanese Navy, Minolta started to develop and produce optical glass at Itami, near Kobe City, in 1942. The first consumer Rokkor was the 75 mm. f/3.5 on the 1946 Minolta Semi IIIA camera, which was also the first Japanese lens with an anti-reflection coating.

Nikon.
(Nippon Kogaku Kogyo Kabushiki Kaisha).

Three companies were consolidated in 1917 to form Nippon Kogaku Kogyo, to meet the needs of the Imperial Japanese Navy in World War I. The component corporations were the optical division of Tokyo Keiki Seisaku Sho, Iwaki Glass Seisaku Sho and Fuji Lens Seizo Sho. In 1921, eight German engineers and scientists were given five year contracts to advance optical technology at Nippon Kogaku: Max Lang, optical design; Hermann Dillman, optical computing; Ernst Bernick, mechanical engineering; Heinrich Acht and Otto Stange, product design and drafting; Adolf Sadtler and Karl Weise, lens grinding and polishing, and Albert Ruppert, prism grinding and polishing.

Heinrich Acht remained at Nippon Kogaku until 1928, and during his last three years he designed and produced lenses from 75 mm. to 500 mm., with apertures from f/2 to f/6.8. Acht's 500 mm. f/4.8 was named Flieger Objective, and these designs became the first lenses made by Nippon Kogaku. In 1929, after Acht left, Kakuno Sunayama designed an improved 500 mm. f/4.8 aerial lens, called the Trimar, and a 120 mm. f/4 Tessar type, for 6.5 x 9 plate cameras, called the Anytar.

In 1932, all of the company's lenses were called Nikkors, and they were supplied as original equipment on a number of Japanese cameras, including all Canons before World War II. The first Nikon camera was marketed in October, 1948, and the 1950 50 mm. f/1.4 Nikkor was the first mass- produced, high quality lens for a 35 mm. camera. In subsequent years, Nikon lenses were supplied as original equipment on other cameras, and were designed for large format cameras and for enlarging, as well as for Nikon cameras.

Olympus Optical Company, Limited.
(Olympus Kogaku Kogyo Kabushiki Kaisha).

Olympus began in 1929 as Takachiho Seisaku Sho, a microscope manufacturer. In June, 1936, Olympus made its first photographic lens, a 75 mm. f/4.5 copy, as were most Japanese lenses of the time, of the Zeiss Tessar. A company-wide contest was won by the name Zuiko, which remains the trade name for lenses with an excellent reputation for optical performance and construction. Zuiko lenses were supplied on cameras made by a number of Japanese firms, including Mamiya, Elmo, Aires and Walz. The company changed its name to Olympus in 1949.

Petri Camera Company.

Petri began in 1907 as Kuribayashi Seisaku Sho, a photographic accessory manufacturer. The first camera was made in 1919, the first lens in 1942. Before World War II, the company made First cameras and lenses, and after the war its products were called Orikkor and Orikon. Later, the camera and the company names were consolidated and changed to Petri. The company declared bankruptcy in 1977, and was operated by company union members until 1979.

Tokyo Optical Company, Limited.
(Tokyo Kogaku Kikai Kabushiki Kaisha).

Tokyo Optical began in September, 1932, under the direction of the Imperial Japanese Army. The optical division of the Seikosha factory of Hattori Tokei, a clock and watch manufacturer, was merged with Katsuma Kogaku Kikai Seisaku Sho, a sub-contractor to Hattori Tokei. The new company was formed to manufacture photographic lenses and precision optical and mechanical instruments. By 1934, it had produced two triplet photographic lenses, the State and Toko, in f/6.3 and f/4.5 apertures. In 1937, Tokyo Optical made its first Tessar design, which it called the Simlar.

In 1940, the company made a 50 mm. f/1.5 which copied the front of the Zeiss Sonnar and the back of the Zeiss Bitar, and it was also called a Simlar. The designer, Ryoji Tomita, made a 50 mm. f/0.7 design in 1944, which was later sold to the U.S. Occupation forces.

Tokyo Kogaku lenses were supplied on pre- and post-war Minions, and for the 1954 Leotax F the name was changed to Topcor. All of the company's Topcon single lens reflexes were fitted with Topcor lenses.

Tomioka Optical Company, Limited.

In 1924, Masashige Tomioka founded Tomioka Kogaku Kenkusho in the Shinagawa district of Tokyo to develop photographic lenses. After a long period of trial and error, he produced the Lauser, a 4-element f/4.5 Tessar design made with Japanese glass. In 1932, the laboratory became a manufacturing facility, Tomioka Kogaku Kikai Seizosho, and made original equipment lenses for camera companies.

After the war, Tomioka developed a triplet, the Tri-Lausar, for the Pigeon 35, Toyoca 6, Beautycord S and Yashimaflex B. By 1949, Tomioka had become the exclusive supplier for the Yashica Company, Ltd., and currently produces most Yashica lenses.

Lens Manufacturers. 1970 to 1985.

By 1984, there were more than twenty Japanese lens manufacturing firms, in addition to camera companies, producing interchangeable lenses, largely for 35 mm. single lens reflexes. In alphabetical order, they were:

Company	Brand
Ace Optical Co., Ltd.	Acetar
Cima Kogaku Co., Ltd.	Cimko
Kawakami Seiki Seisakusho, Ltd.	Kawanon
Kenlock Corporation	Kenlock
Kimura Seimitsu Kogyo Co., Ltd.	Kimunor
Kino Precision Industries, Ltd.	Kiron; Panagor
Komine Co., Ltd.	
Kowa Co., Ltd.	Kowa
Makina Optical Co., Ltd.	Makinon
Mitake Optical Co., Ltd.	Eyemik
Nakadai Kogaku Co., Ltd.	
Nissin Koki Co., Ltd.	Promura; Hi-Lux
Ozone Optical Co., Ltd.	Ozunon
Sankeisha and Co., Ltd.	
Sanko Optical Co., Ltd.	Sankor
Seimax Corporation	Seimax; Seimar
Sigma Corporation	Sigma
Soligor Corporation	Soligor
Sun Lens, Inc.	Sun
Tamuron Co., Inc.	Tamuron
Tokina Optical Co., Inc.	Tokina
Yamasaki Optical Co., Ltd.	Congo, Alto

Chapter Sixteen

Historically Significant Japanese Cameras. 1903 to 1985.

Compiled by Takashi Hibi

Since its inception, the Japan Camera and Optical Instruments Inspection and Testing Institute, JCII, a technical organization which inspected the quality of cameras for export and tested the safety of electrical photographic appliances as required by law.

Over the years, JCII built up a definitive collection of photographic and cinematographic instruments. Initially, the collection was designed to provide historical references for the work of the Institute, and to provide documentation of design and change. In 1969, on the 15th anniversary of JCII, the founder and president of the Institute, Kinji Moriyama, designed a scholarly public exhibition of a significant portion of the collection. Almost 450 photographic and cinematographic devices were displayed in an exhibition hall on the Institute's sixth floor.

Mr. Moriyama's scholarship was the basis of a continuing effort to define the historical significance of technological development in the Japanese photographic industry. As the influence of Japanese camera design and the number of Japanese cameras on world markets increased exponentially after World War II, the complexity of determining standards for historical significance, and selecting the cameras themselves, increased substantially.

To engage the issue, the Japanese Historical Camera Screening Committee was formed. The original members were Michifusa Otagi, a camera researcher; Kakugoro Saeki, of Camera Maninichi Magazine; Tatsuo Shirai, of Asahi Camera Magazine; Hachiro Suzuki, from the Pentax Gallery; Masao Tanaka, a camera repair specialist; Kazuo Hayashi, from the Tokyo College of Photography; Hajimu Miyabe, from the Chiba Institute of Technology; and from JCII, Kinji Moriyama, Takeshi Fujita, Masahiro Tano, Tomisaburo Oda and Takashi Hibi.

The committee met frequently, beginning in November, 1969, and produced its first preliminary selection in June, 1970. When the relevant companies were notified, the list was published in several camera magazines. A significant public response yielded a wide range of opinions, suggestions and nominations, as well as a number of generous offers of cameras and other photographic apparatus.

The committee's final screening regulations are reproduced below. Among the general premises on which the committee finally determined its selections were the requirements that cameras had to have been made in Japan, and to have been of technical significance to the development of the Japanese camera industry.

For these purposes, technical significance was determined to refer to an aspect of the optical, mechanical or electrical functions which was demonstrably the first of its kind in Japan, or in the world. The committee determined to refer to fully manufactured, production models of cameras, excluding prototypes and experimental models.

After two other intermediary selections, the final list of historically significant Japanese cameras was announced in June, 1973.

Screening Regulations.

An historical camera will be the first Japanese camera incorporating an aspect of technical significance as defined below. For this purpose, cameras are dated according to the date of sale, or the date of export inspection, whichever is earlier. Cameras also may be determined to have been historically significant because of an influence on the industry or the marketplace.

Cameras will be classified according to the following criteria.
1. Classification by the shape of the camera or the picture format.
2. Classification by the lens.
3. Classification by the finder or the focusing mechanism..
4. Classification by the exposure mechanism or exposure adjustment mechanisms, including
   4.a. Shutter
   4.b. Diaphragm
   4.c. Exposure meter
   4.d. Flash
5. Classification by the method of holding sensitized materials or by the operating device for winding and rewinding film.
6. Classification by the construction and operation of the camera body.

Historically Significant Japanese Cameras.

Date	Camera	Type	Film or Format	Manufacturer
1903				
September	Cherry Portable	Box	Meishi	Konishi Honten
1904				
January	Cherry Portable	Box	Tefuda	Konishi Honten
	Champion Portable	Box	Tefuda	Konishi Honten
1906				
July	Sakura Pocket Prano Portable	Hand	Tefuda	Konishi Honten
1907				
January	Sakura Owner Portable	Box	Nimaekake	Konishi Honten
	Sakura Owner Portable	Box	Cabinet	Konishi Honten
February	Sakura Prano Portable	Hand	Nimaekake	Konishi Honten
	Sakura Prano Portable	Hand	Cabinet	Konishi Honten
April	Sakura Reflex Prano	Single Lens Reflex	Nimaekake	Konishi Honten
	Sakura Stereo Prano	Hand	Nimaekake	Konishi Honten
1908				
January	Sakura Noble Portable	Hand	Cabinet	Konishi Honten
1909				
January	Pearl Portable	Hand	Tefuda	Konishi Honten
April	Idea Telephoto	Box	Tefuda	Konishi Honten
1911				
April	Minimum Idea	Folding	Meishi	Konishi Honten
1912				
	Radio	Special	31 mm.	Ueda Camera Store
1913				
	Flex	Box	25 mm. Tintype	F.M.P. Society
1914				
October	Korok	Folding	Meishi	Konishi Honten

Date	Camera	Type	Film or Format	Manufacturer
1915				
August	Idea Snap	Hand	Daimeishi	Konishi Honten
1916				
January	Lily II	Hand	Daimeishi	Konishi Honten
1918				
	Sweet	Hand	Sweet	Sone Shunsui-do
1923				
August	Pearl II	Hand	120	Konishiroku Honten
	Secrette	Special	Sweet	Sone Shunsui-do
1924				
	Secrette	Special	Atom	Sone Shunsui-do
1925				
June	Pearlette	Folding	127	Konishiroku Honten
1926				
October	Record	Box	35 mm.	Konishiroku Honten
December	Idea Spring	Folding	Cabinet	Konishiroku Honten
	Neat Reflex	Single Lens Reflex	Tefuda	Konishiroku Honten
1930				
January	Tougo	Box	30 mm. x 40 mm.	Tougodo
December	Nifca-Dox	Folding	Daimeishi	Nichidoku
1931				
April	Sakura	Box	127	Konishiroku Honten
August	Sakura	Box	120	Konishiroku Honten
	Pearl	Hand	120	Konishiroku Honten
	Arcadia	Hand	Daimeishi	Molta Goshi Kaisha
	Happy	Hand	Daimeishi	Molta Goshi Kaisha
1933				
April	Pearl 8th Year	Folding	120	Konishiroku Honten
1934				
April	Olympic Jr.	Miniature	127	Olympic Camera Works

Date	Camera	Type	Film or Format	Manufacturer
May	Baby Pearl	Folding	127	Konishiroku Honten
June	Minolta	Press	Daimeishi	Molta Goshi Kaishi
November	Minolta Vest	Folding	127	Molta Goshi Kaishi
	Auto Minolta	Press	Daimeishi	Molta Goshi Kaishi
1935				
April	Super Olympic	Miniature	135	Asahi Bussan
July	Semi Minolta I	Folding	120	Molta Goshi Kaishi
August	Sun Stereo	Stereo	120/8 pairs	Yamashita Tomojiro Shoten Limited
September	Hansa Canon	Miniature	135	Seiki Kogaku
October	Picny	Miniature	127	Minagawa Seisakusho
1936				
January	Hansa Rollette Reflex	Twin Lens Reflex	120	Omiya Photo Supply
March	Nippon	Miniature	120	Mizuno Camera Store
April	New Lily	Folding	Daimeishi	Konishiroku Honten
	Semi First	Folding	120	Kuribayashi Camera
July	Rosen Four	Folding	127	Proud Company
September	First Speed Pocket	Folding	127	Kuribayashi Camera
October	Mulber Six	Folding	120	Kuwada Shokai
November	Minolta Six	Folding	120	Molta Goshi Kaishi
	First Six	Folding	120	Kuribayashi Camera
1937				
January	Roll Light	Twin Lens Reflex	120	Ohashi Koki
March	Meisupi	Twin Lens Reflex	30 mm. x 40 mm.	Tougodo
May	Midget	Subminiature	14 mm. x 14 mm.	Misuzu Shokai
July	Prince Flex	Twin Lens Reflex	120	Fukada Shokai
	Sakura Camera	Miniature Box	127	Konishiroku Honten
August	Clover Baby Reflex	Twin Lens Reflex	127	Hagi Kogyo

Date	Camera	Type	Film or Format	Manufacturer
September	Super Semi Proud	Folding	120	Proud Company
	Weha Chrome Six	Viewfinder	120	Yamamoto Camera Store
	Auto Semi Minolta	Folding	120	Chiyoda Kogaku Seiko
	Auto Press Minolta	Press	Daimeishi	Chiyoda Kogaku Seiko
December	Minolta Flex I	Twin Lens Reflex	120	Chiyoda Kogaku Seiko
1938				
April	Minion	Spring	127	Tokyo Kogaku
May	Guzzi	Subminiature	18 mm. x 18 mm.	Earth Optical Company
	Tsubasa Super Semi	Spring	120	Optochrome Company
July	Baby Super Flex	Single Lens Reflex	127	Kikodo
August	Boltax	Viewfinder	24 mm. x 24 mm.	Minagawa Seisakusho
September	Riken Camera	Viewfinder	127	Riken Kogaku
December	Hammond B	Special	127	Maruso Kogaku
1939				
February	Canon Jr.	Viewfinder	135	Seiki Kogaku Kogyo
September	Lyrax	Viewfinder	120	Fuji Kogaku
1940				
January	Leotax	Rangefinder	120	Showa Kogaku
	BB Semi First	Folding	120	Kuribayashi Camera
	Meikai	Twin Lens Reflex		Tougodo
September	Mamiya Six I	Folding	120	Mamiya
	Shinkoflex	Single Lens Reflex	120	Yamashita Shokai
1941				
September	Auto Keef	Rangefinder	127	Kokusaku Seiko
December	Mamiya Six III	Folding	120	Mamiya
	Minoltaflex Automat	Twin Lens Reflex	120	Chiyoda Kogaku Seiko
1946				
August	Minolta Semi IIIA	Folding	120	Chiyoda Kogaku Seiko

Date	Camera	Type	Film or Format	Manufacturer
1947				
May	Steky	Subminiature	10 mm. x 14 mm.	Riken Kogaku
	Minolta 35	Rangefinder	135	Chiyoda Kogaku Seiko
November	Bolty	Spring	24 mm. x 24 mm.	Chiyoda Shokai
1948				
May	Minion 35	Viewfinder	135	Tokyo Kogaku
July	Petal	Special	5 mm.	Petal Optical
August	Mamiyaflex Jr.	Twin Lens Reflex	120	Mamiya
	Olympus 35 I	Viewfinder	135	Takachiyo Kogaku Kogyo
September	Hansa Jupiter	Box	135	Omiya Photo Supply
October	Nikon I	Rangefinder	135	Nippon Kogaku Kogyo
	Mamiya 35	Rangefinder	135	Mamiya
1949				
February	Canon IIB	Rangefinder	135	Canon
March	Minolta 35	Rangefinder	135	Chiyoda Kogaku Seiko
July	Nikon M	Rangefinder	135	Nippon Kogaku Kogyo
	Mamiyaflex Automat A	Twin Lens Reflex	120	Mamiya
August	Nicca III	Rangefinder	135	Nippon Camera
	Snappy	Subminiature	14 mm. x 14 mm.	Konishiroku Shashin Kogyo
	Fujica Six IBS	Spring	120	Fuji Photo Film
September	Minolta Memo	Viewfinder	135	Chiyoda
	Yallu	Twin Lens Reflex	135	Yallu Optical
November	Look	Rangefinder	135	Look Camera
	Gemflex	Twin Lens Reflex	14 mm. x 14 mm.	Showa Kogaku
	Cooky	Viewfinder	135	Kashiwa Seiko
1950				
January	Ricohflex III	Twin Lens Reflex	120	Riken Kogaku

Date	Camera	Type	Film or Format	Manufacturer
March	Konan 16 Automat	Subminiature	10 mm. x 14 mm.	Chiyoda
April	Firstflex P-1	Twin Lens Reflex	120	Tokiwa Seiki
July	Taniflex	Single Lens Reflex	120	Taniyama Camera
August	Teleca	Subminiature	10 mm. x 14 mm.	Toko Shashin
September	Mamiya 16 Super	Subminiature	10 mm. x 14 mm.	Mamiya
1951				
October	Binox	Twin Lens Reflex	120	Binoca
November	Echo 8	Special	6 mm. x 6 mm.	Suzuki Kogaku
	Tomic	Spring	120	Toko Shashin
1952				
February	Asahiflex I	Single Lens Reflex	135	Asahi Kogaku Rogyo
April	Olympus Chrome Six III	Spring	120	Olympus Optical
	Tomy	Special	120	Ars Seiki
May	Koniflex	Twin Lens Reflex	120	Konishiroku
	Minoltaflex IIB	Twin Lens Reflex	120	Chiyoda
	Airesflex Z	Twin Lens Reflex	120	Aires Camera Works
June	Pigeon 35 III	Rangefinder	135	Shinano Koki
July	Nicca III-S	Rangefinder	135	Nicca Camera
October	Panon	Special	120	Panon Camera Company
	Arco 35	Folding Rangefinder	135	Arco Photo Industries
November	Rich-Ray Six	Special	120	Rich-Ray Shokai
1953				
January	Konilette I	Folding	30 mm. x 36 mm.	Konishroku
May	Richlet	Box	35 mm. Paperbacked	Rich-Ray Shokai
June	Canon IVSb	Rangefinder	135	Canon

Date	Camera	Type	Film or Format	Manufacturer
August	Mammy	Box	24 mm. x 28 mm.	Mamiya
	Press Van	Folding	120 and 135	Suzuki Optical Company
September	Laurelflex	Twin Lens Reflex	120	Tokyo Kogaku
October	Topcon 35	Rangefinder	135	Tokyo Kogaku
	Windsor	Viewfinder	135	Toko Photo Company
November	Ricohflex VII	Twin Lens Reflex	120	Riken Kogaku
	Lord 35I	Rangefinder	135	Okaya Kogaku
December	Asahiflex IA	Single Lens Reflex	135	Asahi Kogaku Kogyo
1954				
January	Stereo Alpen	Stereo	135	Hachiyo Kogaku
April	Riken 35	Rangefinder	135	Riken Kogaku
May	Fujicaflex Automat	Twin Lens Reflex	120	Fuji Photo Film
July	Olympus 35IVa	Compact	135	Olympus Optical
	Alarm Six	Spring	120	Alarm Koki
	Doryu-2	Special	10 mm. x 10 mm.	Doryu Camera Company
August	Koniflex II	Twin Lens Reflex	120	Konishiroku
October	Aires 35II	Rangefinder	135	Aires Camera Works
November	Asahiflex IIB	Single Lens Reflex	135	Asahi Kogaku Kogyo
	Firstflex 35	Single Lens Reflex	135	Tokiwa Seiki
	Escaflex	Single Lens Reflex	120	Yashima Optical Company
1955				
February	Stereo Rocca	Stereo	120/24 pairs	Rokuwa
March	Stereo Hit	Stereo	127/8 pairs	Tougodo Sangyo Company
April	Auto Terra	Spring	135	Teraoka Seisakusho
	Pentaflex	Single Lens Reflex	135	Tokiwa Seiki
	Minolta A	Rangefinder	135	Chiyoda

Date	Camera	Type	Film or Format	Manufacturer
	Neoca 35 I-S	Rangefinder	135	Neoca Camera
May	Primoflex VA	Twin Lens Reflex	120	Tokyo Kogaku
July	Waltz 35	Viewfinder	135	Waltz Shokai
August	Miranda T	Single Lens Reflex	135	Orion Seiki Manufacturing
September	Olympus Wide	Viewfinder	135	Olympus Optical
October	Minolta Autocord L	Twin Lens Reflex	120	Chiyoda Kogaku Seiko
	Lord 35IVB	Compact	135	Okaya Kogaku
December	Mamiya Six Automat	Spring	120	Mamiya
	Hofman	Press	Tefuda Sheet	Hofman Camera Company

1956

Date	Camera	Type	Film or Format	Manufacturer
January	Ricohflex	Twin Lens Reflex	120	Riken Kogaku
February	Topcon 35S	Rangefinder	135	Tokyo Kogaku Kikai
March	Konica IIA	Rangefinder	135	Konishiroku
April	Konica III	Rangefinder	135	Konishiroku
October	Mamiyaflex C Professional	Twin Lens Reflex	120	Mamiya
November	Rittreck	Single Lens Reflex	120	Musashino Koki

1957

Date	Camera	Type	Film or Format	Manufacturer
February	Mamiya Magazine 35	Rangefinder	135	Mamiya
	Minolta Auto-wide	Rangefinder	135	Chiyoda Kogaku Seiko
	Amano 66	Single Lens Reflex	120	Amano Special Machinery
	Mamiya Elca	Rangefinder	135	Mamiya
March	Minolta Super A	Rangefinder	135	Chiyoda Kogaku Seiko
April	Nikon Fish Eye Camera	Special	120/50 mm.	Nippon Kogaku Kogyo
	Minolta 16	Subminiature	10 mm. x 14 mm.	Chiyoda Kogaku Seiko
May	Fujipet	Viewfinder	120	Fuji Photo Film
	Fujica 35M	Rangefinder	135	Fuji Photo Film

Date	Camera	Type	Film or Format	Manufacturer
September	Nikon SP	Rangefinder	135	Nippon Kogaku Kogyo
November	Topcon R	Single Lens Reflex	135	Tokyo Kogaku
1958				
February	Canon VL	Viewfinder	135	Canon
April	Minolta V2	Viewfinder	135	Chiyoda Kogaku Kogyo
	Zunow	Single Lens Reflex	135	Zunow Optical Industry
	Miranda B	Single Lens Reflex	135	Miranda Camera Company
	Konica III-A	Rangefinder	135	Konishiroku
	Yashica 44	Twin Lens Reflex	127	Yashima Optical Company
	Primo Jr.	Twin Lens Reflex	127	Tokyo Kogaku
May	Asahi Pentax K	Single Lens Reflex	135	Asahi Optical Company
August	Minolta SR-2	Single Lens Reflex	135	Chiyoda Kogaku Kogyo
October	Aires 35V	Viewfinder	135	Aires Camera Works
	Panorax 35Z-1	Panorama	24 mm. x 238 mm.	Panorax Kogyo
1959				
January	Kallo T	Viewfinder	135	Kowa Optical
March	Konica IIIM	Viewfinder	135	Konishiroku
	Mamiya Sketch	Viewfinder	24 mm. x 24 mm.	Mamiya
	Yashica Y16	Special	10 mm. x 14 mm.	Yashica
April	Nikon F	Single Lens Reflex	135	Nippon Kogaku Kogyo
	Zenza Bronica	Single Lens Reflex	120	Zenza Bronica
May	Widelux	Panorama	24 mm. x 60 mm.	Panon Camera Shokai
July	Kallo 180	Viewfinder	135	Kowa Koki
	Septon Pen	Subminiature	12 mm. x 13 mm.	Okamoto Koki
August	Ramera	Subminiature	10 mm. x 14 mm.	Kowa Optical

Date	Camera	Type	Film or Format	Manufacturer
September	Kallo 140	Viewfinder	135	Kowa Optical
	Olympus Pen	Half Frame	135	Olympus Optical
	Ricohmatic 44	Twin Lens Reflex	127	Riken Kogaku

1960

Date	Camera	Type	Film or Format	Manufacturer
January	Lord Martian	Viewfinder	135	Okaya Kogaku
	Aires Viscount M2.8	Viewfinder	135	Aires Camera
February	Nikkorex 35	Single Lens Reflex	135	Nippon Kogaku Kogyo
	Konica F	Single Lens Reflex	135	Konishiroku
	Minolta Uniomat	Rangefinder	135	Chiyoda Kogaku Seiko
April	Polaroid Land 120	Spring	Polaroid Land	Yashica
	Olympus Auto Eye	Viewfinder	135	Olympus Optical
	Aires Radar-Eye	Viewfinder	135	Aires Camera Company
July	Minolta V3	Viewfinder	135	Chiyoda Kogaku Seiko
August	Miranda Automex	Single Lens Reflex	135	Miranda Camera
September	Topcon Wink Mirror	Single Lens Reflex	135	Tokyo Kogaku

1961

Date	Camera	Type	Film or Format	Manufacturer
February	Yashica Rapide	Half Frame	135	Yashica
	Canonet	Compact	135	Canon
	Fujipet EE	Rangefinder	120	Fuji Photo Film
March	Viscawide-16	Panorama	10 mm. x 52 mm.	Taiyo Koki
	Asahi Pentax S3	Single Lens Reflex	135	Asahi Kogaku Kogyo
April	Tower 39	Box	135	Mamiya
July	Graphic 35 Jet	Compact	135	Kowa Optical
September	Canon 7	Compact	135	Canon
October	Ricoh Auto 35V	Compact	135	Riken Kogaku
November	Fujica 35 Auto M	Compact	135	Fuji Photo Film
December	Minolta Hi-matic	Compact	135	Minolta

Date	Camera	Type	Film or Format	Manufacturer
1962				
March	Olympus Pen EES	Half Frame	135	Olympus Optical
	Yashica Sequelle	Half Frame	135	Yashica
April	Taron Marquis	Compact	135	Taron
July	Minolta SR-7	Single Lens Reflex	135	Minolta
December	Nikkorex Zoom 35	Single Lens Reflex	135	Nippon Kogaku Kogyo
	Konica FSW	Single Lens Reflex	135	Konishiroku
1963				
February	Konica Eematic	Single Lens Reflex	135	Konishiroku
March	Olympus Pen F	Single Lens Reflex	135	Olympus Optical
	Canon Demi	Half Frame	135	Canon
	Topcon Super	Single Lens Reflex	135	Tokyo Kogaku
	Kowa H	Single Lens Reflex	135	Kowa Optical
August	Nikonos	Special	135	Nippon Kogaku Kogyo
October	Canon Dial 35	Half Frame	135	Canon
December	Minolta Hi-Matic 7	Compact	135	Minolta
1964				
April	Ricoh Auto Shot	Compact	135	Ricoh
June	Argus 260 Automatic	Instamatic	126	Mamiya
July	Ricoh EE Rapid	Half Frame	Rapid	Ricoh
	Kowa SW	Compact	135	Kowa Optical
	Asahi Pentax SP	Single Lens Reflex	135	Asahi Kogaku Kogyo
	Ricoh 35K Rapid	Compact	Rapid	Ricoh
	Fujicaflex II	Single Lens Reflex	135	Fuji Photo Film
November	Topcon Uni	Single Lens Reflex	135	Tokyo Kogaku

Date	Camera	Type	Film or Format	Manufacturer
1965				
February	Koni-Omega Rapid	Press	120, 220	Konishiroku
March	Minolta Autocord	Twin Lens Reflex	120, 220/12	Minolta
	Canonet QL17	Compact	135	Canon
	Canon Pellix	Single Lens Reflex	135	Canon
April	Minolta 24 Rapid	Rapid	Rapid	Minolta
	Canon Demi C	Half Frame	135	Canon
May	Yashica Electro Half	Half Frame	135	Yashica
June	Yashica Half 17EE Rapid	Half Frame	135	Yashica
	Yashica Lynx 14	1Viewfinder	135	Yashica
	Olympus Pen EM	Half Frame	135	Olympus Optical
October	Olympus LE	Viewfinder	135	Olympus Optical
November	Konica EE Matic S	Compact	135	Konishiroku
	Fotochrome	Special	53 mm. x 72 mm.	Petri Camera
	Yashica EZ-Matic 4	Instamatic	126	Yashica
	Yashica Atoron	Subminiature	8 mm. x 11 mm.	Yashica
December	Argus 264 Automatic	Instamatic	126	Mamiya
	Konica Autorex	Single Lens Reflex	Dual 135	Konishiroku
1966				
March	Minolta SR-T101	Single Lens Reflex	135	Minolta
May	Keystone Reflex K1020	Single Lens Reflex	126	Mamiya
June	Yashica Half 14	Half Frame	135	Yashica
July	Marshall Press	Press	120, 220	Marshall Koki
	Ricoh Super Shot 24	Compact	135	Ricoh
August	Minolta Autopak 500	Instamatic	126	Minolta
September	Miranda Sensorex	Single Lens Reflex	135	Miranda Camera

Date	Camera	Type	Film or Format	Manufacturer
1967				
March	Yashica EZ-Matic	Instamatic	126	Yashica
	Olympus Pen FT	Single Lens Reflex	135	Olympus Optical
June	Koni-Omega Rapid M	Press	120, 220	Konishiroku
August	Konica EE Matic Deluxe F	Compact	135	Konishiroku
October	Mamiya Sekor 1000DTL	Single Lens Reflex	135	Konishiroku
1968				
January	Yashica Lynx 5000E	Compact	135	Yashica
March	Koni-Omegaflex M	Twin Lens Reflex	120, 220	Konishiroku
	Rittreck Six	Single Lens Reflex	120, 220	Musashino Koki
	Konica FTA	Single Lens Reflex	135	Konishiroku
April	Kowa Six	Single Lens Reflex	120, 220	Kowa Optical
July	Teflex	Half Frame	135	Nichiryo
	Perma Matic 618	Box	126	Taron
	Petri Color 35	Compact	135	Petri Camera
August	Canon EX EE	Single Lens Reflex	135	Canon
October	Fujica G690	Rangefinder	120, 220	Fuji Camera
	Yashica TL Electro-X	Single Lens Reflex	135	Yashica
1969				
April	Olympus 35SP	Compact	135	Olympus Optical
	Bell and Howell Autoload 342	Instamatic	126	Canon
July	Ricoh 126C Flex	Single Lens Reflex	126	Ricoh
	New Canonet QL17	Viewfinder	135	Canon
	Pentax 6 x 7	Single Lens Reflex	120, 220	Asahi Kogaku Kogyo
August	Minolta Hi-Matic 11	Compact	135	Minolta

Date	Camera	Type	Film or Format	Manufacturer
October	Minolta 16MG-S	Subminiature	12 mm. x 17 mm.	Minolta
December	Konica Electron	Compact	135	Konishiroku
1970				
March	Ricoh TLS 401	Single Lens Reflex	135	Ricoh
April	Convertible Horseman	Single Lens Reflex	120, 220	Komamura Shokai
May	Mamiya RB67 Professional S	Single Lens Reflex	120, 220	Mamiya
June	Sakura Pak 100	Instamatic	126	Konishiroku
	Fujica ST701	Single Lens Reflex	135	Fuji Photo Film
September	Canon F-1	Single Lens Reflex	135	Canon
	Canodate E	Compact	135	Canon
	Yashica Atoron Electro	Subminiature	Minox	Yashica
	Exacta Twin TL	Single Lens Reflex	135	Cosina
November	Nicnon S	Special	18 mm. x 24 mm.	Nichiryo
December	Astral S20	Instamatic	126	Sedic
1971				
October	Olympus 35EC-2	Compact	135	Olympus Optical
November	Asahi Pentax ES	Single Lens Reflex	135	Asahi Kogaku Kogyo
1972				
January	Zenza Bronica EC	Single Lens Reflex	120, 220	Zenza Bronica
	Minolta 16 QT	Subminiature	12 mm. x 17 mm.	Minolta
February	Argus Electronic 355X	Instamatic	126	Sedic
March	Canon EX Auto	Single Lens Reflex	135	Canon
April	Miranda Sensoret	Compact	135	Miranda Camera
June	Chinon M-1	Single Lens Reflex	135	Chinon
	Kowa UW190	Single Lens Reflex	135	Kowa Optical

Date	Camera	Type	Film or Format	Manufacturer
July	Ricoh 35 Electronic	Compact	135	Ricoh
	Olympus M-1	Single Lens Reflex	135	Olympus Optical
September	Sedic Pocket Carefree 110	Subminiature	110	Sedic
1973				
February	Minolta XM	Single Lens Reflex	135	Minolta
March	Cosina Hi-Lite EC	Single Lens Reflex	135	Cosina
	Minolta Autopak 400X	Instamatic	126	Minolta
April	Fujica ST801	Single Lens Reflex	135	Fuji Photo Film
	Leica CL	Compact	135	Minolta
1974				
February	Fujica ST901	Single Lens Reflex	135	Fuji Photo Film
May	Vivitar 602	Subminiature	110	West Electric
September	Canon 110ED	Subminiature	110	Canon
	Mamiya RB67 Professional S	Single Lens Reflex	120, 220	Mamiya
December	Konica C35EF	Compact	135	Konishiroku
1975				
June	Zenza Bronica EC-TL	Single Lens Reflex	120, 220	Bronica
	Mamiya M645	Single Lens Reflex	120, 220	Mamiya
August	Pocket Fujica 200F	Subminiature	110	Fuji Photo Film
November	Contax RTS	Single Lens Reflex	135	Yashica
	Olympus OM-2	Single Lens Reflex	135	Yashica
	Fujica Date	Compact	135	Fuji Photo Film
1976				
January	Sedic Tele Focal	Subminiature	110	Sedic
March	Pocket Fujica 350 Zoom	Subminiature	110	Fuji Photo Film
April	Zenza Bronica ETR	Single Lens Reflex	120, 220	Bronica

Date	Camera	Type	Film or Format	Manufacturer
May	Canon AE-1	Single Lens Reflex	135	Canon
	Osanon Digital 750	Single Lens Reflex	135	Yashima Optical Company
	Minolta 110 Zoom	Single Lens Reflex	110	Minolta
September	Cosina Hi-Lite	Single Lens Reflex	135	Cosina
November	Flash Fujica Date	Compact	135	Fuji Photo Film
December	Hanimex VEF	Subminiature	110	Sedic
	Asahi Pentax ME	Single Lens Reflex	135	Asahi Kogaku Kogyo
1977 April	Sunpak SP-1000	Subminiature	110	Sunpak Corporation
May	School 110	Subminiature	110	Sedic
July	Vivtar 742 XL	Subminiature	110	West Electric Company
August	Minolta XD	Single Lens Reflex	135	Minolta
	Minolta XG-E	Single Lens Reflex	135	Minolta
November	Konica C35 AF	Compact	135	Konishiroku
1978 March	Zenix TL-5	Subminiature	110	Zenix Industries
	Canon A-1	Single Lens Reflex	135	Canon
April	Pocket Fujica 550 Auto	Subminiature	110	Fuji Photo Film
	Konica C35 EFD	Compact	135	Konishiroku
May	Vivitar 35EM	Compact	135	Nitto Kogaku
	Minimax 110EE	Subminiature	110	Sugaya Optical
July	Asahi Pentax Auto 110	Single Lens Reflex	110	Asahi Kogaku Kogyo
August	Art Panorama 240	Panorama	120	Tomiyama Manufacturing
September	Coca Cola	Novelty	110	Sedic
October	Zenix Zoom TS	Subminiature	110	Zenix Industries
	Yashica Autofocus	Compact	135	Yashica

Date	Camera	Type	Film or Format	Manufacturer
November	Fujica GW690 Professional	Rangefinder	120, 220	Fuji Photo Film
	Konica FS-1	Single Lens Reflex	135	Konishiroku
December	Plaubel Makina 67	Press	120	DOI International
	Ricoh FF-1	Compact	135	Ricoh
1979				
January	Nikon F2 H-MD	Single Lens Reflex	135	Nippon Kogaku Kogyo
February	Flash Fujica Auto Focus	Compact	135	Fuji Photo Film
March	Cosina VAF Auto Focus	Compact	135	Cosina
April	Hanimex 35 Reflex Flash	Single Lens Reflex	135	Sedic
	Olympus XA	Compact	135	Olympus Optical
	Contax 139 Quartz	Single Lens Reflex	135	Yashica
June	Fujica XA-5	Single Lens Reflex	135	Fuji Photo Film
	HD-1 Fujica	All-Weather	135	Fuji Photo Film
July	Ricoh AD-1	Viewfinder	135	Ricoh
October	Minolta Weathermatic A	All-Weather	110	Minolta
	Minolta 110 Zoom Single Lens Reflex Mark II	Single Lens Reflex	110	Minolta
	Mamiya ZE	Single Lens Reflex	135	Mamiya
November	Asahi Pentax ME Super	Single Lens Reflex	135	Asahi Kogaku Kogyo
	Canon AF 35M	Compact	135	Canon
December	Carena EF-250	Compact		Zenix Industries
1980				
February	Nikon F3	Single Lens Reflex	135	Nippon Kogaku Kogyo
April	Olympus XA-2	Compact	135	Olympus Optical
	Contax 137 MD Quartz	Single Lens Reflex	135	Yashica
June	Asahi Pentax LX	Single Lens Reflex	135	Asahi Kogaku Kogyo

Date	Camera	Type	Film or Format	Manufacturer
July	Chinon Bellami	Compact	135	Chinon
August	Agfa Selectronic 2	Single Lens Reflex	135	Chinon
	Zenza Bronica SQ	Single Lens Reflex	120, 220	Bronica
September	Mamiya ZE-2 Quartz	Single Lens Reflex	135	Mamiya
November	Hanimex 35 Micro Flash	Single Lens Reflex	135	Fuji Koeki
1981				
February	Minolta CLE	Compact	135	Minolta
March	Minolta Hi-Matic AF-D	Compact	135	Minolta
	Konica C35-EF3	Compact	135	Konishiroku
April	Raynox FC-35 Auto Flash	Compact	135	Hosoi Seisakusho
June	Makinon MK	Single Lens Reflex	135	Makina Kogaku
	Canon AF35ML	Compact	135	Canon
July	Mamiya ZE-X	Single Lens Reflex	135	Mamiya
	Ricoh XR-S	Single Lens Reflex	135	Ricoh
September	Fujica Auto 7	Viewfinder	135	Fuji Photo Film
	Canon New F-1	Single Lens Reflex	135	Canon
October	Chinon Infrafocus AF	Viewfinder	135	Chinon
	Fuji Instant Camera F-10	Rigid	Instant	Fuji Photo Film
	Fuji Instant Camera F-50S	Folding	Instant	Fuji Photo Film
	Minolta X-700	Single Lens Reflex	135	Minolta
November	Asahi Pentax ME-F	Single Lens Reflex	135	Asahi Kogaku Kogyo
1982				
January	Nikon FM2	Single Lens Reflex	135	Nippon Kogaku Kogyo
March	Telepac TS-35	Single Lens Reflex	135	Yashio and Company
April	Contax Preview	Special	Polaroid Land	Yashica

Date	Camera	Type	Film or Format	Manufacturer
May	Mamiya RZ 67 Professional	Single Lens Reflex	120, 220	Mamiya Koki
August	Zenza Bronica SQ-AM	Single Lens Reflex	120, 220	Bronica
	Chinon CE-5 AF	Single Lens Reflex	135	Chinon
October	Minolta AF-C	Compact	135	Minolta
November	Fujica DL-20	Compact	135	Fuji Photo Film
	Fujica DL-100	Compact	135	Fuji Photo Film
	Olympus OM30	Single Lens Reflex	135	Olympus Optical
	Osram Flash Disc Autowinder	Subminiature	Disc	Fuji Koeki
December	Nimslo-3D	Stereo	135	Sunpak Corporation
	Fuji Instant Camera F55-V	Folding	Instant	Fuji Photo Film
1983				
January	Canon T-50	Single Lens Reflex	135	Canon
	National Macro Camera C-M30	Subminiature	110	West Electric
February	Enica SX	Subminiature	Minox	Niko Kogyo
	Vivitar TEC35 Autofocus	Compact	135	West Electric
March	Minolta Disc 7	Subminiature	Disc	Minolta
	Goko UF	Compact	135	Sansei Koki
May	Konica Disc 15 Auto Focus	Subminiature	Disc	Konishiroku
June	Minolta AF-SV	Compact	135	Minolta
	Fuji Disc Camera 70	Subminiature	Disc	Fuji Photo Film
August	Nikon FA	Single Lens Reflex	135	Nippon Kogaku Kogyo
	Chinon CP-5 Twin Program	Single Lens Reflex	135	Chinon
September	Olympus OM-4	Single Lens Reflex	135	Olympus Optical
October	Olympus Quick Flash AFL	Compact	135	Olympus Optical
	Fujica GS 645W Professional	Viewfinder	120, 220	Fuji Photo Film

Date	Camera	Type	Film or Format	Manufacturer
1984				
February	Ricoh XR-P Multi Program	Single Lens Reflex	135	Ricoh
	Pentax PC 35AF-M	Single Lens Reflex	135	Asahi Kogaku Kogyo
May	Yashica T AF-D	Compact	135	Kyocera
	Fuji Instant Camera 800X	Folding	Instant	Fuji Photo Film
June	Pentax 645	Single Lens Reflex	120, 220	Asahi Kogaku Kogyo
October	Fuji DL-200	Compact	135	Fuji Photo Film
December	Minolta 7000AF	Single Lens Reflex	135	Minolta
1985				
January	Canon T-80	Single Lens Reflex	135	Canon
March	Kodak VR35 K-10	Compact	135	Chinon
	Fuji Auto 8QD	Single Lens Reflex	135	Fuji Photo Film
	Ricoh FF-70D	Single Lens Reflex	135	Ricoh
	Fuji TW-3	Half Frame	135	Fuji Photo Film

Appendix

Eras and Dynasties in Japan.

The Tokugawa Era. 1603-1867.

Also known as the Edo period. Tokugawa Ieyasu was appointed shogun in 1603, and made the small fishing village of Edo his headquarters. Edo was renamed Tokyo during Meiji. Edo was also known as the period of Tokugawa Isolation, because Japan was sealed against trade with the entire world except the Dutch and Chinese between 1639 and 1834. Commodore Perry's visit in 1854, during which he made a gift of three daguerreotypes by Brown to his hosts, is considered influential in bringing about the end of the Isolation.

The Meiji Era. 1868-1911.

The Meiji Restoration was a period of modernization in Japan, made possible in part by the Meiji Constitution of 1889. The Meiji government created a state capable of directing and guiding economic and industrial planning, permitting the country to operate as a cohesive entity in world markets. Japan's 1895 defeat of China brought what was previously considered a small feudal state to the attention of Western political powers. By the Paris Exposition of 1900, when Japanese cameras were brought to the attention of the West, the country was emerging into the European consciousness.

The Taisho Era. 1912-1925.

The tragedy of Taisho was the Kanto earthquake, which levelled Tokyo and killed more than 100,000 people. Postwar imports of cameras, particularly from Germany, and the growth of photographic enterprises in Japan, contributed to a rising popularity of the medium. Taisho is considered the beginning of the modern Japanese photographic industry.

The Showa Era. 1926-1988.

Emperor Hirohito. Within a decade of the end of World War II, the Liberal Democratic Party was formed and Japan had joined the United Nations. By 1969, Japan's economy had overtaken Western Europe. As the country became a dominant force in world economic matters, Japan excelled in the development of a number of technologies, and in a wide range of consumer electronics, including photographic and video cameras. From 1970, as photographic cameras incorporated more electronic sensing and control elements, to 1988, when electronic still video cameras were being introduced, the convergent optical and electronics technologies were clearly all elements of Japanese expertise.

Formats.

These formats appear in the text, and the corresponding notations for inches and millimeters are not precise, they are rounded to the nearest conventional unit in traditional photographic nomenclature. In some cases, plate format refers to a size in which manufacturers supplied both dry plates and sheet films.

Atom Format. ($1^5/_8$ x $2^1/_4$ in.), (45 x 60 mm.).
   A plate format which became a sheet film and a roll film format.
   One-fourth of the Continental wallet size (90 x 120 mm).

Brownie Format. ($2^1/_4$ x $3^1/_4$ in.), (60 x 90 mm.).
   8 exposures on 117, later renamed 120 film.

Cabinet Format. (5 x $6^1/_2$ in.), (129 x 165 mm.). Plate format.

Continental Wallet Format. ($3^1/_2$ x $4^3/_4$ in.), (90 x 120 mm.). Plate format.

Dai Meishi Format. ($2^1/_2$ x $3^1/_4$ in.), (65 x 90 mm.).
   Dry plate format which became a roll film format.

Meishi Format. ($2^1/_4$ x $3^1/_8$ in.), (57 x 83 mm.). Plate format.

No. 0, Sweet Format. ($1^5/_8$ x $2^1/_8$), (45 x 55 mm.). Film format.
   One-fourth of Tefuda and Anglo-American Wallet formats ($3^1/_4$ x $4^1/_4$ in.).
   The 1901 Ueda Camera Store catalogue indicated that the Britannia No. 0,
   and the 1896 Pocket Kodak used a similar format.

Postcard Format. (4 x 5 in.), (102 x 127 mm.) Also Two Plate and 4 X 5 format.

Roll Film Formats. 120 and 220 Film formats.
   A group of formats use the $2^1/_4$ inch, 6 cm. width of 120 and 220 film.
   They are conventionally referred to in abbreviations of their
   measurements in centimeters. In ascending order, they are:

   645: ($2^1/_4$ x $1^5/_8$ in.), (6 x 4.5 cm.). This horizontal format is oriented across
   the width of the film, provides 15 or 16 exposures on 120 lengths. The
   format is the largest portion of a 6 x 6 which will crop to the proportions
   of 8 x 10.

   6 x 6: ($2^1/_4$ x $2^1/_4$ in.), (6 x 6 cm.). The ubiquitous square format uses a
   length of film equivalent ot its width, provides 12 and 24 exposures on
   120 and 220, respectively.

   6 x 7: ($2^1/_4$ x $2^3/_4$ in.), (6 x 7 cm.). Sometimes called Ideal Format, it is
   oriented along the width of the film in proportion to 8 x 10. Usually
   provides 10 exposures on 120 film.

   6 x 9: ($2^1/_4$ x $3^1/_4$ in.), (6 x 9 cm.). Originally a Brownie format on 127 film,
   close to Dai Meishi, in the same proportion as full frame 35 mm. 8
   exposures on 120 film.

Tefuda Format. ($3^1/_4$ x $4^1/_4$ in.), (83 x 108 mm.). Dry plate format.

Two Plate Format. (4 x 5 in.), (102 x 127 mm.). Plate format.

Vest Format. ($1^5/_8$ x $2^1/_2$ in.), (40 x 65 mm.). Roll film format.
   In Japan, format of the U.S. Vest Pocket Kodak et. al., eight exposures on
   127 film.

Editor's Acknowledgements

In the year and a half it has taken to rewrite, design and produce this book, I have had the good fortune to be able to call upon a number of talented and skilled friends for assistance. Each of them resolved technical issues, corrected errors of varying magnitude, and lent clear thinking and broad understanding to what began as a substantial effort indeed. They, and I, take great solace in knowing that the remaining errors are entirely the responsibility of Philip Condax, Senior Curator of Technology Collections, at the International Museum of Photography, George Eastman House, whom eagle-eyed readers should address directly in those regards.

Philip Baker, Director, Product Development, Seiko Instruments U.S.A., was particularly generous with his time. An inventive camera and optical designer and a wonderfully original thinker, Phil often led off down curious research paths that proved to go directly to clarification. Dave Andresen of Sarasota, Florida, the country's best camera repairman, provided thoughtful technical assistance.

Polaroid Corporation, through Sam Yanes, Director of Corporate Communications, generously provided the gloriously long-scale Type 52 film with which the original illustrations were reproduced to size. Steve Mosch, Professor of Photography and Chairman of the Photography Department, Savannah College of Art and Design, provided valuable assistance with that project.

Edward K. Kaprellian, research and design consultant, and David A. Gibson, Curator, Patent Museum, Eastman Kodak Company, reviewed the Fujimura's original translation and made many helpful suggestions and corrections. Takashi Hibi and Tomisaburo Oda at JCII provided thoughtful comments, additions and clarifications which immeasurably enhanced the work.

In addition to those who contributed their efforts, a number of others worked on this book. Paul Rossmann is a consummate professional at both design and diplomacy: to this day he has let me believe that I designed the book and he simply, well, *adjusted* it as he page by page gave it the graceful look of which we are all so proud.

Jennifer Janson brought to proofreading and editorial correction of the manuscript and galleys, and to the preparation of the index, such skill that she is clearly destined to follow in the auspicious footsteps of her grandparents, H.W. and Dora Jane Janson. Betsy Michaels provided exceptional effort and Daria Clarke labored tirelessly. Alfred Ellis provided prescient contractual and financial advice, and Joan and Pam Hesse at Pam Hesse Composition were a font of helpful enterprise.

Gary Gurwitz at Mercantile Printing has consistently produced the most lovely books for this and many other publishers and museums with consummate skill, the keenest of craftsmen's eyes, and superhuman tolerance for the frailty of editors.

Gordon Lewis
Charleston, South Carolina

Index

Cameras are listed by both tradenames and manufacturer. Position is frequently determined by a subjective evaluation of the most common reference. When a tradename has been used by more than one manufacturer, for instance *First*, there is a separate listing which includes all products bearing the name. A number of companies have changed names at least once (see Chapter 15, pg. 182). The index notation is appropriate to the time of manufacture. In the text, every effort has been made to use full trademarks in the initial reference, while resorting to the authors' common designations in subsequent references. This index reflects references as they appear in the text, and may address common rather than trademark useage.